THE NEW INTERNATIONAL COMMENTARY ON THE NEW TESTAMENT — F. F. BRUCE, *General Editor*

THE EPISTLE OF JAMES AND JOHN

THE EPISTLES

OF

JAMES AND JOHN

by

ALEXANDER ROSS, M. A., D. D.

Pastor at Burghead, Morayshire, Scotland
Formerly Professor of New Testament
in the Free Church College, Edinburgh.

WM. B. EERDMANS PUBLISHING COMPANY
GRAND RAPIDS, MICHIGAN

THE EPISTLES OF JAMES AND JOHN
BY ALEXANDER ROSS, D.D.

WM. B. EERDMANS PUBLISHING COMPANY
GRAND RAPIDS, MICHIGAN, U.S.A.

First published in 1954
Second printing, March 1964
Third printing, January 1967

Note: Upon the death of Ned B. Stonehouse, November 18, 1962, F. F. Bruce accepted the publishers' invitation to become General Editor of this series of New Testament commentaries begun under the very able and faithful scholarship of Professor Stonehouse.

The Publishers

The Scripture text used in this commentary is that of the American Standard Version of 1901. This text is printed in full for the sake of readers who do not read Greek; the expositions are, however, based upon the Greek text.

PHOTOLITHOPRINTED BY GRAND RAPIDS BOOK MANUFACTURERS, INC.
GRAND RAPIDS, MICHIGAN
1966

EDITOR'S FOREWORD

The opportunity of introducing this work from the pen of Dr. Alexander Ross affords me very particular pleasure. Appearing almost simultaneously with the work of F. F. Bruce on Acts, it brings into prominence the international character of the company of scholars who are united in this undertaking, and in particular demonstrates again the significant part taken by representatives of the British Isles.

Ross, like Bruce, is a Scot, also claims Aberdeen as his alma mater, and is associated in the editorship of *The Evangelical Quarterly*. Among their differences, however, is the fact that the career of the present author has been one of direct service to the Church rather than to university education. For many years Ross has held an influential and highly respected place among the ministers of the Free Church of Scotland. From 1937 to 1952 he was Professor of New Testament Exegesis in the theological seminary of that Church, the Free Church College of Edinburgh. But Ross has always loved preaching and the work of the pastorate in general, and in 1952 he resigned his post in Edinburgh to respond to an urgent call that had been extended to him by the congregation of Burghead in Morayshire.

Following his graduation from Aberdeen (from which he holds both an M.A. and a B.D. degree) he served churches in both Scotland and Canada. In 1950 he was awarded the D.D. degree by the Presbyterian College of Montreal. Among his writings are articles on "The Life of Christ," "The Teaching of Christ," and "The Epistle to the Hebrews" in the *New Bible Handbook* published by the Inter-Varsity Fellowship of Great Britain in 1947. He is also the author of a commentary on The Epistle to the Galatians in the *New Bible Commentary* recently published in England by the same organization and issued by Eerdmans in America.

Dr. Ross thus has brought to the preparation of this work on the Epistles of James and John an extraordinarily rich background as teacher and preacher, editor and author. But the reader will also discern other qualifications of a specifically spiritual kind that add immeasurably to the impact of this volume. For he is disclosed throughout as a man who loves Christ and His Word with a consuming passion and who therefore is by no means indifferent to the reception given his commentary. His commitment to the authority of the Word is such, however, that his treatment is faithfully expository. He never descends to a loose or partisan handling of Scripture.

Highly desirable as such qualities of mind and heart are in all exegetical writing, they seem to be especially fruitful in the exposition of these epistles. Doctrinal issues and questions are everywhere present or presupposed but the practical thrust of the New Testament is nowhere more conspicuous or emphatic than here, and Ross, the scholar-preacher and devout Christian man, appears to be exactly the person to expound their meaning for the present day. Luther stumbled at the "faith and works" religion of James, but Ross, following in the God-centered line of the Reformed tradition, shows how significant and essential this teaching is to a thorough understanding of the Scriptures. Similarly his treatment of the Johannine Epistles captures their moving message of faith in the Incarnate One and of love which expresses itself in keeping his commandments. One may anticipate accordingly that with the attainment of the overall purpose of increase of knowledge there may also be an advancement of doing of the truth.

NED B. STONEHOUSE,
General Editor

Philadelphia, U.S.A.

CONTENTS

ABBREVIATIONS

ASV — American Standard Version (1901)
AV — Authorized Version (1611)
CGT — Cambridge Greek Testament
DAC — Dictionary of the Apostolic Church (Hastings)
DB — Dictionary of the Bible (Hastings)
DCG — Dictionary of Christ and the Gospels (Hastings)
EGT — Expositor's Greek Testament
ICC — International Critical Commentary
LXX — The Septuagint
Mof — The Moffatt Translation
RSV — Revised Standard Version (1946)
Wey — Weymouth Version

THE EPISTLE OF JAMES

INTRODUCTION TO THE
EPISTLE OF JAMES

I

Reception of the Epistle

The voice of Church tradition speaks in rather an inconclusive fashion here. Origen (about 230 A.D.) is the first Church writer who explicitly quotes this Epistle as Scripture, and he ascribes it to James, the Lord's brother, though, in another place, he refers to it as "the Epistle which goes under the name of James." Ascending the stream of tradition, we find traces, dubious in the opinion of some scholars, more or less certain in the opinion of others, of the existence of this Epistle. The earliest book which can be regarded, with some degree of certainty, as echoing some of its teaching, is that early Christian writing which has been called a kind of primitive *Pilgrim's Progress,* and which is known as "The Shepherd of Hermas." It has been variously dated, in the period 100—150. In the Shepherd, quotations from either the Old or the New Testaments are not very numerous, but some verses in it remind us of James' Epistle, and, according to Dr. George Salmon, in his *Introduction to the New Testament,* the great number of the coincidences incline us to believe that they are not accidental. Some of the themes which James deals with are dealt with by Hermas, in some detail. The teaching of the opening verses of James is several times echoed by Hermas — that we must ask God for wisdom, ask in faith without doubt or hesitation. He who is afflicted with doubt in his prayer life is called by James a double-minded man (Jas. 1:8), and the cognate noun occurs frequently in Hermas. All through one part of Hermas there runs what seems to be a reference to the contrast which James draws between the

11

wisdom which cometh from above, and the wisdom which is earthly (3:15—17). Hermas uses the word "synagogue" for a place of Christian worship, as James does (2:2), and other words in the vocabulary of James which he uses are the verb "to bridle" (1:26), the verb "to speak against" (4:11), and the adjective "full of pity" (5:11).

Some have discovered allusions to the Epistle of James in the Epistle of Clement of Rome, written about the year 96. There are several coincidences of language which Salmon thinks are best explained as indicating that Clement used the Epistle of James, though he does not venture to say that any of them amounts to positive proof. Indeed, they cannot be so regarded, and the evidence here is somewhat dubious, but, in a book of the New Testament which was written some time in the latter part of the seventh decade of the First Century, we have some striking coincidences of language with the Epistle of James. In James 1:3 we have a phrase which is identical with a phrase in 1 Peter 1:7, and it is a rather unusual phrase, while the resemblance between James 4:7 and 1 Peter 5:8, 9 is striking: see commentary. We have also "manifold trials" in Jas. 1:2 and 1 Peter 1:6. Keeping in view the strong arguments which will be considered later on which seem to point to an earlier date for the Epistle of James than the date of First Peter, we seem to have here an indication that, at least as early as the year 66 or 67 or a few years earlier, the Epistle of James was known in the Church and was regarded as Scripture.

II

Internal Evidence and the Authorship

The voice of Church tradition, as is evident, speaks with varying degrees of clearness, but the internal evidence, the evidence afforded by the Epistle itself, provides quite a number of good reasons for attributing it to James, the Lord's brother. The writer was undoubtedly a Jew, and,

INTRODUCTION

possibly, a Jew who wrote in Palestine. His home land is the same as that which is written of in Deut. 11:14, "I will give the rain of your land in its season, the former rain and the latter rain, that thou mayest gather in thy grain, and thy new wine, and thine oil," for he illustrates patience by the example of the farmer who waits for the precious fruit of the earth, and has long patience until he receive the early and the latter rain (5:7). Wine and oil, too, were among the natural products of his land, as is shown by his question, "Can a fig tree yield olives, or a vine figs" (3:12). The hot burning wind which withered the grass (1:11), is the same as that of which Ezekiel speaks, when he asks (17:10), "Shall it not utterly wither when the east wind toucheth it?" It was the same wind which withered the gourd of Jonah, the same probably whose approach our Lord said those wise in weather lore could forecast (Lk. 12:55, "a scorching heat").

That the writer was a Jew can be deduced from the fact that he speaks of Abraham as "our father" (2:21), from the fact that he uses the Jewish word "synagogue" for a Christian place of worship in 2:2, from his reference to "Gehenna" in 3:6, and from his use of the specifically Jewish name for God in 5:4. That he wrote for Jewish *readers* seems also clear. The opening words of the letter state explicitly for whom it was intended, the Jews of the Dispersion; that is to say, the letter was written by a Jew whose home, probably, was in Palestine, to his fellow-Jews who had gone to various parts of the Roman Empire for purposes of trade and commerce, men who often migrated from one city to another (4:13). The Jews who are addressed, however, are all Christian Jews. He describes himself as a servant of the Lord Jesus Christ, and addresses his readers as brethren, who shared with him "the faith of our Lord Jesus Christ" (2:1). They had experienced the miracle of regeneration (1:18). He speaks of the worthy Name which had been invoked upon them in Baptism (2:7). He exhorts them to wait in patience for the Coming of the Lord (5:7), looking for the crown which He promised to them that love

Him (1:12). The Book of Acts tells us of a migration of Christian Jews from Jerusalem which was brought about by the persecution which followed the death of Stephen (Acts 11:19). Thus, there could quite easily have been Christian Jews of the Dispersion to whom, at an early date, this letter might have been written.

Who, then, was the Jew who wrote this letter? Who was this James? Three men in the New Testament bear that name, but two of them can safely be left out of account. The disciple of Jesus, James the son of Alphaeus, seems to have been an obscure and undistinguished person. James, the son of Zebedee, died early as a martyr, in the year 44, as we are informed in the 12th. of Acts. The third James, who is mentioned in the 17th. verse of that chapter, James the Lord's brother, is the only one of the three whose claims here really call for any investigation.

There are three interesting points in connection with the internal evidence which can, at least, be said to support the belief that the Epistle was written by James, the Lord's brother.

(1). There are some coincidences of language between the Epistle and both the speech of James at the famous Jerusalem Council of the year 50, at which James presided, and the Council's letter, which was probably drawn up by James with, it may be, the assistance of other members of that Council. At the beginning of the Council's letter we have a form of greeting which occurs also in Jas. 1:1 and elsewhere in the N. T. only in Acts 23:26, where, again, an actual letter is being accurately quoted. The speech begins thus: "Brethren, hearken unto me"; we have a parallel in Jas. 2:5. The expression "your souls", in the Council's letter, is a Hebraic expression: we find it also in Jas. 1:21; cf. also Jas. 5:20. The verb "to turn", for conversion, occurs in Acts 15:19, in the speech of James, and also in Jas. 5:19, 20. The expression "upon whom My Name is called" occurs in Acts 15:17, in the speech of James, in a quotation from Amos; cf. Jas. 2:7. To go outside Acts 15, we have in Acts

14

21:24 the verb "to spend" used by James; we have it also in Jas. 4:3. We have the verb "to purify" used by James in Acts 21:24 and 26; we have it also in Jas. 4:8. Such coincidences of language, though not absolutely convincing, tend to show that we are all the time in contact with one and the same mind. It is certainly striking that in the rather restricted scope afforded by the short passage in Acts 15 and the short passage in Acts 21, we should discover so many points of similarity with the vocabulary of the Epistle.

(2). The Epistle is the work of just that type of mind which all the mentions of James in the N. T. and in Church tradition reveal him to be. Hegesippus, the earliest historian of the Christian Church, who flourished in the period 140—175, says that James was known as "the Just." He drank no wine, he ate no animal food. No razor ever touched his head. Hegesippus also says that James spent so much time on his knees in prayer in the Temple that they became as hard as horny camel's knees. It is doubtful if we can rely on all these statements. Hegesippus says that James alone was allowed to enter into the Holy of holies, and that seems rather a tall story and may cast some doubt on the other statements of that old historian. There is no doubt about James' strong attachment to the Jewish Law. That attachment is evident in the report of the Jerusalem Council and in Acts 21 also; it may be gathered also from Gal. 2:12, where it would appear that his name could be used by fanatical Judaizers to serve their own purposes. His rigid keeping of the requirements of the Jewish Law won for him the admiration even of unbelieving Jews, according to Josephus, who tells us of the admiration in which he was held at the time of his death, which, according to Josephus, took place just after the death of the Roman procurator, Festus, in the year 62. According to Eusebius, James was beaten to death with a club. A more highly coloured account of his death is given by Hegesippus, who says that he was hurled from the pinnacle of the Temple.

It is easy to imagine a man like James writing an Epistle

like this. The writer has been called "an austere moralist," who has some terribly severe things to say about those who make loud professions of faith, but live lives which are sadly out of harmony with their professions. In his second chapter he rings the changes with unwearied pertinacity on the thesis, "Faith without works is dead." It seems fairly evident that the writer is a Jewish Christian, a man who is deeply rooted in the ancient Jewish faith, but who calls men to obey the old God-given Law as interpreted and transfigured by Jesus, who has, in the deepest sense, *fulfilled* it. The Law of God, as thus interpreted and transfigured, is "the perfect Law, the Law of liberty" (1:25), "the Royal Law" (2:8), which James enunciated as Jesus did, "Thou shalt love thy neighbour as thyself." That the writer has his roots deep in O. T. prophecy ought to be obvious to every reader. We seem to catch echoes of the stern, uncomprising teaching of Amos in words like those in the first six verses of his fifth chapter. Isaiah is the direct inspiration of the graphic words in 1:10. In his wellknown definition of "pure religion and undefiled" in 1:27 he may be said to have summed up in unforgettable words some of the most striking features of the ethical teaching of the O. T. prophets. One thing which marked out James from his fellows, according to Church tradition, was earnest prayer, and in the Epistle we have the great words in 5:16, which Weymouth translates thus, "The heartfelt supplication of a righteous man exerts a mighty influence."

(3). There is a third fact to be considered here, the exact significance of which should be carefully estimated. This Epistle contains more verbal reminiscences of the teaching of Jesus than all the other apostolic writings taken together. Specially noteworthy are its undoubted echoes of the Sermon on the Mount. Compare Jas. 1:22 with Mt. 7:20 and 24, Jas. 3:12 with Mt. 7:16, Jas 2:5 with Mt. 5:3, Jas. 4:11, 12 with Mt. 7:1. "Your riches are corrupted, your garments are moth-eaten," this writer cries (5:2), and Jesus says, "Lay not up treasures...." (Mt. 6:19). When this writer says, "Swear not, neither by heaven, neither by the earth, neither by any oath, but let...." (5:12), he is quite consciously and deliberately repeating a word of Jesus (Mt. 5:34—37).

How are we to interpret such phenomena? Surely they must be regarded as proving that the writer had been, somehow or other, in close contact with Jesus. The instances are too numerous, as Salmon says, to allow us to think of chance resemblances. They are not cases of quotations from the Synoptic Gospels, but have all the appearance of being independent testimony to our Lord's teaching. Salmon hazards the conjecture that a great deal more of this Epistle may be founded on sayings of our Lord than we now have the means of identifying, and, in particular, that what is said in 1:12 may refer to an unrecorded saying of Jesus. Prof. J. A. Robertson, in his *Hidden Romance of the New Testament,* says that we must note "the fact that the writer never expressly says that he is quoting Jesus, nor does he acknowledge any indebtedness to the Gospels. Indeed, hardly in any case can he be said to be quoting at all." "We can, in fact," Prof. Robertson declares, "scarcely resist the conclusion that we are listening to the reproduction of thoughts from a mind that had lived and laboured for years alongside the Master-mind which created and gave them perfect utterance. They drop out freely and spontaneously, as from a mind that had so absorbed them that they had become part and parcel of its very self. Had James not listened to Jesus' talk, as they wrought side by side, at the bench in Nazareth, and half-unconsciously, half-reluctantly, all his thinking had become moulded by it?" See another quotation from Prof. Robertson in the commentary on 3:17.

The three points which we have considered tend to confirm us in the belief that the Epistle was written by James, the Lord's brother. The writer occupies a position so important and so distinguished that the mere name "James" is sufficient to identify him to his readers. James, the Lord's brother, did occupy an important and distinguished position in the Church at Jerusalem, as the Book of Acts makes clear. Compare the first verse of the Epistle of Jude.

III

The Greek of the Epistle

The Greek of the Epistle we may regard as approaching more closely the standard of classical purity than that of any other N. T. book, with the exception of the Epistle to the Hebrews and the Preface to the Third Gospel. The vocabulary may be described as a rich one, thirteen words apparently occurring here for the first time in Greek literature, words like "double-minded" in 1:8 and 4:8, "religious" in 1:26 and the adjective "gold-ringed" in 2:2. The language of the writer, as Zahn says, "is comparatively free from gross mistakes, and even shows some feeling for the euphony and rhythm of the Greek tongue," as in 1:17. The question may well arise here, Could a Jew of Galilee of comparatively limited education, such as one surmises James to have been, have written such remarkable Greek? Josephus wrote his book on the *Wars of the Jews*, first in Aramaic, and subsequently translated it into Greek. It has been conjectured by some quite orthodox scholars that it is not impossible that James wrote the Epistle in Aramaic, and someone else translated it into Greek. On that point, J. B. Mayor says: "The rich vocabulary is not unlike that which may have been professed by a professional interpreter, but is very remarkable, if we attribute it an unlearned Jew, writing perhaps the earliest book of the N. T."

But, while such conjectures are interesting, they may, perhaps, underestimate the extent of James' education. Zahn says that "to assume that from the position which James occupied in Jerusalem he would have had no opportunity to acquire the facility in the use of Greek which the author of this letter had, or that he lacked the ability to acquire it, is entirely arbitrary. Assuming that the letter was written between 44 and 51, the author had been from fifteen to twenty years a member, and for a number of years the official head, of this Jerusalem Church, which very early in its history had more Hellenists than Hebrews in its membership." In daily contact with such Hellenists James could, in the course of the years, have attained to considerable proficiency in the use of the Greek tongue.

IV

The Date of the Epistle

This Jewish writer evidently writes under a profound sense of a great crisis that is approaching his nation, a judgment of God upon it: see the commentary on 5:3, 7 and 9. This judgment was the fall of Jerusalem in the year 70, and the heartless oppression of the poor by the rich for many years before the year 70, as described with great fulness by Josephus, harmonises well with this writer's stern denunciation of the rich farmers in 5:1—5. But, the date of the Epistle, many hold, can be pushed back to a considerably earlier date than the years immediately preceding the year 70. If James was the author, it must have been written before the year 62, when he died. How much further back beyond that year can we push the date of this Epistle?

There is no reference in the epistle to the non-Jewish world. There is no mention whatever of the existence of men of Gentile birth in the Church; not one word of allusion to the controversies to which, according to the Book of Acts, their admission led with regard to their relation to the Jewish ceremonial Law. It is often, as Salmon reminds us, one of the surest criteria of the date of a document to notice what were the controversial interests of the writer. In the case before us, there is not the faintest allusion to the serious dispute that led to the summoning of the Jerusalem Council in the year 50, the dispute of which echoes can be heard in the Epistles to the Romans and the Corinthians, namely, the terms of the justification of the Gentile believer, and the extent to which he was obliged to observe the Jewish Law. Such considerations point to a date before the year 50, so that this Epistle may be the earliest N. T. writing. The persecution begun in Jerusalem in the year 44 (Acts 12) had spread to the Christian Jews of the Dispersion, the Diaspora, and in various places unbelieving Jews were dragging believers before their tribunals (2:6). "It is inconceivable," says a writer on the Epistle in Hastings' DAC., "that an Epistle to Jewish Christians of the Diaspora after 50 should contain no reference to the burning question," which was discussed at the Council of that year, and the writer adds that he is not aware that any satisfactory answer has ever been given to that objection. Strong arguments in favour of the early date will be found set forth in Salmon's *Introduction to the N. T.*, in Zahn's *Introduction to the N. T.*, and in J. B. Mayor's commentary on the epistle. Even so radical a scholar as Dr. A. T. Cadoux, in his little book on *The Thought of St. James*, published in 1944, favours the early date, pointing out that arguments in support of it are the simplicity of the greeting, the use of "synagogue" for a Christian place of worship, and the mention of "elders" only (5:14) as officials of the Church.

V

General Characteristics

The style of the writer is a sharp and incisive one. An outstanding example of his vigorous manner of speech and of his rich vocabulary, too, is to be found in what he says about the evils wrought by the tongue, in 3:1—8. The Epistle leaves on us the impression that it comes from a vigorous personality, a strong, immoveable personality, a real pillar of the Church, as James was declared by Paul to be (Gal. 2:9). "The author," says the writer of the article in Hastings' DAC., already quoted, "plunges at once into his subject with a bold paradox, and his short, decisive sentences fall like hammer strokes. His rebukes contain some of the sharpest invective in the N. T. (4:1—6, 5:1—6), and he knows when irony will serve him best. In 2:19 you have what is perhaps the most tremendous and shattering irony in the N. T.: You believe that God is one; and you are quite right; evil spirits also believe and shudder." As J. B. Mayor says: "The flashes of irony which break through Paul's splendid vindication of his apostolic authority in 2 Corinthians seem passionless and pale, contrasted with the volcanic energy which glows beneath the denunciations of James."

It is good to have so direct, so pungent and so practical a message coming to us from the very early days of Christianity. The practical side of Christian truth is one that some sound Evangelicals have sometimes been in danger of forgetting, but we neglect it to our grave loss. But, while the Epistle is so refreshingly practical, and while the whole tone of it is severely ethical, James cannot be regarded as an ethical teacher and no more. His practical exhortations have their roots in deeper things, in the vital truths of Christian theology, though these roots, as is natural, are, to a large extent, hidden from the eye. There is a good deal of what may be called "compressed theology" in the Epistle, in expressions like "Of His own will He brought us forth" (1:18), "the implanted word...." (1:21), "the perfect law of liberty" (1:25), "heirs of the Kingdom...." (2:5), etc. See the commentary on some remarkable words written in 2:1.

Dr. A. S. Peake, in his book, *The Bible, its Origin, Significance, and its Abiding Worth,* refers to this Epistle as "a relatively insignificant book," but close study of it shows that to be a very shortsighted dictum. It is often asserted that Luther called it "an Epistle of straw," but that

21

seems to be a distortion of what he actually said. He did not, as a matter of fact, call it "an Epistle of straw" outright, but, contrasting it with John, Romans, Galatians and 1 Peter, he wrote in 1522 what he did not reprint in later editions of his Bible: "St James' Epistle is a right strawy Epistle *as compared with them;* for it has no real Gospel character." There is here, as Zahn says, "a degree of unfairness, which is as easily accounted for as it is regrettable." Luther thought, of course, that some words in the second chapter of the Epistle contradicted the Pauline doctrine of Justification by faith. An attempt is made in the commentary, at the appropriate points, to show that for this idea there is really no foundation whatever.

VI

Contents of the Epistle

It is difficult to analyse the contents of the Epistle, as it is not a formal treatise. Possibly, information had reached James with regard to certain things in the life of the Jewish-Christian Churches of the Dispersion which needed to be corrected, so that he is moved to write informally some weighty words of counsel to them. But, before he writes any words of stern warning, he has some strong words of good cheer to address to them in their persecutions and their varied trials, or temptations. Carr (Camb. G. T.) suggests that two of the main themes of the Epistle are (a). Resistance to temptation, or "endurance" (1:3 and 5:7), and (b). Activity in the Christian graces, of which "faith" (1:6; 2, *passim;* 5:15) and "mercy" (2:13 and 3:17) are leading examples. One of the most clearly marked features of the Epistles certainly is the stress which James lays on the absolute necessity of cultivating the Christian graces, of cultivating practical godliness. None need to be reminded of that more than do Christian teachers, and, as is suggested in the exposition, some of the sternest words written about the tongue seem to have been intended specially for them.

INTRODUCTION

The contents of the Epistle may be analysed as follows:

1. *A salutation* (1:1).

2. *Trials from without* (1:1—12).

3. *Trials from within: the heart of man is the source of sin, God is the source of all good, and, especially, He is the bestower on the soul of the new life, through the operation in it of the Word of truth* (1:13—18).

4. *The Word of truth must be treated in the right way: (a) we must be doers of the word (1:19—25) and (b) our religion must be one of active benevolence and not one of mere words (1:26, 27).*

5. *All unmerciful conduct will be punished mercilessly by the God of love. At His judgment seat the merciful man alone will have cause for rejoicing* (2:1—13).

6. *Faith and Works: the general theme is that faith is worthless unless it be accompanied by works* (2:14—26).

7. *The sins of the tongue, with special reference to some of the dangers which beset Christian teachers* (3:1—12).

8. *The false and the true wisdom* (3:13—18).

9. *You are very far from possessing the peace which is the harvest of the true wisdom. Too many of you are ruled by wordly desires and have been guilty of spiritual adultery. Repent of your sins and humble yourselves before God* (4:1—12).

10. *The uncertainty and brevity of human life should lead us to humble dependence on the will of God* (4:13—17).

11. *The rich oppressors of the Church are to meet with a terrible doom* (5:1—6).

12. *Exhortations to the Church to stand firm and to be forbearing in view of the Coming of the Lord and in view of the great examples of the prophets and of Job (5:7—12).*

13. *Various activities of the Church, prayer, praise, visitation of the sick, confession of sins and the restoration of backsliders (5:13—20).*

CHAPTER I

TRIALS FROM WITHOUT

1:1—12

1 James, a servant of God and of the Lord Jesus Christ, to the twelve tribes which are of the Dispersion, greeting.

2 Count it all joy, my brethren, when ye fall into manifold temptations;

3 knowing that the proving of your faith worketh patience.

4 And let patience have its perfect work, that ye may be perfect and entire, lacking in nothing.

5 But if any of you lacketh wisdom, let him ask of God, who giveth to all liberally and upbraideth not; and it shall be given him.

6 But let him ask in faith, nothing doubting: for he that doubteth is like the surge of the sea driven by the wind and tossed.

7 For let not that man think that he shall receive anything of the Lord;

8 a double-minded man, unstable in all his ways.

9 But let the brother of low degree glory in his high estate;

10 and the rich, in that he is made low: because as the flower of the grass he shall pass away.

11 For the sun ariseth with the scorching wind, and withereth the grass; and the flower thereof falleth, and the grace of the fashion of it perisheth: so also shall the rich man fade away in his goings.

12 Blessed is the man that endureth temptation; for when he hath been approved, he shall receive the crown of life, which the Lord promised to them that love him.

1 James introduces himself to his Christian readers of the Dispersion as a Jew who had entered into voluntary bond-service to God and who, recognising in Jesus Christ God Incarnate, had given to Him exactly similar bond-

25

service, such glad, wholehearted service as God alone has the right to demand.[1]

In vv. 2—12 James deals with *outward* trials.

2 James hails his readers as brothers, because he and they are bound together by a tie which is both racial and religious. The frequent recurrence of this affectionate form of address, as Farrar says, "shows that the wounds which James inflicts are meant to be the faithful wounds of a friend." His first word to them is one of strong encouragement. They were, no doubt, being persecuted, many of them (2:6), but persecution was not the only thing that troubled them; they were surrounded[2] by "manifold[3] trials." Peter has the same phrase, and he would have his readers place over against their trials "the manifold grace of God" (1 Peter 1:6 and 4:10). James says that joy should be the supreme emotion in the mind of his readers as trials confront them, and their joy should be deep joy. Some would take "all joy" as meaning "pure joy, nothing but joy." Mayor points out that James does not say that trial *is* all joy; he bids us *count* it all joy, "that is, look at it

---

[1] The phrase "servant of God and of the Lord Jesus Christ" occurs only here. Paul, Peter and Jude have "servant of Jesus Christ." (Rom. 1:1; Phil. 1:1; 2 Pet. 1:1; Jude 1). What has been called the "bracketing" of God and Christ, as in so many other salutations in the N. T. Epistles, is deeply impressive and is of far-reaching theological significance. Christ stands on the divine side of reality, over against the men who are His servants. In the LXX "Lord" occurs frequently as the Greek equivalant of "Jehovah." The Greek word διασπορά the "Dispersion," is used in LXX of the Jews dispersed among foreign nations (Deut. 28:25; Ps. 147:2, etc.). It occurs again in N. T. only in Jn. 7:35 and 1 Pet. 1:1.

[2] *Fall into (περιπέσητε)* occurs again in N. T. only in Lk. 10:30. It may convey the idea of falling into trials, so as to be *surrounded* by them.

[3] *Manifold (ποικίλοις)* means, literally, "many-colored." Trials have many aspects, and they may change their appearance from day to day. The same thing may be said about the grace of God and the wisdom of God, to which the same adjective is applied (1 Pet. 4:10 and Eph. 3:10).

from the bright side, as capable of being turned to our highest good." These Jewish believers *know* something that ought to induce them to look at their trials from a different standpoint from that which is taken by those who have never studied in the school of Christ.

3 What they know is that trials will test their faith, and, if the issue of the trial is that their faith is proved to be genuine faith,[4] that will mean a strengthening of their character; trials, rightly taken, will produce in them the sterling quality of *endurance*.[5] Endurance is that *staying power* which enables a man to persevere steadfastly through the most adverse circumstances. The Greek word does not denote such a *passive* quality as the English word "patience" often denotes; "it is a noble word," says Trench in his *New Testament Synonyms;* "it does not mark merely passive endurance but the brave patience with which the Christian contends against various hindrances, persecutions and temptations that befall him in his conflict with the outward and inward world." The word occurs again in 5:11, and the corresponding verb occurs in v. 12 of this chapter, in 5:11, in Mt. 10:22, etc. Our Lord manifested this quality in its fulness (2 Thes. 3:5). The use of the word by our Lord in Lk. 21:19 is interesting; "in your endurance" of suffering

---

4   τὸ δοκίμιον ὑμῶν τῆς πίστεως is rendered by *the proving of your faith.* The great English Church exegete Hort held that the meaning required here is "what is genuine in your faith," and specimens of the vernacular discovered in the sands of Egypt have shown the soundness of that supposition. In some of these specimens the word used here is found qualifying the word "gold" — "standard gold". The thought of James seems to be that the child of God comes out of his trials with his faith proved to be of standard quality. The same phrase is found in 1 Pet. 1:7, where note the metaphor of the purging of gold; cf. Job 23:10.

5   ὑπομονή. The meaning of this word is explained in the exposition, here and on 5:7, but it might be well to note that it occurs frequently in Paul's Epistles, and in one particular passage, Rom. 5:3, we have an interesting and an instructive parallel to the words of James here.

without giving way, "ye shall win your souls." It is well to note that this early emphasis laid by James on faith indicates that he would not be likely to undervalue its proper use.

4 This quality of endurance, however, must have its full effect, it must attain its *end*. It may be rendered incomplete by our impatience or our needless repining when things go wrong with us. It is vitally important to attend to this, because the attaining of this sterling quality of endurance will set us on the way to a mature and ripened character, one that *lacks nothing*.[6]

5 The word "lack" links together vv. 4 and 5. You are far from possessing that mature and ripened character, and, especially, some of you are lacking in wisdom,[7] the wisdom that you need in order that you may deal with your trials in the right way. You need it in other realms as well, for, as Moffat says, this wisdom is "the divine endowment of the soul by which the believing man recognizes and realises

---

[6] The end is that they may be *perfect and entire (τέλειοι καὶ ὁλόκληροι)*. The perfect are those who attain to the *end* for which they were created. The word often describes full-grown men as opposed to babes, Christians who have attained to maturity of character and understanding, as in 1 Cor. 2:6; Eph. 4:13; Phil. 3:15 (on which Lightfoot has an illuminating note); Col. 1:28 and Heb. 5:14. In 1 Cor. 14:20, "In mind be men" is found in contrast with the immaturity of children. The word "entire" occurs again in N. T. only in 1 Thess. 5:23. It means "complete in all its parts." It often had sacrificial associations and was used by Jewish writers like Josephus and Philo of a body without defect or blemish, whether that of priest or victim.

[7] σοφία. The distinction between mere knowledge and the divinely-inspired wisdom is an important one. We recall Tennyson's words, "Knowledge comes, but wisdom lingers." In 1 Cor. 13:8 Paul speaks of knowledge as being "done away"; he does not say that about the true wisdom of which he had written in 1 Cor. 2:6. We have good reason for asserting that in Scripture "wisdom" is ascribed only to God and to good men, except in an ironical sense, when it is usually accompanied by some qualifying phrase, e.g., "the wisdom of this world" (1 Cor. 1:20), "of this age" (1 Cor. 2:6).

28

that divine rule of life called righteousness (see 1:20, 3:18), either in intercourse with others, or, as here, in the management of his own conduct." This wisdom, which James describes so fully and richly in 3:17, we may regard as the inward attitude of a soul that has found a better Teacher than any of the Jewish Rabbis, who had their Wisdom Literature, or any of the Greek philosophers. This wisdom is the "principal thing" (Prov. 4:7). It is more than knowledge. "If any man lack knowledge, let him go to College," but, if any man lack wisdom, that is an entirely different matter. For it he must go to the eternal Fountain of wisdom, and, if he goes there, he will not be disappointed. God gives liberally,[8] with open hand, in the realm of Nature (Ps. 145:16); He gives with still richer liberality in the realm of Grace. And He does not upbraid or reproach the recipient as being utterly unworthy of the boon bestowed on him. In the *Wisdom of the Son of Sirach* we read (41:12): "After thou hast given, upbraid not." God never does that. "He bestows on us what we need without asking embarrassing questions about our deserts," to quote Moffat again, "and without a hard word, never harping on the benefit or treating prayer as presumption." The great example here is Solomon (1 Kings 3:9—12), but James lays stress on the glad fact that God gives to *all* who ask, not to a Solomon or people of similar character merely.

6 Our prayer, however, must be the prayer of faith; cf. 5:15. "Only let him ask in faith, with never a doubt." (Mof) The word "surge" occurs only once again in the New Testament, in Lk. 8:24, where we have "the *raging* of the water," and it is rather interesting to observe that in the next verse there in Luke, we have our Lord's question, "Where is your faith?" The doubting man, as Mayor

---

[8] ἁπλῶς. This adverb occurs here only in N. T., and its literal meaning is "simply." The gift is unconditional. The idea of generous giving, however, harmonises well enough with such an idea. The cognate noun occurs in the sense of liberality, in Rom. 12:8, 8:2 and 9:11.

suggests rather strikingly, is described as like a cork floating on the wave, now carried towards the shore, now away from it. Or, the thought may be simply that of the instability of a billow, changing from moment to moment, as the wind blows upon it. The verb which corresponds to the noun "surge" occurs in Eph. 4:14, where we have *"tossed to and fro* and carried about by every *wind* of doctrine."

7 The kind of man described by James will not receive *anything* from the Lord, neither wisdom nor anything else.

8 He is virtually a man with two souls,[9] which are in conflict with each other; cf. our phrase, "to be in two minds;" cf. also Ps. 12:2 (in the Hebrew) "with a heart and a heart do they speak." Farrer quotes a saying of a Jewish Rabbi, "Let not those who pray have two hearts, one directed to God, one to something else." Such a man is unstable[10] and unreliable in all his ways, and not merely in the realm of prayer. James will suggest later on another reason why some prayers are not answered (4:3).

9 Whatever the character of our outward circumstances, we can find reasons for exultation in them. When a brother of low degree, a poor man such as is described in 2:2, receives saving faith, he is exalted spiritually, his "high estate" carrying with it both a present and a future dignity, all that is involved in being rich in faith and heir of the Kingdom (2:5).

10 About the contrasted case of the rich brother James writes more at length. He is to exult in the fact that

---

9 Doubleminded *(δίψυχος)*. The adjective used here is not to be found in the Greek Classics, and it does not occur in LXX. It occurs only here in N. T., and it was possibly coined by James. See Introduction, under "External Testimony."

10 *ἀκατάστατος* occurs in N. T. only here and in 3:8. It occurs once in LXX, in Isa. 54:11, "tossed with tempest." It occurs frequently in Greek writers, Demosthenes using it of the Greek democracy, whose shifting, unreliable policy he compares to winds at sea. The corresponding noun is translated "confusion" in 3:16, where see commentary. This noun was used by Greek writers to describe political instability and confusion.

he has been made low. The pride which once he had in his wealth has been shattered and he has been led to rate riches at their true value. Above all, he has come to see the perishableness of all worldly glory, which is certain to wither away like the loveliest of the flowers. Let him exult because he has learned such lessons in the school of the heavenly wisdom, and because he has thus escaped the fate that is to overtake the ungodly, unconverted rich man.

11 This fate is described by James in very graphic language, which rests on the words of Isa. 40:7, 8. James thinks of what he had often witnessed in Galilee, when the sirocco or the scorching wind[11] that blows from the desert and the blazing sun of summer so swiftly withered the fair flowers that they fell.[12] Isaiah's words are quoted again in 1 Peter 1:24, and there we have, as in Isaiah, a contrast between the fading flowers and the unfading, imperishable, eternal Word of God. As surely as the flowers, will the ungodly rich man fade away "in his goings," suddenly, it may be, in the course of his journeys for trade (4:13), or, "while still on the move," as Hort suggested.

Let the converted rich man exult in that he has escaped such a doom, and let him also exult in the fact that, whatever humiliation may have been his experience, whether by losing some of his wealth or in other ways, he has been made possessor of "the true riches" (Lk. 16:11), which he shares in common with the brother of low degree.

12 Both the brother of low degree and the rich brother will have to reckon with temptation, though their temp-

---

11 $\varkappa\alpha\acute{\upsilon}\sigma\omega\nu$ occurs often in LXX to describe the sirocco, or scorching south-east wind of Palestine, which comes blowing from the desert: see Jer. 18:17, Hos. 13:15, Jonah 4:8, etc. The word occurs again in N. T. of the burning heat of the sun, in Mt. 20:12 and Lk. 12:55.

12 $\grave{\epsilon}\xi\acute{\epsilon}\pi\epsilon\sigma\epsilon\nu$: more literally, falls *out*, or falls *away*, "a beautifully exact word to describe the dropping of the petals or corona out of the calyx, as an effect of drought, which would be more strikingly sudden under the hot eastern sun than in a temperate climate like ours" (C.G.T.).

tations may take different forms. James seems to be gliding quietly here from the idea of temptation as outward trial to the more sinister idea of temptation as inward incitement to evil, which, at any rate, is the dominant idea in the following verses. Before describing the spiritual tragedy of the man who succumbs to temptation, James describes in remarkable words the man who bravely endures temptation and emerges from it victorious. Having stood a test[13] which was far more severe than the test of fire that is applied to gold (1 Peter 1:7) and having shown that, by the grace of God, he has the pure gold of heaven in his character, he is crowned with the crown of life,[14] the crown which consists of life in all its range and fulness. This crown has been promised by the Lord to those who love Him, who love Him through all their trials, outward and inward, and in spite of them. "Love begets patience," says Bengel. Love to God in the soul tends to produce greater staying power in the soul, and this staying power strengthens the conviction that "all things work together for good to them that love God." (Rom. 8:28).

---

13   *Approved (δόκιμος)*. This word was often used by Greek writers to describe coins which have been tested and shown to be genuine: cf. the metaphor used in 1 Thess. 5:21. It is used here of persons, also in Rom. 14:18, Rom. 16:10 ("approved in Christ"), 2 Tim. 2:15 etc. The adjective with an opposite meaning, *not standing the test, rejected,* is applied to soil in Heb. 6:8 and to persons in 1 Cor. 9:29, etc.

14   *τὸν στέφανον τῆς ζωῆς*. This is what is called a genitive of apposition—the crown which *is* life, in all the fulness of the meaning of that great word; cf. the crown which *is* righteousness in all the fulness of its realisation (2 Tim. 4:8) and the crown which *is* glory in all the fulness of its manifestation (1 Pet. 5:4). Note the contrast between such crowns and the fading away of earthly prosperity, referred to in the preceding words. "Crown" in such N. T. passages as 1 Cor. 9:25 and 2 Tim. 4:8 is clearly a metaphor derived from the Greek games, the wreath of victory. But, in a writer so thoroughly Jewish as James, and in view of 2:5, the crown meant here is, perhaps, that of sovereignty or royalty. There may be an allusion here to a saying of Jesus which is not recorded in our Gospels, like the saying quoted by Paul in Acts 20:35.

1:13—18

13 Let no man say when he is tempted, I am tempted of God; for God cannot be tempted with evil, and he himself tempteth no man:

14 but each man is tempted, when he is drawn away by his own lust, and enticed.

15 Then the lust, when it hath conceived, beareth sin: and the sin, when it is fullgrown, bringeth forth death.

16 Be not deceived, my beloved brethren.

17 Every good gift and every perfect gift is from above, coming down from the Father of lights, with whom can be no variation, neither shadow that is cast by turning.

18 Of his own will he brought us forth by the word of truth, that we should be a kind of first fruits of his creatures.

13 James repudiates with horror the idea that God can ever incite[15] any one to sin. Such ideas as those expressed in so subtle a way in the poisonous honey of Omar Khayyam,

O Thou who didst with pitfall and with gin,
Beset the path I was to wander in,

are swept ruthlessly aside. James is thinking of some who might argue that, because trials come from God, then from God comes also the temptation to sin which is often aroused by the outward trial. This, however, is not true, and that because the very nature of God forbids such a blasphemous thought, "God is incapable of being tempted by evil" (Mof) "to do evil." (Wey.), neither does he, the all-holy One,

---

15 *Tempted (πειραζόμενος)*. This verb means sometimes to *test* with a *good* motive, as in Jn. 6:6, 2 Cor. 13:5 and Rev. 2:1, and in this good sense it is used of God's sending of trials, as in 1 Cor. 10:13, Heb. 11:17 and Rev. 3:10. It means at other times to *test* with a *bad, sinister* motive, in order to perplexity or failure (Mt. 19:3, Lk. 11:16, Jn. 8:6) or in order to lure into sin (1 Cor. 7:5, 1 Thess. 3:5 and here).

tempt any man. That temptation issues in spiritual disaster in many cases is due to the corrupt heart of man.

14 There is something in the corrupt heart of man, "his own desire," which responds to the bait which has been so cunningly placed in the trap of temptation by the arch-enemy of our souls.[16] He is beguiled and allured by his own desire, attracted by the bait. The well-known analysis given by Thomas à Kempis of the same kind of reaction to temptation as that described by James may be quoted: "First comes to mind a simple thought, then a strong imagination, afterwards delight and an evil movement and assent." This corresponds, says Moffat, "to what James means by illicit *desire*, the imagination toying with a forbidden idea, and then issuing in a decision of the will."

15 The mere fact of our being tempted does not involve in itself anything sinful. It is when the desire of man goes out to meet and embrace the forbidden thing and an unholy marriage takes place between these two, that sin is born. Once sin is born, it grows, and, unless it be counteracted and mastered by the grace of God, when it is full-grown, it brings forth death, death in all the breadth of the meaning of that dread word, death spiritual and death eternal, the death that lies beyond physical death for the ungodly. Thus, we have here the two destinies of man, in v. 12 the fulness of life that is to be the portion of those who love God and the death that is to be the inevitable doom of the persistent haters of God.

16 "Make no mistake about this, my beloved brothers" (Mof).

17 Nothing but good can come from God. He is the

---

16 *Drawn away and enticed (ἐξελκόμενος καὶ δελεαζόμενος).* The first verb, which occurs only here in N. T., contains a metaphor taken from hunting, and means "to lure forth," as game is lured from its covert. The second verb means "to entice as by a bait," a metaphor from hunting or from fishing. It is used often in the Greek Classics with the sense of enticing or seducing. It occurs again in 2 Peter 2:14 and 18.

Father of lights, first no doubt, as the Creator of the heavenly bodies, but also, and most of all, as the Source of all moral and spiritual light. God is unchangeable[17] in His being and in His attributes. As Horatius Bonar sings:

> "Light of the world! for ever, ever shining,
>   There is no change in Thee."

Nothing but good can come from Him who "knows no change of rising and setting, who casts no shadow on the earth" (Mof).[18] The "light that leads astray" is never "light from heaven," though Robert Burns sought to delude himself into the convenient belief that it sometimes is. How can the Father of lights ever lead His creatures into darkness? Think of the glorious perfections of the ever-blessed God and you can never entertain so pernicious an idea. "The moon is not always at the full," says Plummer, "the sun is sometimes eclipsed, and the stars suffer changes in

---

[17] *Variation (παραλλαγή)* This word conveys the idea of passing from one condition to another, and may here perhaps mean simply the change from light to darkness. We may find a contrast suggested between the natural sun, which varies its position in the sky from hour to hour and from month to month and the Eternal Source of light, who is absolutely unchangeable.

[18] *Shadow that is cast by turning (τροπῆς ἀποσκίασμα).* The word "shadow" suggests the idea of a shadow projected *from* one body to another, or in any way caused by the movements of a body. Thus, this phrase may mean, either (1) the shadow of night caused by the rotation of the earth, or (2) the shadow of eclipse caused by the revolution of a planet. The word "turning" is used by Homer and other Greek authors of the movements of the heavenly bodies, and it occurs, with similar associations, in LXX, in Deut. 33:14 and Job 38:33. This phrase may convey the thought that the Eternal Source of light casts no shadow on the earth, according to Moffat's translation, or perhaps more likely the idea that no change anywhere in the created universe can cast a shadow on *Him*, on His eternal brightness. Mayor suggests the translation, "overshadowing of mutability," and takes the whole passage to mean that God is alike incapable of change in His own nature, and incapable of being changed by the action of others.

like manner. In Him there is no change, no loss of light, no encroachment of shadow. There is never a time at which one could say that through momentary diminution in holiness it had become possible for Him to become a tempter."

18 God is always bestowing good gifts on men, and the most precious of all His gifts is the gift of a new heart. *Of His own will*, so to speak, putting His whole heart into it, He bestowed this gift on us, and it ill accords with that will, that holy will, which planted in us the seed of a new life of holiness, to say that we are ever tempted to *sin* by God. We have had already in v. 15 a terrible "bringing forth," now we have this blessed "bringing forth" which ushers us into a new world of thought and experience. Born again by the Word of truth,[19] by the Word of God (1 Peter 1:23), by the Word of the truth of the Gospel, which always bears fruit (Col. 1:5, 6), we have before us this destiny, that of being a kind of firstfruits[20] of the creatures of God. In Jer. 2:3 Israel is described as "holiness to the Lord and the firstfruits of His increase." Philo speaks of the Jews as being "set apart from the entire human race as a kind of first-fruits to their Maker and Father." The New Testament Church is God's Israel (Phil. 3:3, etc.), and it falls heir to the honour ascribed to Israel according to the flesh in Jer. 2:3. Just as the fruits which ripen first herald the new season of ingathering, so those who had been born again by the Word of truth announce a new order of things in the spiritual world, and they are the pledge and the prophecy of a golden world-wide harvest yet to be gathered in.

---

[19] $\lambda\acute{o}\gamma\omega$ $\dot{\alpha}\lambda\eta\theta\epsilon\acute{\iota}\alpha\varsigma$ means the word or message which conveys the saving truth of the Gospel to the soul: cf. 2 Cor. 6:7, Eph. 1:13 and Col. 1:5, 6.

[20] $\dot{\alpha}\pi\alpha\rho\chi\acute{\eta}\nu$. This idea, which rests on Lev. 23:9, 10, occurs with a variety of applications in N. T., as, e.g., in Rom. 8:23, Rom. 16:5, 1 Cor. 16:15, and 1 Cor. 15:20 and 23.

19   Ye know this, my beloved brethren. But let every man be swift to hear, slow to speak, slow to wrath:

20   for the wrath of man worketh not the righteousness of God.

21   Wherefore putting away all filthiness and overflowing of wickedness, receive with meekness the implanted word, which is able to save your souls.

22   But be ye doers of the word, and not hearers only, deluding your own selves.

23   For if any one is a hearer of the word and not a doer, he is like unto a man beholding his natural face in a mirror:

24   for he beholdeth himself, and goeth away, and straightway forgetteth what manner of man he was.

25   But he that looketh into the perfect law, the law of liberty, and so continueth, being not a hearer that forgetteth but a doer that worketh, this man shall be blessed in his doing.

26   If any man thinketh himself to be religious, while he bridleth not his tongue but deceiveth his heart, this man's religion is vain.

27   Pure religion and undefiled before our God and Father is this, to visit the fatherless and widows in their affliction, and to keep oneself unspotted from the world.

The Word of truth must be treated in the right way. We must be doers of the Word (vv. 19—25) and our religion must be one of active benevolence and not one of mere words (vv. 26, 27).

19 *You know this*[21] — act upon your knowledge. It is by the Word of truth that we have been regenerated, the Word that brings to us the deepest truth about God and

---

21   *You know this (ἴστε).* In the English A. V. we have, instead of these words, the word "wherefore," which represents a reading found in some of the later MSS. In ℵ ABC, Vulg., etc., we have the reading adopted here.

37

man and everything. We must listen continually to that Word, and not spend so much time in airing our own views and listening to the sound of our own voices. We have here the first of the things that James has to say about the evil that is often wrought by the tongue, but what he says here is mild in comparison with what he will have to say later on, especially in his third chapter. It is possibly the case that, in all that he has to say about the tongue, James has in his mind especially the harm that is often done to the cause of God through the uncontrolled use of the tongue by *teachers in the Christian Church*. There are far too many loud and voluble talkers, both in the Church and the world, he would have us realise. If we listen more and talk less, we will not be so ready to fall into that wild and passionate wrath which serves no good purpose. Ceaseless talkers may easily degenerate into fierce controversialists, and may indulge in wild denunciations of those who oppose them, denunciations in which they may sometimes fancy they are doing God service, but which really do more harm than good.

20 Such wrath hinders the spread and triumph of God's righteousness, both in the individual soul and in the world at large. There is such a thing as righteous wrath, but there is also a wild and uncontrolled wrath which works much mischief. It does not really advance the best interests of the cause of God.

21 James now proceeds to give a deeply suggestive description of the way in which the Word of God should be heard and received. Moffat translates here, "so clear away all the foul rank growth of malice, and make a soil of modesty for the Word . . . .",i.e., he thinks that we have only one metaphor here, that of the soil. It seems, however, that "putting away" is a metaphor derived from the laying aside of clothes, as it is in Rom. 13:12, Eph. 4:22, Col. 3:8, and Heb. 12:1 (stripping for the race). The metaphor is continued in "filthiness"; cf. 2:2, "vile clothing," where the corresponding adjective is used. But this metaphor does glide

here into the other methaphor of the soil. The Word is a
seed, and it must have a clean soil. All filthiness caused by
the overflowing malice of the heart — so we may combine
the two expressions used by James — must be got rid of.
On Col. 3:8 Lightfoot says that "malice", at least in the
New Testament, does not describe vice generally, but the
vicious nature which is bent on doing harm to others, and
he says that it is well defined by Calvin (on Eph. 4:31) as
the depravity of a mind which is opposed to humanity and
just dealing. The Word must be received with *meekness*,
with a truly docile mind, however sharp the prickings of
the Sword of the Spirit may sometimes be, as we are made
uncomfortable through the exposure of the sin of our lives
and of our hearts. James describes the Word as the *implanted* Word, the Word "which roots itself inwardly with
power to save your souls," as Moffat has it. For an example
of such "receiving" compare Acts 17:11.

22 Hearing the Word is not enough. *"Become doers,
show yourselves* doers of the Word." The distinction
between hearing and doing is emphasised in the Parable of
the Sower, and, following on our Lord's interpretation of
that Parable, as given in Luke's Gospel, we have our Lord's
words which are recorded in Luke 8:21. To stop short at
hearing and to fail to go on to doing leads to self-deception,
the worst kind of deception. Yet no delusion is so common
among hearers of the Word in this age, as in all ages. It is
greatly to be feared that there are multitudes of "sermon-
tasters," to use a striking old Scotch phrase, who have never
yet tasted that the Lord is gracious. If we content ourselves
with sentimental admiration of the preacher, or simply with
the enjoyment of an emotional and mental treat, and if the
sermon does not move us to do something to our lives that
sadly needs to be done, we are indeed in a parlous spiritual
state. That is the point of the simile of the mirror, and a
very caustic simile it is.

23 The mirror James had in mind was a piece of bur-
nished metal, usually made of a mixture of copper and tin.

The word he uses occurs once again, where Paul says in 1 Cor. 13:12, according to Moffat's translation, "At present we only see the baffling reflections in a mirror." Paul is there contrasting the imperfect knowledge of truth which we get through the reflection in a mirror with direct knowledge of the reality. Here in James we have the more familiar idea of a man seeing his natural face, literally, the face of his birth, the face he brought into the world with him, in a mirror. The mirror of the Word of God reveals man to himself; it shows him that there is something seriously wrong with the nature which he brought into the world with him.

24 Two classes of hearers are now described. We have first the man who glances into the mirror and then goes his way and at once forgets what he saw, so that no lasting impression is made upon him. He beheld himself and went away, an aorist tense followed by a perfect tense, indicating the suddenness of the action and the permanence of the result. Just a glance and he is off, and he has stayed away — that is the force of the graphic language of James here. The mirror of the Word of God never flatters; that is why some do not like to gaze too long or too often into it. We may recall the story that is told of an African princess. When for the first time she looked into a small mirror and saw what she looked like, in a sudden rage she dashed it to the ground so that it was broken in pieces.

25 Here, however, is another man who seems to be described as bending over the mirror, as peering into[22] it, in order to examine more minutely what it reveals to him. He gazes intently into it and continues gazing. That leads us into a line of thought that is somewhat different from the thought of James here, but is quite in harmony with other

---

22 *He that looketh into (ὁ παρακύψας)*. The verb used here contains the idea of a man bending over a mirror, in order to examine more minutely what it reveals, peering into it. It is used of John and Mary looking into the empty sepulchre (Jn. 20:5 and 11). It occurs also in that remarkable verse, 1 Pet. 1:12.

parts of Scripture, a line of thought that is suggested by
John Bunyan, when he writes of the wonderful glass which
the Shepherds of the Delectable Mountains showed to
Christiana and Mercy. "Now the glass was one of a thou-
sand. It would present a man, one way, with his own
features exactly; and turn it but another way, and it would
show one the very face and similitude of the Prince of
pilgrims Himself. Yea, I have talked with those that can
tell, and have said they have seen the very crown of thorns
upon His head by looking into this glass; they have therein
also seen the holes in His hands, in His feet, and His side."
The man who continues looking into the mirror of God's
Word sees in it things far more wonderful than his own
face. He sees not only his filthy garments, not only the spots
and stains on his life; he sees in it Christ, the Christ of the
thorn-crowned brow, the Christ of the Cross, his Saviour,
whose blood cleanses him from all sin.

James here has not quite the same line of thought, but
it comes to the same thing in the end. He says that this
man finds that he is looking into the perfect law, namely,
the law of liberty, the "royal law," as James calls it in 2:8.
This man realises very speedily how far he has come short
of the divine standard, he sees his deep, dark, defiling sin.
That moves him to take action, he repents, he turns to God,
he is cleansed and forgiven, and then he becomes, not a
hearer that forgetteth,[23] but a doer of the work, a practical
doer of righteousness, and he is blessed in his doing. Such
a man is not a forgetful hearer but a doer who works, and
he seeks to conform his life more and more to the law of
liberty: as he sees Christ more and more clearly in the
Word, he is changed more and more into His image, "from
one degree of radiant holiness to another' (2 Cor. 3:18,

---

23 *A hearer that forgetteth* (ἀκροατὴς ἐπιλησμονῆς) is, quite
literally, "a hearer of forgetfulness," a hearer marked by forgetfulness,
a Greek construction which we find also in a phrase like "judge of
unrighteousness" in Lk. 18:6 and in 2:4, "judges of evil thoughts."

Wey.). This man regards the Law of Christ as *perfect*, because it is final and complete, as contrasted with the Law of Moses which was not that; he regards it as the law of *liberty*, because he finds in it the expression of a Father's love for His children, and not the announcement of the stern precepts of a despot. While the Law of Christ in no way relaxes the stern demands of the law of unchangeable righteousness, it speaks in the heart as the Law of a Father whose service is perfect freedom, and that makes the yoke easy and the burden light.

26 We come now to another example of self-deception, that of the man who thinks that he is religious[24] when he is not. The words of James here are of quite general application, but they may well convey a special warning to all preachers and teachers in the Church. It is painfully easy to degenerate into one like Mr. Talkative, whose portrait is painted with such biting satire by John Bunyan. He was "the son of one Saywell, who dwelt in Prating Row, and notwithstanding his fine tongue, he is but a sorry fellow." The man who does not bridle[25] his tongue may very easily deceive his own heart, as, for example, by the dangerous delusion that fine talk can make up for the absence of practical, godly living, or by being careless in his speech, fancying that words matter very little, forgetting one of Our Lord's most solemn utterances (Matt. 12:36, 37), or, if he be a preacher, by pouring out a great flood of words with little reality of personal experience in them. Such religion is futile.

---

24 *Religious ... religion.* The first word *(θρησκός)* occurs only here in N. T., the second *(θρησκεία)* occurs twice here, and again in Acts 26:5 and Col. 2:18. As is explained in the exposition, it refers to the outward manifestation of religion.

25 *Bridle (χαλιναγωγῶν).* This verb, which occurs again in 3:2, seems to have been used by James for the first time in Greek literature. The metaphor suggests that the tongue can rush us away into far more dangerous regions than a runaway steed.

27 Pure and unsoiled religion[26] in the presence of the God who is our Father is a very different thing from a religion which has its chief manifestation in elaborate outward washings, and it is also a very different thing from the religion that is mere talk. James does not intend here to describe the whole of religion. The word he uses is used by Josephus to describe the public worship of God, and it indicates the outward manifestation of religion. The things mentioned by James, as Trench says, are "the body of which godliness, or the love of God, is the informing soul." In contrast to the outwardly religious Pharisee who devoured widows' houses (Mk. 12:40), Christians should visit orphans and widows in their affliction in order to point them to Him who is the Father of the fatherless and the Judge of the widow (Ps. 68:6). In Old Testament times the fatherless and widows were specially cared for and protected by Jehovah: see Deut. 27:19; Ps. 94:6; Ps. 146:9; Jer. 7:6; Mal. 3:5; etc. It is not surprising, therefore, that in New Testament times we should find the fatherless and widows cared for with even deeper tenderness; in one of the earliest scenes of First Century Church life widows have a place in the daily giving of relief (Acts 6:1). In the discharge of such charitable tasks there might sometimes be a danger of moral and spiritual pollution, and, therefore, the Christian is also exhorted by James to keep himself unspotted from "the contagion of the world's slow stain." There must be no selfish isolation of himself from all contact with the woes of humanity, but, at the same time, he must seek earnestly to maintain personal purity in all his intercourse with others.

---

26 *Undefiled* and *unspotted*. The first adjective ($\dot{\alpha}\mu\dot{\iota}\alpha\nu\tau o\varsigma$) is used to describe the inheritance of the redeemed in 1 Pet. 1:4, and it is used with reference to our Lord as our Great High Priest in Heb. 7:26. It occurs once again, in Heb. 13:4. The other adjective ($\ddot{\alpha}\sigma\pi\iota\lambda o\nu$) is found in 1 Tim. 6:14, 1 Pet. 1:19 and 2 Pet. 3:14; cf. "not having spot" in Eph. 5:27.

CHAPTER II

UNMERCIFUL CONDUCT AND THE MERCIFUL MAN

2:1—13

1 My brethren, hold not the faith of our Lord Jesus Christ, the Lord of glory, with respect of persons.

2 For if there come into your synagogue a man with a gold ring, in fine clothing, and there come in also a poor man in vile clothing;

3 and ye have regard to him that weareth the fine clothing, and say, Sit thou here in a good place; and ye say to the poor man, Stand thou there, or sit under my footstool;

4 do ye not make distinctions among yourselves, and become judges with evil thoughts?

5 Hearken, my beloved brethren; did not God choose them that are poor as to the world to be rich in faith, and heirs of the kingdom which he promised to them that love him?

6 But ye have dishonored the poor man. Do not the rich oppress you, and themselves drag you before the judgment seats?

7 Do not they blaspheme the honorable name by which ye are called?

8 Howbeit if ye fulfil the royal law, according to the scripture, Thou shalt love thy neighbor as thyself, ye do well:

9 but if ye have respect of persons, ye commit sin, being convicted by the law as transgressors.

10 For whosoever shall keep the whole law, and yet stumble in one point, he is become guilty of all.

11 For he that said, Do not commit adultery, said also, Do not kill. Now if thou dost not commit adultery, but killest, thou art become a transgressor of the law.

12 So speak ye, and so do, as men that are to be judged by a law of liberty.

13 For judgment is without mercy to him that hath showed no mercy: mercy glorieth against judgment.

All unmerciful conduct will be punished mercilessly by the God of love. At His judgment seat the merciful man alone will have cause for rejoicing (2:1—13).

1 James has been dealing with some faults that are to be found sometimes among hearers of the Word of truth, and he now proceeds to refer to another serious fault that may mar worship in the Christian assembly. He begins his exhortation by using once again his favourite form of address, "My brothers," and it is very appropriate here, as he is about to deal with a glaring example of the lack of Christian love and brotherhood. We note that the man who has been supposed by some to depreciate faith here calls Christianity "the faith of our Lord Jesus Christ."

Our Lord seems to be called here "the Glory."[1] That is how the words are understood by Bengel, Mayor, Moffat, Warfield and others: "our Lord Jesus Christ, the Glory." In 1 Cor. 2:8 Paul designates Jesus "the Lord of glory," the One whose eternal home is the Glory of God, but James does not here associate the word "glory" with "Lord." It seems likely that there is in the words of James a reference to the Shekinah, which, according to Rabbinical teaching, was the visible glory of God's presence (the cloud, or the light in the cloud) resting above the Cherubim or filling the Temple: see 1 Kings 8:10, etc. In Zech. 2:5 we read: "I, saith Jehovah, will be unto her a wall of fire round about, and I will be the Glory in the midst of her." As Warfield says, in his book *The Lord of Glory,* "Jesus was, in a word, the Glory of God, the Shekinah. It is thus that James thought

---

[1] $\tau\tilde{\eta}\varsigma$ $\delta\delta\xi\eta\varsigma$. In an article entitled "Glory," in Hastings' DCG., it is said that the phrase "the glory of God" "must mean His essential and unchanging Godhead as revealed to man. And the familiar ascription 'Glory to God' would imply not only a right human praise, but the assigning to God of what He truly *is,* for nothing higher can be given Him." God is "the God of glory" (Acts 7:2), and the word "glory" as used here by James, lifts our thoughts into the realm of the eternal, in the manner suggested in the exposition. For James, as for Paul, the glory of God was radiant on the face of Christ (2 Cor. 4:6, Weymouth).

and spoke of his own brother, who died a violent and
shameful death while still in His first youth!" No wonder
Warfield adds the remark "Surely there is a phenomenon
here which may well awaken enquiry." Westcott says on
John 1:14, "Christ, the Light of the world, is seen by the
believer to be the manifested Glory of God." Moffat says
that, in the word "glory" as used by James, we have "a
striking term for Christ as the full manifestation of the
presence and majesty of God." In *His* presence such scenes
as the one about to be described ought to be impossible.
All distinctions between rich and poor are less than nothing
in the blaze of the glory which shines in Him, in which the
fine clothes of the rich man and the shabby clothes of the
poor man seem very little different.

2-3 In this little vignette of First Century Church life
we see very clearly indeed these two men, the gold-ringed
man,[2] possibly with many rings flashing on his fingers, in fine
clothing,[3] and the poor man in his shabby clothing; both
of them it would appear, unbelievers. The rich man is
given a comfortable seat, while the poor man has either to
stand or to sit on the floor. James accuses those who can
stoop to such base conduct of indulging in respect of
persons,[4] that is, of treating the two men according to their
outward appearance.

---

[2] ἀνὴρ χρυσοδακτύλιος. The Parable of the Prodigal Son indicates
that the wearing of rings was not unknown among the Jews. G. F.
Watts, in one of his great paintings, shows us the Rich Young Ruler
turning his back on Jesus, and on one of his fingers a ring can be seen
flashing.

[3] ἐν ἐσθῆτι λαμπρᾷ. The adjective here used is used of a star in
Rev. 22:16. It is used with the sense of clear or transparent in
Rev. 22:1. Here it means splendid or magnificent. We find it com-
bined with "clothing," as here, in Lk. 23:11 and Acts 10:30.

[4] προσωπολημψίαις. Three times Paul says that there is no respect
of persons with God (Rom. 2:11; Eph. 6:9 and Col. 3:25). Peter
has the cognate adjective in Acts 10:34 and the cognate adverb in
1 Pet. 1:17. There is a plural used here, which may be taken to
indicate the various occasions and instances in which this fault may

4 You are making the wrong kind of distinction between human beings and thus proving that you are judges with evil, thoughts.

5 Bring your false estimates into the light of the Gospel. The distinction that God makes between human beings is of a very different kind. The electing love of God has laid hold of many who are poor as to the world, poor in earthly goods,[5] and has made them rich with the true riches which means being rich towards God (Lk. 12:21), rich in faith and heirs of the Kingdom which He promised to them that love Him, as He promised to them the crown of life (1:12). To be loved by God and to love Him in return is to be rich indeed, it is indeed to possess "all things," as Paul says in Rom. 8:32 and 1 Cor. 3:21—23. Paul says in 1 Cor. 1:26 that *not many* men of good birth have been effectually called, he does not say that not *any* have been called. James here does not say that no rich men are ever chosen, nor does he say that all the poor are chosen.

6 But you, in marked contrast to God, have dishonoured the poor man. And, why show such favour to your rich fellow-Jews? Are they not among the most bitter and cruel enemies of Christ and His people? Do they not oppress[6] you and drag[7] you into court?

---

reveal itself. To respect persons is, quite literally, to *receive faces*, that is, to judge men by something external and not by their real character.

[5] τοὺς πτωχοὺς τῷ κόσμῳ. (*Poor as to the world*). This is the reading in ℵ ABC, etc. The reading "poor of this world" has very slight support.

[6] καταδυναστεύουσιν is a very strong word, and in the only other place where it is found in N. T. (Acts 10:38), it refers to oppression by the *devil*. Weymouth translates here, "yet is it not the rich who grind you down?" It is used in LXX, in Amos 8:4 (oppression of the poor), Jer. 7:6 (oppression of the stranger, the fatherless and widows) and in Ezek. 18:12 (oppression of the poor and needy).

[7] ἕλκουσιν is used elsewhere, as here, of dragging with force and violence, as in Acts 16:19 and 21:30. But in two great verses in the Fourth Gospel it means to draw gently by sweet inward influence and power (Jn. 6:44 and 12:32).

7 Do they not blaspheme that fair name that was invoked upon you, that is, in Baptism? As our Lord is called the Good Shepherd, so He bears the good, the beautiful Name, "the Name high over all, in heaven and earth and sky." The Name of Christ came to be specially spoken of as *the Name* (Acts 5:31). In the Old Testament it is frequently said of Israel that the Name of Jehovah was named upon them (Deut. 28:10, Jer. 14:9, Amos 9:12, etc.). The idea conveyed by the phrase is that of dedication to the service of God. In the Shepherd of Hermas the same phrase is used of those who had been baptized into the Christian Church. In the New Testament it occurs only once again and then on the lips of James, as he quotes the words of Amos 9:12 at the Jerusalem Council (Acts 15:17).

8 It may be that you will make a feeble attempt to defend your conduct by saying that, in showing such respect to the rich man, you are only trying to obey the Royal Law, the Law which rules as sovereign over all Laws, the Law of love. If you could make good your claim that you have acted from such a motive, your conduct would be shown to be praiseworthy, but it is quite impossible to make good such a claim.

9 You cannot shelter under such a plea, because you have clearly been guilty of respect of persons, and have thus broken the Royal Law, which surely demands equality of treatment for rich and poor. You thus stand condemned as law-breakers, who are exposed to the just judgment of God.

10-11 The Law of God is a unified whole and disregard[8] of one commandment means that you are disobedient to the Lawgiver. So, do not entertain the delusion that the keeping of one isolated commandment of the Decalogue will compensate for the breach of some other of

---

8 *Stumble (πταίση)* For this word used to describe transgressions of the Law of God cf. 3:2 and Rom. 11:11. To cross over the line which marks the "way" is to become a transgressor (verse 9), and the picture here may be that of a transgressor tripping over the border which marks the way (EGT).

its requirements. As Farrar says, "To break one commandment is to break all, for it is to violate the principle of obedience, just as it matters not at what particular point a man breaks his way out of an enclosure, if he is forbidden to go out of it at all."

12 The conception of the Law of God which James is condemning is the conception which thinks of it as a collection of unconnected rules. That may fittingly be regarded as a slavish conception, and the Law of Christ is a law of liberty: it calls for the free manifestation in the outward conduct of the loving spirit within. We shall be judged at the final Assize, not so much by the observance or neglect of this or that external rule as by the degree in which our heart and life have been dominated by the spirit of love.

13 The callous treatment meted out to the poor man in the service was one manifestation of the merciless spirit. James now deals with the general question of harshness, and not merely harshness shown to the poor. His words remind us of some of our Lord's words (Mt. 5:7; Mt. 18:35; Lk. 6:36). The merciless will receive no mercy. If, by the grace of God, and as imitators of our Father (Lk. 6:36), we show mercy in our behaviour to our fellowmen, we shall experience mercy in God's judgment of us, and mercy glorieth against judgment, which may be taken to mean that mercy, full of glad confidence inspired in the soul by the love of God poured out there (Rom. 5:5), has no fear of judgment. Love, says John, has boldness in the day of judgment (1 John 4:17).

14 What doth it profit, my brethren, if a man say he hath faith, but have not works? can that faith save him?

15 If a brother or sister be naked and in lack of daily food,

16 and one of you say unto them, Go in peace, be ye warmed and filled; and yet ye give them not the things needful to the body; what doth it profit?

17 Even so faith, if it have not works, is dead in itself.

18 Yea, a man will say, Thou hast faith, and I have works: show me thy faith apart from thy works, and I by my works will show thee my faith.

19 Thou believest that God is one; thou doest well: the demons also believe, and shudder.

20 But wilt thou know, O vain man, that faith apart from works is barren?

21 Was not Abraham our father justified by works, in that he offered up Isaac his son upon the altar?

22 Thou seest that faith wrought with his works, and by works was faith made perfect;

23 and the scripture was fulfilled which saith, And Abraham believed God, and it was reckoned unto him for righteousness; and he was called the friend of God.

24 Ye see that by works a man is justified, and not only by faith.

25 And in like manner was not also Rahab the harlot justified by works, in that she received the messengers, and sent them out another way?

26 For as the body apart from the spirit is dead, even so faith apart from works is dead.

From this point to the end of this chapter James deals with the subject of faith and works, and the general theme is that faith is worthless unless it be accompanied by works.

14 James has already exhorted his readers to become

doers of the Word, and, as Moffat says, having already touched this string, "he now strikes some resonant chords from it." You have *faith* in our Lord Jesus Christ, you say (v. 1), but is it a living, operative faith, the faith which works by means of love (Gal. 5:6)? Can the faith that is not accompanied by moral character and conduct save any one at the judgment seat of a God who is merciless to the man who shows no mercy?

15-16 If you coolly dismiss with pious good wishes a shivering[9] and starving fellow-Christian,[10] one who is as poor as the man in shabby clothes already described, and take no practical steps to help such, what is the use of any faith that you may have? In 1 John 3:17, 18 a similar picture of heartless conduct is drawn, but the language of James is, perhaps, more incisive.

17 Your faith is a dead faith, inwardly dead as well as outwardly inoperative. A living faith always manifests itself in deeds.

18 "Yea a man will say, some one will say...." The man whom James imagines as breaking in on the argument is possibly, as Farrar suggests, "a Gentile Christian who makes a perfectly true criticism of the worthlessness of an idle orthodoxy." Select any man at random in the Christian brotherhood, and he will make such a criticism. This Gentile Christian says to the exponent of a barren orthodoxy, "Thou hast faith and I have works (as well); show me thy faith apart from the works — which you cannot do — and I by my works will show thee my faith." James adopts this argument as his own. It is utterly im-

---

9 *Naked (γυμνοί)* has here the force of "ill-clad," as in Mt. 25:36, ff. Peter was probably clad only in his under-garment, when he wrapped his outer garment around him and cast himself into the sea on a memorable occasion (Jn. 21:7).

10 The specific mention of "sister" is worthy of notice; it shows that we are dealing here with a Christian document. Sisters must receive equality of treatment with brothers in the Church of Him with whom there is neither male nor female (Gal. 3:28).

51

possible for one man to set up, so to speak, as a specialist in faith and another man to set up as a specialist in works. That kind of separation between faith and works is quite illogical. Faith and good works must always go together. As Paul says, when we are saved by faith and not by works, we are regenerated men, *created in Christ Jesus unto good works* (Eph. 2:8—10).

19 The mere acceptance and holding of a sound creed is not enough. It was the proud boast of the Jew that he was a monotheist. One of the grandest declarations of the Law of Moses was this: "Hear, O Israel: Jehovah our God is one Jehovah." It is good to believe that, but what ought to be the fruit of that belief in our lives? "And thou shalt love Jehovah thy God with all thy heart, and with all thy soul, and with all thy might" (Deut. 6:4, 5). Thou believest that God is one, but remember that the demons believe and shudder.[11] Their belief in the existence of God begets in them only a shivering fear and a horrible dread; it does not lead them to trust in God and it does not inspire in them loving service to Him. The verb "shudder" means properly to bristle, to stiffen, like hair standing on end, as in Job 4:15 (LXX), but it may also express a high degree of awe or terror, as in Dan. 7:15 (LXX). A mere acknowledgment of the first article of the creed does not carry us very far in the realm of spiritual experience. The faith that produces the kind of mental reaction manifested by the demons is poles apart from the faith of the Christian believer, who has peace with God (Rom. 5:1), who exults in God (Rom. 5:11), who ought to have the perfect love which casts out fear (1 John 4:18).

It may be fairly argued that, if James is contradicting

---

11 φρίσσουσιν. We may think of how the demons in the Gospels exhibited terror in the presence of the Son of God (Mk. 5:7, Mt. 8:29, etc.). These words of James seem to have made a deep impression on some of the early Christian writers; e.g. Justin Martyr, in his *Dialogue with Trypho the Jew*, speaks of even the demons "shuddering" at Jesus.

here Paul's doctrine of Justification by Faith, he goes about his refutation in a strange way. The Pauline doctrine centres in the death and resurrection of Jesus, not in a mere conviction regarding the existence of the one living and true God. The plain truth is that Paul and James deal with entirely different subjects. Paul, in his teaching on Justification, is combating Jewish legalism; James is making his protest, in the interests of morality, against Antinomianism. We may put it like this: they are not antagonists facing each other with crossed swords; they stand back to back, confronting different foes of the Gospel.

20 James now addresses the exponent of a barren orthodoxy still more pointedly, and he deals with him rather drastically. He addresses him as an "empty man," as the Greek means quite literally, an empty-headed man. The "empty man," says Trench, "is one in whom the higher wisdom has found no entrance, but who is puffed up with a vain conceit of his own spiritual insight." "You senseless fellow" is Moffat's translation. Can you not get this into your head, James says to this man, that faith without works is an utterly barren[12] thing, producing no harvest of virtue in the life? He then gives two illustrations from the O. T. of the great truth that it is by good works that the presence and the reality of a living faith are demonstrated.

21-24 The first case is that of Abraham's offering up his son upon the altar.[13] He is held up as an outstanding

---

12 *Barren (ἀργή)* is probably the true reading, not "dead." This word means, literally, *without work*, producing nothing of any importance. It is translated "idle" in Mt. 20:3 and 6, in 1 Tim. 5:13, in Titus 1:12 ("idle gluttons," which is certainly better than "slow bellies" in English A. V.). It occurs again in 2 Pet. 1:8, where English A. V. has "barren." In Mt. 12:6 our Lord speaks of idle *words*: see commentary on 5:12.

13 *θυσιαστήριον*. Abraham in a very real sense did offer Isaac, on the altar of his own will, having proved his willingness to surrender Isaac to God. The word here used is used in Mt. 5:23 of the altar of burnt-offering and in Lk. 1:11 of the altar of incense. A different word is used once (Acts 17:23) to describe a heathen altar.

example of faith by the writer of the Epistle to the Hebrews
(11:8—19) and by Paul in Rom. 4:3 and Gal. 3:6—9. In
Heb. 11:17—19, as here in v. 21, reference is made to the
offering up of Isaac by Abraham. Paul twice quotes Gen.
15:6 (Rom. 4:3 and Gal. 3:6), as James does here in v. 23.
Again the fact may be stressed that there is no real contradiction between the teaching of Paul and that of James,
though James lays special stress on the fact that Abraham's
faith was *perfected* in one signal work that was inspired by
his faith. Faith co-operated with his works (v. 22) and was
perfected by them, we may say, as the tree is perfected by
its fruits, which show that the tree is a living tree. Abraham's
faith, says Luther, "was *completed,* not that it had been
imperfect, but that it was consummated in its exercise."
"If," says Ropes, "when the test came, the faith had not
been matched by works, then it would have been proved
to be an incomplete faith." The remarkable words of
Heb. 11:17 may be noted: *"He who had received the
promises* offered up his only-begotten son." It looked as
though by the offering up of Isaac he would for ever make
it impossible for the promises to be fulfilled, but, because
they were the promises of *God,* on which Abraham's faith
rested, they encouraged him to proceed with that crowning
act of obedience to God.

Thus the words of Gen. 15:6 were fulfilled, their full
meaning was brought out. Luther called that verse the
greatest verse in Genesis. As the result of this great experience, Abraham was brought into closer fellowship with God,
and he was called the Friend of God. He is not so described
in Genesis, but we find that lofty title bestowed on him in
2 Chron. 20:7 and Isa. 41:8. It is said that among the Arabs
Abraham is known to this day as "Friend of God," sometimes, simply, as "the Friend." You see, James proceeds to
say (v. 24), no longer addressing the "vain man," but the
whole body of Christian believers, that by works a man is
justified and not by faith *alone.* Lightfoot says of Paul's
words in Gal. 5:6, already quoted, that they "bridge over

the gulf which seems to separate the language of St. Paul and St. James. Both assert a principle of practical energy, as opposed to a barren inactive theory." We have noted several times that James has no desire whatever to deny the value of faith, and it is not likely that he has the faintest desire to do so here, with Gen. 15:6 in mind. It is quite wrong to regard James as teaching here that faith makes no contribution to Justification, but it must be a right faith, he insists; not a faith severed from works, but a faith which proves its reality and vitality in works. According to a saying of the Reformers, we are justified by faith alone, but not by the faith that is alone.

25 The second O. T. illustration is vastly different, and has to do with a person who was vastly different from Abraham. He was a Jew, Rahab was a Canaanite: he was the great pioneer of faith, "the father of all them that believe" (Rom. 4:11). She had none of the spiritual privileges enjoyed by Abraham, she was as a matter of fact, a woman stained by gross sin, yet she, too, by the grace of God, walked in the steps of the faith of Abraham (Rom. 4:12). Her faith is also extolled in Heb. 11:31, she finds a place in the Genealogy of our Lord in the first chapter of Matthew, and her case shows how wide is the application of the principle which James is illustrating, and it also proves that differences of sex, differences of character and differences of social rank matter nothing in the realm of grace. Rahab claimed that she had "dealt kindly" with the messengers of Israel (Josh. 2:12), and her action was inspired by a true faith in Israel's God. She had heard of the great works of Jehovah in connection with the Exodus and what followed on it, and they had inspired in her not merely a mere belief that such a God existed (that God is one), but that He was God in heaven above and in the earth beneath, who would faithfully keep all His promises (Josh. 2:9—11). She wanted to be identified with the Israel of God, and the reality of her faith in Israel's God came out in this, that she received the messengers, hid them, and sent them out another way, by a window instead of the door, and to the mountain instead of straight back to the camp of Israel, thus enabling them to escape the danger zone, where her fellow townsmen might be on the lookout for the invaders (Josh. 2:15, 16 and 22). Such were the works that proved the reality and the strength of her recently-born faith.

26 James concludes his argument here by making use of this figure of the body and the soul. When body and spirit are separated, death and putrefaction result: so, if faith be separated from works, it is a dead faith; it is "dead in itself" (v. 17). Faith of that kind indicates the absence of all real spiritual life, and shows that spiritual death and corruption still reign.

CHAPTER III

BRIDLING THE TONGUE

3:1—12

1 Be not many of you teachers, my brethren, knowing that we shall receive heavier judgment.

2 For in many things we all stumble. If any stumbleth not in word, the same is a perfect man, able to bridle the whole body also.

3 Now if we put the horses' bridles into their mouths that they may obey us, we turn about their whole body also.

4 Behold, the ships also, though they are so great and are driven by rough winds, are yet turned about by a very small rudder, whither the impulse of the steersman willeth.

5 So the tongue also is a little member, and boasteth great things. Behold, how much wood is kindled by how small a fire.

6 And the tongue is a fire: the world of iniquity among our members is the tongue, which defileth the whole body, and setteth on fire the wheel of nature, and is set on fire by hell.

7 For every kind of beasts and birds, of creeping things and things in the sea, is tamed, and hath been tamed by mankind:

8 but the tongue can no man tame; it is a restless evil, it is full of deadly poison.

9 Therewith bless we the Lord and Father; and therewith curse we men, who are made after the likeness of God:

10 out of the same mouth cometh forth blessing and cursing. My brethren, these things ought not so to be.

11 Doth the fountain send forth from the same opening sweet water and bitter?

12 can a fig tree, my brethren, yield olives, or a vine figs? neither can salt water yield sweet.

The sins of the tongue, with special reference to some of the dangers which beset Christian teachers (vv. 1—12).

1 W. H. Bennett (*Century Bible*) says that "3:1—4:12 expand and expound 1:19, 20. The necessity for the advice given here is shewn by 1 Cor 14:20—33, from which we gather that the eagerness of the Christians to speak in public reduced their meetings to a perfect babel." Moffat translates here: "My brothers, do not swell the ranks of the teachers; remember, we teachers will be judged with special strictness." In what he writes in the first chapter about the tongue (vv. 19, 20 and 26) James had, possibly, Christian teachers chiefly in mind, but here there is no doubt whatever as to the people whom he desires to castigate. We read of teachers in the Church of Antioch (Acts 13:1); a true teacher is one of the gifts of the Ascended Lord (Eph. 4:11). It can be inferred here that there was a desire among believers known to James, as at Corinth, to aspire too lightheartedly to the work of teachers without considering with sufficient seriousness the tremendous responsibility involved. Teachers, among whom James includes himself, will be judged with special strictness, he says, and that sobering reflection may well solemnise a preacher every time he enters a pulpit. According to an old saying, no one should become a minister of the Gospel, unless he can't help it, unless he has something of the spirit of Paul when he said, "Necessity is laid upon me." (1 Cor. 9:16). "Do not swell the ranks of the teachers," says James. We wonder if he meant to suggest quietly that there were too many empty windbags among them already.

2 In many things we stumble, all of us, and in nothing more frequently or more seriously than in speech. Not to stumble in speech, which is a most necessary virtue in a teacher, is tremendously difficult. A story is told about a young man who put himself into the hands of a Christian teacher of ancient times, in order to be trained in knowledge and virtue. The first lesson given to him was to learn by heart the first verse of the 39th Psalm, "I said, I will take heed to my ways, that I sin not with my tongue: I will keep my mouth with a bridle, while the wicked is before me."

At the end of a month he returned to report that he had not yet learned that lesson in all its meaning and implications. Month after month he returned with the same story, until he came to see that the bridling of the tongue involves a lifelong discipline. James says, in his graphic and vigorous style, that really to master the tongue is to bridle the whole body, so that it will not run away with us, like a runaway horse. If anywhere under the sun there could be found a man who had perfectly bridled the tongue, he would be a perfect man, or a man who is spiritually mature.

3 James uses two figures, which can be found in combination also in some old Greek writers. The first figure is suggested by "bridle" in the preceding verse. The bridle, though it is so small, exerts its curbing influence over the whole body of the strong horse, so that it pursues a straight and not an erratic course, a course that is determined by its rider.

4 The second figure is that of the ship and its rudder. The *so great*[1] ship is opposed to the *very small* rudder.[2] The man who has command of the very small rudder, which in an ancient ship was a kind of oar or paddle, working in a rowlock or port-hole, can influence the movement of the big ship, whatever winds may beat upon that ship.[3] It is not the winds, however strong and fierce[4] they may be, but

---

[1] This adjective occurs again in 2 Cor. 1:10, Heb. 2:3 and Rev. 16:18.

[2] πηδάλιον. This word occurs once again in N. T., in the story of Paul's voyage to Rome, in Acts 27:40. A second century writer, describing one of the Alexandrian grain ships, such as the one on which Paul sailed, says: "The crew was like a small army. And they were saying she carried as much corn as would feed every soul in Attica for a year. And all depends for safety on one little atom of a man who controls that great rudder with a mere broomstick of a tiller" (quoted by Cobern in *The New Archaeological Discoveries*, p. 580).

[3] *Driven (ἐλαυνόμενα):* this verb is used of clouds driven by winds in 2 Pet. 1:17, of sailors propelling a ship by oars in Mk. 6:19, of demons driving to some place a man whom they possessed in Lk. 8:29.

[4] *Rough winds:* Moffat has here "stiff winds" and Weymouth

the impulse[5] of the man at the helm[6] that determines the ship's course. Is James thinking here of the old days on fishing smacks of the Galilean Lake?

5 The tongue is a little member of the body, "that little bit of flesh between the jaws," to quote Luther's description of it, but it can boast great things and it can work much mischief. The same thought is conveyed in the graphic figure of the forest fire, which is a familiar figure in the O. T.: cf. Ps. 83:14, Isa. 9:18, Zech. 12:6, etc. We find this metaphor in other ancient literature, for example, in the Greek poet Euripedes, who compares the incautious revelation of a secret to a spark catching hold of a forest. The English A.V. has here the colourless rendering, "Behold how great a matter a little fire kindleth," whereas the language of James is remarkably graphic. It is, literally, *"What* a fire kindles *what* a forest."[7] Weymouth translates:

"strong gales." The adjective *(σκληρῶν)* is used with the sense of "stern" or "harsh" in Mt. 25:24 and with the sense of "dangerous" in the words spoken by Christ to Paul on the Damascus road (Acts 26:14).

[5] ὁρμή occurs once again in N. T., in Acts 14:5, where it means "a hostile movement or rush of people." Weymouth has here "the caprice of the man at the helm."

[6] τοῦ εὐθύνοντος means, quite literally, "of the man who leads or guides straight." The graphic picture in this 4th verse "gives the impression that the writer gives the result of personal observation" (EGT).

[7] *How much wood:* ὕλη occurs frequently in the Greek Classics, from Homer downwards, in the sense given in the English A. V., "matter," i.e., a mass of materials, timber, firewood, etc. But it is also used, perhaps more often, in the sense of forest. The aptness and the frequency of the illustration of the forest fire in ancient literature favours that interpretation here. Reference is made in the exposition to the frequency of that illustration, both in profane and Biblical literature. Carr (CGT) refers to passages in Virgil's *Aeneid* which describe the terror, the swift progress, and the violence and destructive fury of the forest fire. Carr also reminds us that the life of the individual or of society the tongue has often set aflame by speech that curses (verse 9) or rouses passion or suggests evil or creates slander and suspicion, and he says that "on such words and their results, tragedies like *Othello* and *Romola* are founded."

"Remember how a mere spark may set a vast forest in flames." How often has a little word, carelessly spoken, caused destructive conflagrations in State and Church!

6 Moffat's very vigorous translation may be quoted. "And the tongue is a fire, the tongue proves a very world of mischief among our members, staining the whole body and setting fire to the round circle of existence with a flame fed by hell." This is a deeply interesting verse, and also a startling one, while it contains some things that are rather difficult of interpretation. Manifold are the evils emanating from an uncontrolled tongue, so that it exhibits itself as a very world of mischief[8] in our members, a prolific source of iniquity, a universe of iniquity. Many strong things are said in Scripture about the tongue, in the Book of Proverbs and elsewhere, but none of them is quite so caustic as what James says here. He emphasises the thought of the tongue as *defiling*.[9] Filthy speech spreads its slime over all who listen to it. Paul speaks of *rotten* words (Eph. 4:29) and of the more refined kind of wit, the persiflage that may also, too often, have its tincture of subtly concealed filth in it, the "jesting" which is so closely allied often to "filthiness" and "foolish talking" (Eph. 5:4).

The tongue, James says, may also inflame the wheel of nature, literally, the wheel of birth, the same word as occurs in 1:23, the word occurring elsewhere in N.T. only in

---

[8] *The world of iniquity* (ὁ κόσμος τῆς ἀδικίας). This translation is adopted by most scholars ancient and modern. Carr (CGT) argues for the translation "the adornment" or "embellishment of iniquity," "that which gives it its fair outward show and yet conceals its inner foulness." "The evil tongue," he says, "adorns and embellishes iniquity and yet it defiles and stains the whole body and personality of a man." It may be admitted that that is a possible interpretation, but it is extremely doubtful. It may be noted, however, that *cosmos* means "adornment" in 1 Pet. 3:3, and the cognate verb means "to adorn" in Mt. 12:44, 1 Pet. 3:5, Titus 2:10 and Rev. 21:2 and 19.

[9] σπιλοῦσα. This verb occurs just once again in N. T., in the 23rd verse of the Epistle of Jude. We had the adjective "undefiled," from the same root, in 1:27.

Matt. 1:18 and Luke 1:14. Some take this difficult phrase to mean "the wheel of existence, of life"; we might compare such an English phrase as "the machinery of life." Others take it to mean "the wheel of human origin," which, as soon as men are born, begins to revolve, the *course* of life, or the *round* of life. Moffat, as we have seen, has "the round circle of existence," and Weymouth translates "the whole round of our lives." Our changeful life goes on its way unceasingly like a revolving wheel. J. B. Mayor takes it to mean the wheel of birth, of this earthly transitory life to which birth admits us, "the circle or round of this transitory life, which is easily inflamed and disturbed by misused speech, stirring up man against man, class against class, nation against nation; such speech sets at naught truth, morality and religion and is itself set on fire by Gehenna. . . Surely such a state of things must be limited to this lower existence; it could find no place in heaven."

We have here the only occurrence outside the Gospels of the word "Gehenna." In the Gospels it is found some ten times on the lips of our Lord as describing the place of the future punishment of the wicked, where their worm dieth not and their fire is not quenched (Mk. 9:47). In Mt. 5:22 we have our Lord's words "the Gehenna of fire," and in Mt. 23:33 His words "the judgment of Gehenna." This dread symbolical language seems to be derived from the valley of the children of Hinnom (2 Kings 23:10), where children used to be burned in honour of Moloch. King Josiah abolished these hideous sacrifices, and the Jews came to regard the place with deep abhorrence and they cast into this deep valley on the south east of Jerusalem all manner of refuse, and also, possibly, the dead bodies of criminals who had been executed and the dead bodies of animals. Fires were needed to consume the refuse and this truly awe-inspiring symbol of the ever-burning fire and the crawling worms is used by our Lord to shadow forth dimly the fate that awaits the ungodly. Hell is the rubbish heap of the Universe — is that the idea suggested?

7 Every kind of beasts.... is being tamed,[10] and has been tamed, of mankind: cf. Gen. 1 and Ps. 8, that "lyric echo" of the Creation story, as Delitzsch called it. The two tenses, present and perfect, indicate that man's dominion over the creatures is no new fact, though fresh illustrations of it come to light every day.

8 The tongue is a destructive fire, James has said, and now he describes it as a venemous beast which no man can tame. "It combines," says Plummer, "the ferocity of the tiger, and the mockery of the ape with the subtlety of the serpent." Weymouth translates here: "But the tongue no man or woman is able to tame." That looks more like insinuation than interpretation, and it has the savour of a sarcastic jibe, a somewhat surprising thing to encounter in a serious translation of the N. T. And yet, of course, James quite strictly does mean that no human being can tame the tongue. "The tongue no one of men, no one of the human race, can tame." According to Augustine, "He does not say that no one can tame the tongue, but no one of men; so that, when it is tamed, we confess that this is brought about by the pity, the help, the grace of God." The tongue is a restless evil, like an untameable beast. The same adjective is used here as in 1:8.[11] It occurs in a passage in the Shepherd of Hermas. "Slander is evil: it is a restless demon, never at peace." The tongue is often full of death-bearing[12] venom, like a poisonous snake. Paul quotes in Rom. 3:13 the words of Ps. 140:3, "the poison of asps is under their lips."

9 There is a tragic inconsistency that may appear among

---

[10] δαμάζεται. This verb occurs only once elsewhere in N. T., of the demoniac whom no man had strength to tame (Mk. 5:4). It is used in classical Greek of the taming of horses.

[11] See note on that passage.

[12] θανατηφόρος (*deadly*) occurs only here in N. T., and means, literally, death-bearing. It occurs in LXX, in Num. 18:22, where for, "lest they bear sin and die," LXX reads "to receive a death-bearing sin."

Christians, even among Christian teachers. Out of the same mouth may come, in close succession, blessing and cursing[13] — blessing bestowed on the Lord and Father — a unique phrase — on God in His sovereignty and His love, and curses hurled at men who are made in the image of God. It is good to remind ourselves that, though we have grievously strayed from the way of the Lord, we were made in His image, and some traces of that image still remain in fallen man. As "Rabbi" Duncan used to say, we should sometimes take a walk in Eden, and we should remember that man was created before he fell.

10 Again James pleads affectionately with his readers as his *brothers,* and he implores them to realise that these things *ought not so to be.* This phrase occurs only here in N. T., and it denotes something that is utterly incongruous, something that is quite out of harmony with the nature of things.

11–12 Listen to the voice of Nature, if you have become for the time deaf to deeper voices. The great world around you, with its fruitful trees and its gushing[14] springs,[15] in the beautiful harmony of its operations, rebukes many a time the inconsistencies of human conduct. Such illustrations would suggest themselves naturally to a man who was probably writing in Palestine, where fig trees, vines and olive trees abounded, and where salt springs could be found, on the shore of the Dead Sea and at Tiberias on the Galilean Lake. The parallel with our Lord's words in Mt. 7:16 should be

---

13 "This does not imply a combination of blessing and cursing . . .; it simply means that the mouth which blesses God when uttering prayer, curses men at some other times, *e.g.,* during embittered controversy" (EGT).

14 βρύει (*send forth*). This verb occurs only here in N. T. In Greek literature it usually had an intransitive sense, to gush, to teem with juices, to be full to bursting. It was used sometimes of the swelling buds of plants, and figuratively of various kinds of fulness. Here it is transitive—to cause to burst forth.

15 ὀπή (*opening*). This word occurs elsewhere in N. T. only in Heb. 11:38. In that verse Moffat has "caves and gullies."

noted. "No application of these illustrations is made," says Ropes, "and James turns abruptly to another aspect of the matter. The passage well illustrates his vividness and fertility of illustration, as well as his method of popular suggestiveness, rather than systematic development of the thought."

THE FALSE AND THE TRUE WISDOM

13 Who is wise and understanding among you? let him show by his good life his works in meekness of wisdom.

14 But if ye have bitter jealousy and faction in your heart, glory not and lie not against the truth.

15 This wisdom is not a wisdom that cometh down from above, but is earthly, sensual, devilish.

16 For where jealousy and faction are, there is confusion and every vile deed.

17 But the wisdom that is from above is first pure, then peaceable, gentle, easy to be entreated, full of mercy and good fruits, without variance, without hypocrisy.

18 And the fruit of righteousness is sown in peace for them that make peace.

13 James here specifically addresses the Christian teacher. The word "wise man" was often applied to a teacher, and the word "understanding," which is found only here in N. T., indicates one who is an expert in any subject, so that the first word may describe the possession of wisdom as such, and the second may relate to its application to the practical details of life. As Plummer paraphrases the words of James here: "Who among you professes to have superior knowledge, spiritual or practical? . . . . Let every one who claims to have a superiority which entitles him to teach others *prove* his superiority by his good *life*. Once more it is a call for deeds, and not words — for conduct, and not for professions." How unweariedly does James press home the truth which John Bunyan enunciated in the words, "The soul of religion is the practical part." However deep a man's wisdom, however skilful he may be in applying that wisdom in practical directions, that does not make up for the want of a good life. We have heard, no doubt, of the preacher of inconsistent life to whom one said one day, "What you are speaks so loudly that I cannot hear what you say."

The real proof of the presence of the true wisdom in the teacher is that he shows by his good life[16] his works, in the meekness which this wisdom inspires: thus he will prove that he really possesses the heavenly wisdom which God gives in answer to prayer (1:5). In 1:21 the hearer of the Word was exhorted to receive it with meekness, and now the teacher of the Word is exhorted to manifest this same gracious quality of mind. Paul exhorts Christian teachers not to strive, but to be gentle towards all, in meekness correcting them that oppose themselves (2 Tim. 2:24, 25). Peter, too, says that those who defend the faith should do so with meekness and fear (1 Pet. 3:15). Such meekness will advance the cause of God far more efficaciously than the overbearing temper that tries to shout down opponents or may even move the teacher to hurl curses at the heads of those who oppose themselves to him. Meekness, says Martensen in his *Christian Ethics,* "is the power of *love* to quell the ebullition of anger, to restrain the violent and hasty temper." It is an expression of the love which is not easily provoked (1 Cor. 13:5). Its supreme examplar is our Lord Himself (2 Cor. 10:1).

14 If this meekness be lacking, bitter jealousy and faction,[17] or party-spirit may possess the heart. The word translated "jealousy" has sometimes a good meaning, the meaning of "zeal" of the right kind, as in John 2:19, but it has often the meaning of "jealousy" of a wrong kind, as here and in Paul's list of the "works of the flesh" (Gal. 5:20)

---

16 The word translated "life" (ἀναστροφή) means "manner of life, conduct, behavior." It occurs often in N. T., in such passages as Gal. 1:13, Eph. 4:22, 1 Pet. 1:15 and 18 and 1 Pet. 2:12. It describes the life of movement and action, and the "good life" is the perfect life of action (CGT). In Heb. 13:7 we have the phrase "The issue of their life." "Look back upon the close of their career, and copy their faith" (Moffat).

17 ἐριθεία. On this word see Lightfoot's note on Gal. 5:20.

and in such passages as Rom. 13:13 and 1 Cor. 3:3. The bitterness of this evil thing is far more unpleasant and far more dangerous than the bitterness of the springs of Nature (v. 11, the only other place in N. T. where this word "bitterness" occurs). The word "faction" also occurs in Gal. 5:20, and we have it also in such passages as Phil. 1:14 and 2:3. It means, says Hort, "the vice of a leader of a party created for his own pride; it is partly ambition and partly pride. It may involve the haughty forcing of his own views on others." The Revised Standard Version of 1946 translates "selfish ambition"; both Moffat and Weymouth translate "rivalry." If bitter jealousy and selfish ambition be in your hearts, do not pride yourselves on that, though some do, fancying, it may be, that by their bitter partisanship and their uncontrolled, unintelligent zeal they are helping on the cause of God. That sort of thing, too often, means being false to the truth. It is, of course, the case that the message you proclaim is the Word of truth (1:18) and that to stray from the truth means spiritual ruin (5:19, 20), and, therefore, zeal for the truth is commendable. But we must remember that the truth of Christianity cannot be advanced, or defended worthily, except in a Christian spirit, a fact which keen controversialists have not always remembered. Some ardent Christians may defeat their own ends by doubtful methods; the soundest theology may fail to appeal to the minds of outsiders, if it be advocated by men who are self-seeking partisans or men who are unscrupulous in their controversial activities.

15 The people just described may pride themselves on their wisdom, but the sad fact is that their wisdom, which is utterly lacking in meekness, is not God-inspired. James describes it by three adjectives which form a climax: it is earthly[18] and never rises far above the earth, it is entirely

---

18 $\dot{\varepsilon}\pi\dot{\imath}\gamma\varepsilon\iota o\varsigma$. The false wisdom is earthly because its horizon does not extend beyond this world and because it is inspired entirely by motives which are popular among those who "mind earthly things" (Phil. 3:19).

unspiritual,[19] owing nothing to the inspiration of the Holy
Spirit, and its ultimate source is to be sought in the ma-
lignant demons of the pit.[20] The second adjective is the
most interesting and the most difficult to express with
precision in English. I Cor. 2:14 throws light on its
meaning, and so, even more clearly, does the 19th verse of
the Epistle of Jude, where it is said to describe those who
have not the Spirit. Weymouth translates there, "They are
men of the world, wholly unspiritual." This false wisdom
is demon-like because it is full of pride and malignity and
selfish ambition.

16 The demonic character of the false wisdom is seen
in this, that it results in a condition of anarchy in the
Church. In 1 Cor. 14:33 Paul uses this word "confusion,"[21]
and sets it in contrast with "peace." It is used in Lk 21:9

---

[19] *Sensual.* It is difficult to find an exact English equivalent for
this Greek adjective. It may be taken as describing that which pertains
to the natural life which man and animals share. The word is ψυχικός
and, according to Grimm–Thayer, it means "*governed by the ψυχή,*
i.e., the sensuous nature with its subjection to appetite and passion."
It occurs six times in N. T. In 1 Cor. 15 it is found three times, in
verses 43 and 46, as describing the meanness of our earthly body as
compared with the body which is to be, the spiritual body, the body
which will be a fitting instrument and vehicle for the Holy Spirit.
There this adjective is contrasted with the adjective "spiritual." That
is the case also in 1 Cor. 2:14, where Weymouth translates, "The
unspiritual man rejects the things of the Spirit of God." The precise
nuance of meaning enshrined in this word appears with special clearness in the 19th verse of the Epistle of Jude where the "sensual" man is
declared to be the man who *has not the Spirit,* the man who relies
entirely on the forces and endowments of unregenerate human nature.
Thus, the wisdom which is here in view is, to quote Grimm–Thayer
again, "a wisdom in harmony with the corrupt desires and affections,
and springing from them."

[20] *Devilish (δαιμονιώδης).* Better, perhaps, demonic. Satan is
never spoken of as a demon, but his servants, the evil spirits are, as in
2:19. The false wisdom, James says, pertains to this earth, not to the
world above, to mere nature, not to the Spirit; to the hostile spirits of
evil, not to God.

[21] ἀκαταστασία. See note on 1:8.

of the tumults and commotions of war, but James uses it here of dissensions in the Church, as Paul does in 2 Cor. 12:20. The lack of meekness and therefore of the true wisdom may easily open the door for the entrance into the Church of confusion and every vile deed. The adjective "vile," says Trench in his *New Testament Synonyms,* "contemplates evil under the aspect of its good-for-nothing-ness, the impossibility of any true gain ever coming forth from it"; it occurs again in Jn. 3:20, Jn. 5:29, Rom. 9:11, 2 Cor. 5:10 and Tit. 2:8.

17 This wonderfully full and exhaustive description of the true wisdom, as Dr. James A. Robertson (of Aberdeen) says, in his *Hidden Romance of the New Testament,* "reads like James' veiled picture of the gentle heart of Love that, many a time beside the bench, refused to be provoked by his bitter tongue." As contrasted with the wisdom which is inspired from below, this wisdom is from above, coming down from the upper world of light and glory, as one of the precious gifts of the Father of lights (1:17). It is, first of all, pure, rebuking by its purity that scene of confusion and vile deeds which has just been described. It is pure because it has its origin in the All-holy God and it comes forth from His holy throne, and it always inspires in its recipient a desire to live a holy life, in which the pollution of the world (1:27) and the pollution caused by the tongue (3:6) are escaped. The man who is guided by this wisdom desires to be free from all impure motives and methods, to be free especially, we may say in the light of the context, from wrong headed aggressiveness and quarrelsomeness. Commenting on the adjective which James here uses, as it occurs in 1 John 3:3, Westcott says that it suggests "the notion of shrinking from contamination, of a delicate sensibility to pollution of any kind."

This wisdom is peaceable, because it is not easily provoked into controversy, but is inclined to adopt quieter methods, if that be possible, and if careful attention be paid to the divine order which declares that the heavenly wisdom is

70

first pure, *then* peaceable. We must be pure in heart before we can be true peacemakers (Mt. 5:8, 9). This wisdom is gentle,[22] or sweetly reasonable. The man who possesses the quality of character meant here does not always insist on standing on his own rights. Aristotle, in his *Ethics* contrasts such sweet reasonableness with strict justice. The adjective used here is associated with freedom from contentiousness in 1 Tim. 3:3 and Tit. 3:2. The cognate noun is applied, along with meekness, to Our Lord in 2 Cor. 10:1. This wisdom, further, is easy to be entreated,[23] or *conciliatory*, as Moffat translates. This adjective occurs only here in N. T. Mayor suggests the translations "submissive," "docile," or "tractable." The American R.S.V. has "open to reason." This wisdom is full of mercy and good fruits, not of death-bearing venom (v. 8). We have an example of such good fruits in 1:27, while their absence was condemned in 2:15.

The last two adjectives are translated by Moffat *unambiguous* and *straightforward*. The American R.S.V. has *without uncertainty and insincerity*. The first adjective is found only here in N. T., the second qualifies "love" in Rom. 12:9 and 2 Cor. 6:6, "faith" in 1 Tim. 1:4 and 2 Tim. 1:5, and "love of the brethren" in 1 Pet. 1:22. On the first adjective Dr. R. W. Dale says: "The man who is governed by worldly wisdom is apt to be shifty — what he himself would call politic. He sets his sails to the prevailing wind; speaks well of men of whom he spoke ill yesterday — not because the men themselves are better than they were, but because yesterday he could get nothing by speaking well of them, and to-day he can." We never know where we are

---

[22] ἐπιεικής. This word contains the idea of *yieldingness*. Matthew Arnold suggested for the corresponding noun the translation "sweet reasonableness." This noun is translated "gentleness" in 2 Cor. 10:1 and "clemency" in Acts 24:4. The adjective occurs again in 1 Tim. 3:3, Titus 3:2 and 1 Pet. 2:18, where it is uniformly translated "gentle."

[23] εὐπειθής. It is possible to assign an active sense to this adjective —winning its way by gentleness, persuasive.

with men like that. The second adjective seems to mean that teaching ought never to be equivocal or evasive, but straightforward, literally, free from hypocrisy or pretence. Moffat quotes very aptly some words which Cardinal Newman once wrote in a letter to Cardinal Manning: "I do not know whether I am on my head or my heels when I have active relations with you." Moffat says that "these last two words rule out the habit of using speech to half reveal and half conceal the mind of the speaker, who has something (as we say) at the back of his mind all the time; any subtle reserve or disingenuous dealing in Christian intercourse is certain to create friction and misunderstanding. Whereas, James means, the qualities he has just been praising make for good feeling and mutual harmony in any community."

18 In v. 16 the evil results of the false wisdom were described; now the ultimate result of the true wisdom is declared to be *the fruit which is righteousness;* cf. the crown which is life (1:12), the shield which is faith (1 Thess. 5:8), etc. Man's wrath does not work out God's righteousness (1:20), but the harvest of righteousness will always be reaped some day by those who sow in peace, by those whose lives are indwelt by the peace which James has been praising. Peace is the atmosphere in which, or the conditions under which we may expect the good seed to ripen to the fruit which is righteousness. And the sowers are not merely *lovers* of peace, but *makers* of peace. "The peacemakers who sow in peace reap righteousness" (Mof). It is only they who can ever hope to reap that golden harvest, not the undisciplined talkers who seek by rant and wild denunciation to advance the cause of truth. Dr. Dale says that "not through a fierce and angry temper, by which we ourselves are liable to be betrayed into gross injustice and into many other sins, and which will also provoke other men to sin, but by gentleness, kindness, peaceableness, will righteousness at last come to prevail."

CHAPTER IV

WARNINGS AGAINST WORLDLINESS AND PRIDE

4:1—17

1 Whence come wars and whence come fightings among you? come they not hence, even of your pleasures that war in your members?

2 Ye lust, and have not: ye kill, and covet, and cannot obtain: ye fight and war; ye have not, because ye ask not.

3 Ye ask, and receive not, because ye ask amiss, that ye may spend it in your pleasures.

4 Ye adulteresses, know ye not that the friendship of the world is enmity with God? Whosoever therefore would be a friend of the world maketh himself an enemy of God.

5 Or think ye that the scripture speaketh in vain? Doth the spirit which he made to dwell in us long unto envying?

6 But he giveth more grace. Wherefore the scripture saith, God resisteth the proud, but giveth grace to the humble.

7 Be subject therefore unto God; but resist the devil, and he will flee from you.

8 Draw nigh to God, and he will draw nigh to you. Cleanse your hands, ye doubleminded.

9 Be afflicted, and mourn, and weep: let your laughter be turned to mourning, and your joy to heaviness.

10 Humble yourselves in the sight of the Lord, and he shall exalt you.

11 Speak not one against another, brethren. He that speaketh against a brother, or judgeth his brother, speaketh against the law, and judgeth the law: but if thou judgest the law, thou art not a doer of the law, but a judge.

12 One only is the lawgiver and judge, even he who is able to save and to destroy: but who art thou that judgest thy neighbor?

13 Come now, ye that say, To-day or to-morrow we will go into this city, and spend a year there, and trade, and get gain:

14 wheras ye know not what shall be on the morrow. What is your life? For ye are a vapor that appeareth for a little time, and then vanisheth away.

15 For that ye ought to say, If the Lord will, we shall both live, and do this or that.

16 But now ye glory in your vauntings: all such glorying is evil.

17 To him therefore that knoweth to do good, and doeth it not, to him it is sin.

You are very far from possessing this peace. Too many of you are ruled by wordly desires and have been guilty of spiritual adultery. Repent of your sin and humble yourselves before God (vv. 1—12).

We may well, as Farrar says in his *Early Days of Christianity,* feel surprise at such a picture as James here paints. "Wars, fightings, pleasures that are ever setting out as it were on hostile expeditions, disappointed desires, frustrated envy and even fruitless murder to supply wants which would have been granted to prayer — then, again, prayers utterly neglected or themselves tainted with sin because misdirected to reckless gratification, and because ruined by contentiousness and selfishness — all this spiritual adultery, the divorce of the soul from God to the love of the world — is this indeed a picture of the condition of Christian Churches within thirty years of the death of Christ?" Farrar's idea is that this Epistle was written at some time during the seventh decade of our era, but it was probably written some twenty years earlier than that, and this fact makes the picture still more surprising. See Introduction.

An explanation may be found, partly, in the fact that James was influenced by the state of things around him in Judaea as he writes, and, partly, by the fact that, though he addresses his letter to *Christian* Jews, he does not always draw a fixed line of separation between converted Jews and unconverted Jews. As Lange says: "James puts his Epistle into the hands of the Jewish Christians that he might influence all Jews, as it was a missionary instruction to the

converted for the unconverted, and to the truly converted
for the half-converted." In Judaea strifes about the Law
were fierce and violent, those "legal battles" to which Paul
refers in Tit. 3:9, using the second noun that James uses
in the first verse here. The Temple had become a brigands'
cave (Mt. 21:13). The fanatical sect of the Zealots were at
all times ready to stir up the people to insurrection and
murder. And, as Farrar says, "the dagger of the assassin was
often secretly employed to get rid of a political opponent."
Many of the Christians were, no doubt, being contaminated
by the corrupt atmosphere around them.

1 You are far from living in that atmosphere of peace
that has been described. There is an atmosphere of wars and
battles around you, and whence come these wars and these
battles? They come from the corrupt heart of man (cf. 1:14).
The word "pleasures" used here twice by James, occurs
again in Lk. 8:14, Tit. 3:3 and 2 Pet. 2:13, and in every
case it denotes pleasures of the wrong kind. Desires after
such pleasures war in your members and they always disturb
the peace of your life and the lives of others. Paul writes of
the law of sin in our member which wars against the law
of the mind (Rom. 7:23) and Peter writes of fleshly desires
which war against the soul (1 Pet. 2:11), but the language
of James is of a more general character. These desires for
the wrong kind of pleasures which are at work in your
members, he says, wage ceaseless warfare against everything
that stands in the way of their gratification, and they express
themselves in covetous longings after the wealth and the
possessions of others, and thus strife and bloodshed arise,
and even murders may result.

2 Such a life is an unsatisfied life. You desire and have
not; you murder even and hotly desire to possess, and you
are not able to get what your fevered hearts so hotly long
for; you fight and war, but you never attain to real satis-
faction of soul — in that sense, you *have* not; and the reason
is this, that you have not asked of Him from whom all
blessings flow, of Him in whom alone the soul of man can

find rest and peace. He is the God who gives liberally His good and perfect gifts to all who ask in faith (1:5, 6 and 17) and He will always keep His promises (Mt. 7:7 and 8, Jn. 16:24, etc.).

3 It is possible, however, to ask *wrongly*. "If we ask anything according to His will, He heareth us" (1 Jn. 5:14), but, if we merely seek some material gain which we intend to spend *in* our pleasures, solely in the sphere of activity in which our carnal pleasures can find gratification, we need not expect to have our prayers answered. It is interesting to observe that this verb "spend", which is used of the Prodigal Son in Lk. 15:14, is found, on the lips of James, in Acts 21:24. James has here, first, the active voice of the verb *ask* and then the middle voice, which he also uses in the preceding verse. Mayor seeks to bring out the distinction in this way: "You ask with the lips and receive no answer, because you do not ask with the heart." It is possible sometimes to have the words of the mouth quite correct in prayer while the heart all the time may be fixed on carnal delights. It is not surprising that such prayers are unanswered (cf. Ps. 66:18). There have been many instances of men asking *amiss*. Augustine would ask God to give him chastity, but "not yet." Italian brigands have been known to promise to their saints a share of the profits of their murders. No doubt, James knew men like the Pharisees who were scathingly denounced by Jesus, who could make long prayers, while all the time they were devouring widows' houses (Mk. 12:40).

4 The true reading here seems to be "adulteresses."[1] A

---

[1] The English A. V. has here "ye adulterers and adulteresses," which is the reading in some of the later MSS. The other reading is found in AB and some important Versions, and is probably the correct reading. Its difficulty is in its favor. Some later scribe, possibly, inserted "adulterers," because he thought this verse was to be taken literally, and it seemed strange that James should refer to one sex only. But, in the light of the succeeding context, the words must certainly be regarded as figurative.

familiar Old Testament idea is that Jehovah is the Husband
of His people; see Isa. 54:5, Jer. 3:20 and Hosea, *passim*.
To this corresponds the N. T. idea of the Church as the
Bride of Christ (2 Cor. 11:2; Eph. 5:24—28; Rev. 19:7 and
21:9). Hence, no doubt, the feminine here. Departure from
the living and true God is spiritual adultery, according to
Ps. 73:27 and other O. T. passages. *You* have broken your
marriage vows to God, James says to his readers, if you
are a friend of the world. That is the force of the question
which he asks and the statement which he makes here.
There are two rivals for the love and the allegiance of the
human heart, God and the world. Whoever, then, chooses
to be a friend of the world, comes forward as an enemy of
God. To make pleasure the chief end of life, to be lovers
of pleasures more than lovers of God (2 Tim. 3:4), is
to be on good terms with the persons and forces which are
hostile to God. The question and statement in this verse
lead on directly to the extremely difficult fifth verse.

5 The Scripture[2] never speaks *emptily*, or without
meaning. All it says is said with the utmost earnestness,
and it all has a very purpose and a very definite message.
One of the translations suggested ·in the margin seems to

---

2 ἡ γραφή. λέγει. Lightfoot, on Gal. 3:22, says that " 'the Scripture' (the singular) in N. T. always means a particular passage of
Scripture." Sometimes that is undoubtedly the case, but there are sound
reasons for holding that it is not invariably the case. Warfield in an
article entitled "Scripture" in Hastings' DCG, holds that the prevailing
classical application of "Scripture" to entire documents can also be
seen in N. T., the idea conveyed in some N. T. passages being that of
the O. T. in "its completeness as a unitary whole." He cites about
20 cases in N. T. where that idea seems more natural, this verse being
one of them; other passages are Jn. 2:22, Jn. 10:35 and 2 Pet. 1:20.
James here, quite likely, does not refer to any particular passage, but to
the tenor of several O. T. passages. It may be difficult to know for
certain what these passages are, but that James is appealing to the
authority of Scripture is certain. Carr's assertion that the citation "is
from an unknown source, but the form in which it is made gives the
words an authority equal to that of the O. T." has very little indeed
to commend it.

bring out, more or less clearly, the thought of James here. "That Spirit which He made to dwell in us yearneth for us even unto jealous envy." On the question of the two rivals for the love and allegiance of the heart Scripture says this: "The Spirit which He made to dwell in us,[3] the Holy Spirit, yearns over us with what may be called jealous envy, with an intensity of desire which borders on jealous envy. He longs for the wholehearted undivided love of His people with an intensity which is often present in human jealousy, but, at the same time, with a purity which is, in most cases, absent from human jealousy. The verb "long" or "yearn", where it occurs elsewhere in N. T., always has a good meaning: see Rom. 1:11, Phil. 1:8 and 1 Pet. 2:2. It usually has in it the idea of yearning with strong affection: such an idea is clearly seen in Phil. 1:8 and in such verses as 1 Thes. 3:6 and 2 Tim. 1:4. The longing meant here, then, is not an evil longing of the human spirit, as is suggested in the English A. V., but the earnest longing of the Holy Spirit for the whole heart of the believer. That thought harmonises well with the context here. God is a jealous Lover, and He will tolerate no rival in His child's heart; no spiritual adultery and no alien friendship can be tolerated for a moment by Him.

But, what is the Scripture referred to? It has often been thought that James has here some kind of reference to Exod. 20:5, "I Jehovah thy God am a jealous God." The reference may not be to any particular part of the O. T., but to the tenor of the meaning of many passages, e.g., such a passage as Deut. 6:15 or such a passage as Deut. 32:10 and 11, where the same verb "long" occurs in LXX. In the same chapter, in verses 19—21, we have the idea of the jealousy of Jehovah expressed in view of Israel's unfaith-

---

[3] κατῴκισεν (*He made to dwell*) is the reading in ℵ AB, and it seems to make it clear that the reference is, not to the human spirit, but to the Holy Spirit, who dwells in the spirit of the believer. Cf. Jn. 14:17, Rom. 8:11, 1 Cor. 6:19, etc.

fulness. Scripture, indeed, often expresses such ideas, and it never speaks emptily, it means all it says. "The Spirit given to guide Israel was a Spirit of holiness in the sense that He could not brook sin in those with whom He dealt" (see B. B. Warfield in *Presbyterian and Reformed Review*, Vol. VI, 1895, p. 681).

6 The standard is a lofty one, but He giveth a greater grace, in view of the greater requirement. The Holy Spirit bestows richer supplies of grace in order that the believer may attain to that complete surrender to the yearnings of the Divine Love that is expected of him. It is to the humble that this greater grace is given, that is, to those who realise how far they still come short of the wholehearted devotion that God yearns for. They should be encouraged to expect all needed grace by what Scripture says in Prov. 3:34, a verse which is also quoted in 1 Pet. 5:5. God sets Himself against the proud man, the man who fancies that he is conspicuous beyond others, that he outshines them, as the Greek word suggests, so that the proud man has a very formidable foe indeed, whereas to the humble God comes with reviving grace (Ps. 138:6, Isa. 57:15), with exalting grace (v. 10).

7 Set yourselves, therefore, as under God, His loyal subjects and not His enemies, against whom He sets Himself. *But,* resist the devil,[4] take a bold stand against the devil, the arch-enemy of the Lord. The devil is the *slanderer* who slanders God to man and man to God, and men show that they belong to his family when they live in malice, in envy and hatred. His power is great, but he meets his match in the humble man, the man who is subject to God, who, strong in the "more grace" given him and drawing ever renewed supplies from the fulness that is in Christ (Jn. 1:16), takes a bold stand against him. From such a man the devil *flees,* and that says Bengel, is "A gladsome

---

[4] The personality of Satan, as elsewhere in Scripture, is assumed; cf. Eph. 4:27; 6:16, etc.

word *(laetum verbum)."* Compare 1 Pet. 5:6—9, "humble yourselves.... Keep cool, keep awake (Moffat), for your adversary the devil.... whom resist" (same word as that used by James).

8 The verb "draw near" is used in LXX of the priests offering sacrifices or ministering in the Temple, but also in a wider sense of all worshippers, as in Isa. 29:13 and Hos. 12:6. All believers are priests, and in the 19th verse of the seventh chapter of the Epistle to the Hebrews we read of the "better hope by which we draw near unto God," a verse of which A. B. Bruce says that it is "the dogmatic centre" of that Epistle; cf. the use of this verb in that Epistle in 4:16 and 10:22. Draw nigh unto God, as those who long to come into the closest possible relation to Him, in contrast to those who are His enemies and who keep at a distance from Him. God will then draw nigh unto you, to visit you with His salvation (Ps. 106:4). How should we draw nigh? Cleanse your hands.... The Jewish priests had to wash their hands and feet (Ex. 30:19—21). That was a symbol of moral and spiritual purity (Ps. 26:6; Isa. 1:16). We draw near to God in prayer and the hands were often raised in prayer (1 Tim. 2:8). The hands that had been stained in the fightings and murders referred to by James needed cleansing: cf. Isa. 1:15.

Ye sinners. That sharp term "sinners," which comes in so abruptly is meant to pierce the conscience of the reader, and such also is the intention of the other sharp term which balances it, "ye doubleminded." The doubleminded, as in 1:8, are those who are divided in their heart's love between God and the world. The word "sinners" shows that the cleansing just spoken of is not a mere literal washing of hands. What we have here is really a call to repentance, and, therefore, James adds, "and purify your hearts...."; cf. hands and hearts in Ps. 24:4 and 73:13. In four out of the seven places where this verb "purify" occurs in N. T., it means ceremonial cleansing (Jn. 11:55; Acts 21:24, on the lips of James; Acts 21:26; Acts 24:18). In the other three places (here, 1 Jn. 3:3 and 1 Pet. 1:22) it has an ethical sense.

9 The verb translated "be afflicted" occurs only here in N. T., and it may express the inward feeling of deep misery that is the result of a deep sense of sin, while the mourning and the loud weeping denote the outward manifestation of such heart-sorrow. It is a remarkable fact that the noun "laughter" is found only here in N. T. while the verb "laugh" occurs only twice, in Lk. 6:21 and 25. The N. T. is a deeply serious book, although it is also the most joyful book in the world; the two things are not incompatible. The joy that pervades the N. T. is the fruit of a serious dealing with the things of God and man. Laughter and joy are not evil in themselves, but the Bible speaks of a "laughter of fools" (Eccles. 7:6). The stress here is laid on *your* laughter, *your* joy. What James is reprobating is the hollow merriment of the friend of the world, such laughter and joy as rang through the halls of mirth suggested in 5:5. The word *heaviness*[5] occurs only here in N. T. Literally, it signifies a casting down of the eyes, as in the case of the publican (Lk. 18:13), the outward expression of a heavy heart. Moffat translates "depression" and the American R.S.V. "dejection."

10 In view of the fact that it is the humble who receive grace, we have now an appeal for humility, and the appeal is driven home by the thought that we are all "in the sight of the Lord." Since He is so great in power and we are so weak and frail, since He is so holy and we are so sinful, we ought to humble ourselves before Him. The man who does

---

[5] κατήφεια. The derivation of this word would make it describe the expression of shame and grief, *with downcast eye*. This, says Carr, "is the natural expression of the painfulness of shame," and he quotes these words of Nathaniel Hawthorne: "There is no outrage more flagrant than to forbid the culprit to hide his face in shame, as it was the essence of this punishment (the pillory) to do." We might compare the O. T. phrase, "shame and confusion of face," (Dan. 9:7, 8), and the words of Ezra's penitential prayer (Ez. 9:6, 7).

not dare to lift up his eyes to heaven is raised to heights of glory to which the proud can never come; cf. Lk. 1:32, Lk. 18:14 and 1 Pet. 5:6 for the word "exalt."

11-12 The spirit of humility cannot exist alongside the spirit which speaks against the brethren; such censoriousness in speech leads to one of the worst forms of pride; the man who is guilty of it does not merely criticise his brother but really criticises the Law of God, that is, no doubt chiefly the Royal Law of love (2:8). That kind of thing lands us in moral chaos. It is one of the fundamental axioms of the spiritual life that there is one Lawgiver, who is able to save and to destroy (cf. Mt. 10:28) and the thought of His august majesty and illimitable power ought to restrain the promptings of human pride. The words of our Lord in Mt. 7:1 should be compared. The threefold repetition of the word "brother" in v. 11 is deeply impressive.

4:13—17. The uncertainty and brevity of human life should lead us to humble dependence on the will of God.

13 *Come now.* This expression occurs in N. T. only here and in 5:1. In the English A. V. we have "Go to now," an obsolete English phrase, which is explained in an article on "Go" in Hastings D. B. as meaning "Come, come, take the right course." It is spoken sometimes sarcastically (as here), sometimes encouragingly. There were many Jews engaged in the First Century in commercial enterprise all over the Roman Empire, and that propensity has persisted until our day, so that there is hardly a corner of the world into which the Jews have not penetrated. We see here a group of Jewish traders sitting, it may be, before a map and pointing to the next city they intend to visit, and saying, "To-day.... we will go into *this* city and trade."[6]

---

[6] ἐμπορεύεσθαι occurs in only one other place in N. T., where it means to cheat or to deceive (2 Pet. 2:3). The same word was used for trading and cheating! That is an eloquent commentary on the cheating which too often attended ancient trading, as it too often attends modern trading.

14 Such plans are the height of folly in men who are *of such a nature* that they do not know what shall be on the morrow,[7] much less what will happen a year hence; cf. Prov. 27:1. Of what character is your life? Ye are a vapor[8] that appeareth for a little time, and then disappeareth. You are like that "morning cloud" of which Hosea speaks (6:4), which lies over the woods and fields for an hour or two and vanishes when the sun breaks through. Human life is as frail as that insubstantial mist, and it is as fleeting. Scripture abounds in such thoughts; cf. Job. 7:7; Ps. 39:5, 6; Ps. 90:4—6; 1 Chron. 29:15, etc. In Dr. John Brown's *Rab and his Friends,* we have this passage: "She was walking, alone, though the valley of that shadow, into which we must all enter and yet she was not alone, for we know whose rod and staff were comforting her.... She lay for some time breathing quick, and passed away so gently, that when we thought she was gone, James, in his old-fashioned way, held

---

[7] *Ye know not what shall be on the morrow.* A question emerges here with regard to the reading, a rather interesting question. Should the definite article *(τό or τά)* be retained in the text, as in English A. V. and R. V., in our Version, in RSV, in Moffat and Weymouth, etc., so that the meaning is: "You know not the (things) of to-morrow" *(τὰ τῆς αὔριον)* or, should it be omitted, so that the meaning is: "You know not on the morrow of what nature your life shall be"? Westcott and Hort, relying as usual on the authority of the Vatican MS (B), adopt this latter reading. According to it, James would be made to declare that these traders were ignorant of what the conditions of their life would be on the morrow, whether sickness or health, and so on. In fact, however, the words that follow, *Ye are a vapor,* show that the uncertainty of *life itself* is what he has in mind. The intrinsic evidence, therefore, that is, the evidence of the passage itself, seems to favor some such rendering as we have in our Version. Moffat translates, "You know nothing about to-morrow." Weymouth translates, "You do not even know what will happen to-morrow."

[8] ἀτμίς. Both Moffat and Weymouth translate "mist." The word occurs once again in N. T., in Acts 2:19, which contains a quotation from Joel 2:30 (LXX); we have there the phrase "vapor of smoke," and the word "smoke" occurs in LXX version of Ps. 102:3, "my days consume away like smoke."

the mirror to her face. After a long pause, one small spot
of dimness was breathed out; it vanished away, and never
returned, leaving the blank clear dark of the mirror without
a stain." "What is our life? It is even a vapour, which
appeareth for a little time, and then vanisheth away."

15 The thought of the uncertainty and the frailty of
our life should move us to rest humbly on the will of God;
cf. Acts 18:21, Acts 21:14, 1 Cor. 4:19, Heb. 6:3, etc.

16 But now, in point of fact, instead of manifesting
humility towards God, your attitude is one of boasting.
Vaunting[9] occurs again only in 1 Jn. 2:16, "the vain glory
of life." The cognate adjective "boastful" occurs in
Rom. 1:30 and 2 Tim. 3:2. In Classical Greek this noun
often denotes braggart and boastful talk. All *such* glorying
is evil.[10] There is a glorying which is commendable (1:9
and Rom. 5:2, 3 and 11), but not *such* glorying.

17 The Christian knows the will of God, because God
has showed him what is good (Mic. 6:8), in contrast with
what is evil (v. 16). To know the will of God and not to
do it — we note yet once more the emphasis on doing — involves serious sin.

---

9   ἀλαζονεία. This word, Plummer says, "indicates insolent and
empty assurance; and here the assurance lies in presumptuous trust in
the stability of oneself and one's surroundings. Pretentious ostentation
is the radical signification of the word, and in Classical Greek it is the
pretentiousness which is most prominent, in Hellenistic Greek the
ostentation. There is manifest ostentation in speaking confidently about
one's future; and seeing how transitory everything human is, the ostentation is empty and pretentious."

10   All such glorying, James says in simple words, the very simplicity
of which deepens their severity, is evil *(πονηρά)*. Satan is called "the
evil one" (Mt. 6:13, Mt. 13:38, Eph. 6:16, etc.). and the character and
the source of such glorying ought to be patent to everybody.

CHAPTER V

CONCERNING RICH OPPRESSORS

5:1—6

1 Come now, ye rich, weep and howl for your miseries that are coming upon you.

2 Your riches are corrupted, and your garments are moth-eaten.

3 Your gold and your silver are rusted; and their rust shall be for a testimony against you, and shall eat your flesh as fire. Ye have laid up your treasure in the last days.

4 Behold, the hire of the laborers who mowed your fields, which is of you kept back by fraud, crieth out: and the cries of them that reaped have entered into the ears of the Lord of Sabaoth.

5 Ye have lived delicately on the earth, and taken your pleasure; ye have nourished your hearts in a day of slaughter.

6 Ye have condemned, ye have killed the righteous one; he doth not resist you.

The rich oppressors of the Church are to meet with a terrible doom (vv. 1—6).

1 The rich man in 1:10 is a Christian brother; the rich visitor to the service (2:2) is evidently not a Christian, and the rich men in 2:6 are unbelievers. Here the rich men addressed are quite evidently unbelievers. They are not addressed as brethren. When James has finished with them, he turns with words of encouragement to his Christian brethren (v. 7). From the spirit of godlessness often manifested in commerce he moves here to the consideration of something that is more glaringly iniquitous, tyranny and oppression in the use of wealth. The language of James is stern to an extraordinary degree, and reminds us of many an O. T. prophetic utterance.

Weep. The same word is used in 4:9, but there the weeping is associated with repentance and the mourner has the prospect of having his tears wiped away by the God who deals graciously with the humble. There is no such prospect here; these heartless rich tyrants can expect only "miseries" and "the day of slaughter." James adds a second verb to intensify the utter wretchedness and hopelessness of the future of these men. This second verb, "howl ye," which occurs only here in N. T., is found in several passages in O. T., in close connection with the thought of imminent judgment; see Isa 13:6 (of Babylon), Isa. 15:3 (of Moab) and Isa. 23:1, 14 ("Howl, ye ships of Tarshish"). The word "misery", the cognate noun to the verb "be afflicted" in 4:8, occurs again in N. T. only in Rom. 3:16, in a quotation from Isa. 59:7. The miseries *are coming* upon the rich men — judgment is very near.

2-3 Three verbs are used, all in the perfect tense, to suggest a *state* of corruption in corn and other products of the fields, a *state* of tatters in clothing, like the fine clothing of 2:2, a *state* of rust. "Your wealth," as Ropes interprets, "to any eye that can see realities is already rotten, moth-eaten, rusted." The word "moth-eaten" occurs elsewhere, in Biblical Greek, only in Job 13:28. We are inevitably reminded here of our Lord's words about the clothes-moth in Mt. 6:19. In His words it is clearly implied that clothes form part of the treasure laid up on the earth, and, indeed, in Eastern countries clothes formed a considerable part of wealth; cf. Acts 20:33. Your silver and gold, instead of being used profitably, is being hoarded, and so has been become rusted through and through. Strictly speaking, silver cannot become so corroded as to become worthless and gold does not rust at all, but James' bold figure is not to be understood in too pedantic a fashion. Wealth, when it is not used to good purpose, becomes worthless. To set one's heart on such treasure and to hoard it will bring stern judgment, and, before the judgment sweeps down upon you in the full extent of its awfulness, the rust will bear witness to you regarding the perishability of riches, and, therefore, regarding the certain and complete ruin that will overtake those who have no other ground of confidence. Ropes says that we have here the idea "of rust corroding, and so consuming, human flesh, like the wearing of a rusty iron chain — a terrible image for the disastrous results of treating money as the reliance and the chief aim of life."

You have laid treasure *in the last days*,[1] quite literally, "in last days." These are days of stern crisis, days of judgment. Already the events were shaping themselves that were to result in the Fall of Jerusalem in the year 70, and *that* was *a* coming of the Lord. Our Lord's prophetic discourse in Mk. 13 and parallel passages seems to deal partly with the Fall of Jerusalem and partly with the consummation of all things, of which the Fall of Jerusalem was a forecast and a foreshadowing. To lay up treasure in such days of crisis as were swiftly approaching, James says, is abysmal folly.

4 James now mentions one glaring example of the heartless conduct of some rich men, their holding back of the wages of the farm-laborers who mowed their fields.[2] This

---

1 ἐν ἐσχάταις ἡμέραις. There is a deep sense in which it is true that, in this Gospel dispensation, we are living in the last days. God has spoken His final message to men (Heb. 1:1, 2). Calvin says on 1 Jn. 2:18 that we are now in the last time, "in which all things are so completed that nothing remains except the final revelation of Christ." This present dispensation in which we live is the last on the divine programme; the next will be the Coming of the Lord, in which He will appear in power and glory, to judge the ungodly and to be marvelled at in all them that believe (2 Thess. 1:7—10).

2 χώρας suggests the idea of extensive lands, as it does in the Parable of the Rich Fool (Lk. 12:16). This makes the callous cruelty of the wealthy farmers here all the more heinous. "The men who own such large properties," Plummer says, "are not under the temptations to fraud which beset the needy, and it is scandalous that those who can so well afford to pay what is due should refuse. Moreover, the labour

had been going on for some time and still continued. This was an old story in Israel; the prophets had inveighed against this form of injustice, and in the last of them there is a passage which James may have had in mind here, Mal. 3:5. He may also have had in mind that remarkable verse, Deut. 24:15, where notice the word "hire" (same word as here) and the verb "cry" compared with the noun *cries*[3] here. The Hebrew name for God, "The Lord of Sabaoth," occurs, in N. T. only here and in Rom. 9:29, in a quotation from Isa. 1:9. It describes God as the Almighty Ruler of the hosts of men, the hosts of the stars and the hosts of the angels.[4] The Almighty God has an *ear* for the cries of the

---

of mowing and reaping such fields must be great, and therefore the labourers have well earned their wages." Mowers and reapers are selected as representatives of all hired labourers. Calvin suggests that it is specially iniquitous that those whose hard toil supplies us with food should themselves be reduced to starvation; and to this it has been added, as Plummer remarks, that "the hardheartedness of the grasping employers is indeed conspicuous when not even the joy of the harvest moves them to pay the poor who work for them their hardly earned wage."

3 *Crieth out (κράζει)*. For this idea of sin crying out to God for vengeance compare Gen. 4:10 and Ex. 2:23. In addition to the passages from O. T. quoted in the exposition to show how common in Israel was this oppression of poor labourers by greedy masters, reference may be made to Job 7:2 and 24:5—10. In the apocryphal *Book of Ecclesiasticus* (24:21, 22) we have the words: "The bread of the needy is the life of the poor: he that defraudeth him thereof is a man of blood. He that taketh away his neighbour's living slayeth him; and he that defraudeth the labourer of his hire is a bloodshedder," where "defraudeth" is the same word James uses here.

4 *The Lord of Sabaoth*. This distinctively O. T. name for God does not occur at all in the first eight bocks of O. T. It occurs first in 1 Sam. 1:3 In 1 Sam. 17:45 we have words which may be regarded as furnishing a partial clue to its meaning, "Jehovah of hosts, the God of the armies of Israel." But, as Dr. John D. Davis of Princeton says in his *Dictionary of the Bible*, to interpret this title as meaning merely "the God of the armies of Israel" is "too narrow a generalisation." He goes on to say that "the Greek translators grasped the true meaning of the title and rendered it *Pantokrator*, the Almighty. The word hosts which is used in the title refers to the armies of the universe. The

oppressed, and He makes their cause His own, so that they have a strong Defender indeed.

5 To injustice was added self-indulgence. How extraordinary is the contrast between the festive chamber of the rich suggested here and the starving harvesters of the preceding verse. Moffat translates here, "You have revelled on earth and plunged into dissipation." The first verb occurs only here in N. T., while the cognate noun describes luxurious living in Lk. 7:25 and 2 Pet. 2:13; the second verb is used to describe a voluptuous woman in 1 Tim. 5:6, and in Ezek. 16:49 (LXX) it is used too of the women of Jerusalem, who are compared to the women of Sodom.

On the earth. Their vision is limited to earthly delights, and the thought of the judgment that is to descend on them from heaven, the judgment of the Lord of hosts, has never

---

designation pictures the universe, in its spiritual and material aspects, as forming a vast army, in numerous divisions, of various kinds of troops, in orderly array under the command of Jehovah." The word host or hosts is applied to the angels in 1 Kings 22:19, Ps. 103:21 and Lk. 2:13. The same word is used in connection with the stars in Isa. 40:26. We are thus justified in regarding this divine name as describing Jehovah as the Almighty God, Lord of the hosts of men, Lord of the hosts of angels, Lord of the hosts of the stars, who does according to His will in the army of heaven and among the inhabitants of the earth (Dan. 4:35). The O. T. prophets, who use the title very frequently, seem certainly to attach such a sense to it. As Dr. Davis says: "To the poetic imagination of the Hebrews, with their knowledge of the omnipresent reigning God, the regularity and order everywhere apparent suggested an army in vast, numerous, and varied divisions, acting under the command of one will. The Lord of Hosts, He is the king who alone commands." In LXX, it is sometimes translated *Pantokrator*, an adjective which occurs in N. T. in 2 Cor. 6:18 and 9 times in the Apocalypse. Sometimes it is simply transliterated, as here and in Rom. 9:29. As is suggested in the Introduction, the use of this divine name betrays the hand of a Jewish author. At its first occurrence (1 Sam. 1:3) it is found in close connection with a woman of sorrowful spirit. A Psalmist delights in the thought that the God who counts the number of the stars also heals the broken in heart and binds up their wounds. (Ps. 147:3, 4). This divine name is found here in close association with the woes of the starving harvesters.

once entered into their minds. Or, this thought may be suggested — *on the earth* they may have had abundance of good things, but, when this passing world is done, how will they fare then? As they were laying up treasure in "last days," so they were fattening their hearts in a day of slaughter. The *heart* is here the seat of the appetites and passions; cf. Mt. 15:19 and Lk. 21:34. The pitilessly ironical thought may be suggested that their life of luxurious pleasure was merely a fattening of the ox that it may be fit for slaughter; it still continues to feed placidly on the very day appointed for its slaughter. For *day of slaughter* see Jer. 12:3 and for similar imagery, as describing the day of God's judgment, see Isa. 34:2 and Ezek. 21:15. The words of Josephus, in *The Jewish War*, describing the horrors which attended the Fall of Jerusalem, when the rich Jews were slaughtered without mercy, and often with cruel tortures, provide an illuminating commentary on the words of James.

6 The greatest sin of these godless rich men is now described — they had condemned and slain some of the great men of God who had been sent among them. In Acts 3:14, 7:52, 22:14 and 1 Jn. 2:1, our Lord is called emphatically "The Righteous One", with special reference, quite likely, to the Righteous Servant of Isa. 53. *He* had been condemned and killed, and that was Israel's crowning sin, but we cannot limit the expression thus. This sort of thing had happened many a time in Israel's past; Jerusalem had killed some of the prophets sent to her (Mt. 23:37). James had seen this sort of thing happening in recent days; Stephen had been slain and James the son of Zebedee, and many of the saints (Acts 26:10), who had been condemned before the Jewish tribunals (2:6). James himself was to die as a martyr, according to Church tradition, in the year 62, and, according to tradition, he was known as "James the Just." He doth not resist — the same verb as in 4:6. Leave your persecutors in the hands of God, who *resists* the proud.

5:7—12

7 Be patient therefore, brethren, until the coming of the Lord. Behold, the husbandman waiteth for the precious fruit of the earth, being patient over it, until it receive the early and latter rain.

8 Be ye also patient; establish your hearts: for the coming of the Lord is at hand.

9 Murmur not, brethren, one against another, that ye be not judged: behold, the judge standeth before the doors.

10 Take, brethren, for an example of suffering and of patience, the prophets who spake in the name of the Lord.

11 Behold, we call them blessed that endured: ye have heard of the patience of Job, and have seen the end of the Lord, how that the Lord is full of pity, and merciful.

12 But above all things, my brethren, swear not, neither by the heaven, nor by the earth, nor by any other oath: but let your yea be yea, and your nay, nay; that ye fall not under judgment.

Exhortations to the Church to stand firm and to be forbearing in view of the Coming of the Lord and in view of the great examples of the prophets and of Job (vv. 7—12).

7 James now addresses again his Christian brethren. He urges them to be patient unto the Coming of the Lord. This verb "to be patient" occurs twice in this verse, and we have the cognate noun in v. 10 and also in such verses as Col. 1:11 and Heb. 6:12. The noun translated "patience" in v. 11 would be better rendered "endurance" or "staying power"; it is the word which we have had already in 1:3 and which we have also in such a verse as Heb. 12:2. The quality of character indicated is one of which the people of God have always great *need* (Heb. 10:36). The American R.S.V. has in v. 11, "Behold, we call those happy who were steadfast. You have heard

91

of the steadfastness of Job...." "Patience" is the self-restraint which does not too hastily seek vengeance for a wrong, while "endurance" is the temper which does not easily succumb under suffering. The first word is sometimes translated "long-suffering." The two words occur together in 2 Cor. 6:4 and 6, in Col. 1:11 and in 2 Tim. 3:10, and the contrast between the two corresponding verbs is well brought out in 1 Cor. 13:4 and 7, "Love suffereth long.... Love endureth all things." The long-suffering of God, as He deals with men, is spoken of in Rom. 2:4 and 1 Pet. 3:20, and, as the child of God must imitate his Heavenly Father (Eph. 5:1), he, too, must seek to manifest this lovely quality. In him it is a fruit of the Spirit (Gal. 5:22).

James refers to the Parousia of the Lord. Our Lord used that word three times in the prophetic discourse already referred to (Mt. 24:27, 37 and 39). We find the word elsewhere in Paul's Epistles, in 1 John and in 2 Peter. In the Egyptian Papyri it is found with the meaning of a "royal visit."

The word speaks of the coming of Christ in kingly majesty and glory. Such a "royal visit" took place at the Fall of Jerusalem, when the Divine judgment fell with shattering effect on the Jewish economy.[5]

Some of James's readers would, quite likely, be found among the oppressed harvesters, and he now makes use of

---

[5] *The Coming of the Lord.* Some may be inclined to regard with a certain degree of dubiety the interpretation given in the exposition of the words of James about the Coming of the Lord, and they may even be moved to say that this interpretation involves an explaining away of a difficult passage. It seems to us, however, that the interpretation given can be justified. While we cannot close our eyes to the fact that the N. T. announces a *final* Coming of the Lord, at the consummation of all things, it seems sound enough at the same time to see preliminary comings, in the great moral catastrophes of human history. Dr. R. J. Knowling reminds us how Voltaire made merry at the earthquake of Lisbon. "How absurd to talk about divine judgments! Lisbon is overwhelmed, whilst at the same moment in Paris, a city equally guilty, people were dancing!" "But it has been well pointed out," says

an illustration that would appeal to them. Inhabitants of Palestine would be specially impressed by such an illustration. The *former rains* fall in Palestine towards the end of October, and they loosen the soil which has been hardened and cracked by the long summer heat, so that the farmer can begin ploughing. The *latter rains* are the heavy showers of March and April, which come before the ripening of the harvest and the long summer drought. These two terms are found together in Deut. 11:14, Jer. 5:24, Joel 2:23 and Hos. 6:3.

8 Establish your hearts, or strengthen your hearts, the word used by our Lord in Lk. 22:32. It is often used to describe the Divine working, as in 2 Thess. 2:17 and 1 Pet. 5:10. James says: "Make your courage and purpose firm, but always remember that you cannot do that without the help of God." As already stated, in a very real sense the Lord did come in the Fall of Jerusalem. We recall His own words, *"Henceforth, from this moment onwards,* ye shall see the Son of Man sitting at the right hand of power, and coming on the clouds of heaven." (Mt. 26:64). He thus declares that He is to judge men not merely hereafter but *henceforth,* and we may rightly see His coming to judgment in all the great moral catastrophes of the world's history. We remember how Julia Ward Howe thought of the American Civil War. "Mine eyes have seen the glory of the coming of the Lord.... He is sifting out the souls of men before His judgment seat."

9 *Murmur not.* The verb used here denotes often deep feelings which can hardly be expressed, as in Rom. 8:23; it is used also of a sigh accompanying an earnest prayer, as in Mk. 7:34. Here it may mean murmuring or grumbling. "Do not blame one another for the distress of the

---

Knowling, "that if Voltaire had lived on a few years longer, and witnessed the first great French Revolution and the streets red with blood, he might have seen another illustration of the Lord's parable in Mt. 24:28; he might even have been constrained to exclaim with the Psalmist, 'Verily there is a God that judgeth in the earth!' "

times." You should remember that the Judge is standing before the doors. The Judge, the Lord Christ, who is Judge both of you and your brethren, is as near as that: cf. Mt. 24:33 and Mk. 13:29. As Moffat says: "Like Peter (1 Pet. 4:17) James is alive to the ethical fact that God's judgment will take strict account of the Christian's behaviour as well as that of their persecutors. What! Falling out with one another, when the Judge is standing at the very door!"

10 The word translated "suffering," or "hardship," occurs only here in N. T.; the cognate verb occurs in v. 13 and also in 2 Tim. 2:9 and 4:5; in 2 Tim. 2:3 we have the verb "suffer hardship along with" — "take your share of hardship, as good soldiers of Jesus Christ." The prophets did not escape their share of suffering and persecution: see Mt. 5:12, Mt. 23:34 and 37, Lk. 11:49, Acts 7:52 and 1 Thess. 2:15. You have in the prophets, says James, a splendid example of hardship coupled with patience, and

> The tidal waves of deeper souls
> Into our inmost being rolls,
> And lifts us unawares
> Out of all meaner cares.

11 Those who showed themselves possessed of staying power we pronounce blessed, as James had done in 1:12. The Word of God had said of old, "Blessed is he that endured" (Dan. 12:12, LXX). Indeed, the Word of God was given to us in order to produce in us that robust quality of character (Rom. 15:4). You have *heard,* as the Scriptures were read to you in the synagogue, of the endurance of Job; cf. Mt. 5:21, 27, 33, 38 and 43. This is the only mention of Job in N. T., though the Book of Job is quoted in 1 Cor. 3:19. A hasty survey of the Book of Job might suggest that Job was no outstanding example of what we would call "patience," except in his first acceptance of calamity (1:21 and 2:10). "We would rather say," J. B. Mayor writes, "that his complaint in chap. 3, his indignation against his friends for their want of faith in him, his agony at the thought that God has forsaken him, were symptoms of an extremely sensitive, vehement, impatient character. .... The word means, however, 'endurance' and may well be applied to the persistent trust in God shown in ch. 13:10 and 15, ch. 16:19—21 and ch. 19:25 ff."

In that wonderful story of Job you have seen the *end* of the Lord, you have caught a glimpse of the fact that God has a *purpose* in the chastisement of His children. The chastisement may be severe, but we will see more and more clearly that suffering is not meaningless, that a purpose of grace is being wrought out in it, if we cling to Him and never lose our faith in Him, if patient endurance has its perfect working out in us. (1:4).

> Blind unbelief is sure to err
> And trace His work in vain;
> God is His own interpreter,
> And He will make it plain.
>
> His purposes will ripen fast,
> Unfolding every hour;
> The bud may have a bitter taste,
> But sweet will be the flower.

We must give God time; in the *end* it will be made plainly evident that He is full of pity and merciful; cf. Ps. 30:5, Ps. 103:8, Ps. 145:8, and other O. T. passages, which are echoes of the basic O. T. revelation made to Moses (Ex. 34:6 and 7). The word translated "full of pity" occurs nowhere else in N. T., and the word translated "merciful" occurs again only in Lk. 6:36.

12 But above all things, or especially, do not break out into oaths.[6] We have here a reminiscence of our Lord's

---

[6] *Swear not (μὴ ὀμνύετε).* Plummer seems to be justified in saying that both our Lord and James forbid the use of oaths (1) as an

words in Mt. 5:34—37. James has already exhorted his readers not to blame their brethren for their hardships, and now he warns them against the pernicious habit of irreverently calling upon God in their distress. Feelings of impatience may only too easily lead one to indulge in so-called "strong language," which is usually a sign of grave moral weakness. "It is not to be supposed," says Ropes — and his opinion seems quite sound — "that James had in mind any question of the lawfulness of oaths in a law-court in a Jewish or Christian country. To any Oriental such a saying as this, or Mt. 5:37, would at once suggest ordinary swearing, not the rare and solemn occasions about which some modern readers have been so much concerned." It is the vain, needless, flippant swearing of oaths that is condemned, as a practice which comes dangerously near to profane swearing. Our Lord seems to mean that, in our ordinary everyday intercourse, we should be content with a plain affirmation or denial, because, as He says, "whatsoever is more than these is of the evil one" (Mt. 5:37). Its real inspiration is to be found, not in the God of truth but in the Father of lies. James here, with a seriousness as arresting as that of our Lord, emphasises the fact that this wrong use of language will be judged with the utmost severity by Him who will call men to account for every *idle* word they speak, every word that yields no profit worth while (Mt. 12:36).

---

expression of feeling, (2) as a confirmation of an ordinary statement, and that it is scarcely sound exegesis to say that oaths are entirely and on every occasion forbidden. The Apostles may be taken as the best guides to the understanding of the mind of the Lord. Augustine appeals to Paul in defence of the occasional taking of an oath; Paul sometimes calls God to witness that he is speaking the truth (2 Cor. 1:23 and 11:31; Gal. 1:20; Phil. 1:8). In Heb. 6:16 the fact that men swear oaths to settle disputes is mentioned without any intimation that the practice is wrong. There are serious occasions when an oath may be permissible, but the flippant swearing of oaths in connection with trivial matters is forbidden.

13 Is any among your suffering? let him pray. Is any cheerful? let him sing praise.

14 Is any among you sick? let him call for the elders of the church; and let them pray over him, anointing him with oil in the name of the Lord:

15 and the prayer of faith shall save him that is sick, and the Lord shall raise him up; and if he have committed sins, it shall be forgiven him.

16 Confess therefore your sins one to another, and pray one for another, that ye may be healed. The supplication of a righteous man availeth much in its working.

17 Elijah was a man of like passions with us, and he prayed fervently that it might not rain; and it rained not on the earth for three years and six months.

18 And he prayed again; and the heaven gave rain, and the earth brought forth her fruit.

19 My brethren, if any among you err from the truth, and one convert him;

20 let him know, that he who converteth a sinner from the error of his way shall save a soul from death, and shall cover a multitude of sins.

Various activities of the Church, prayer, praise, visitation of the sick, confession of sins and the restoration of backsliders (vv. 13—20).

13 Suffering in some form or other is sure to come, and the sovereign remedy for all suffering is prayer. The Psalmist says in a remarkable phrase that his one reaction to words of causeless hate is prayer — "but I am (all) prayer" (Ps. 109:4). As Dr. Alexander Maclaren says, "Repelled, his whole being turned to God, and in calm communion with Him found defence and repose." Do not break out into oaths, says James, nor into needless repining and grumbling. Pray, rather. "We kneel how weak, we rise how full of power."

Is any in good spirits? This verb occurs again in N. T. only in Acts 27:22 and 25. On that drifting vessel, buffeted by the winds, Paul calls for cheerfulness. "I will bless the Lord at all times," says the Psalmist (Ps. 34:1). Plummer is, no doubt, quite right when he says that we may with equal truth transpose James's two precepts. "Is any among you suffering? Let him sing praise. Is any in good spirits. Let him pray." "Prayer steadies without dimming the bright flame of cheerfulness; and just as thanksgiving sweetens sorrow, so supplication sanctifies joy." The child of God can sing praise in the most trying circumstances, sometimes even in a prison at midnight (Acts 16:25), but how many there are who, in the noontide of their greatest prosperity, forget to give thanks to the Giver of all good! The verb *sing praise* occurs again in N. T. in Eph. 5:19, Rom. 15:9 and 1 Cor. 14:15.[7] The words of Paul in Eph. 5:19 give us this comfortable assurance that, even though our voice may be little more musical than that of a crow, we can sing praise in our hearts.

14 We have here a remarkably interesting glimpse, though it be only a fleeting glimpse of First Century congregational life. The word "Church" occurs in the Gospels only in Mt. 16:18 and 18:17, in the first case of the Church universal, in the other case of a local congregation. When, at Caeserea Philippi, our Lord spoke of *His* Church, He used a term which had been used in the O. T. of the Jewish Church, the Church of God, so that He was thinking of His disciples as the nucleus of the New Israel. The word "presbyter," or "elder," was also likely taken over from the Jewish into the Christian Church. We read of a council of elders in the Jewish synagoge at Capernaum (Lk. 6:3), and the government of the early Christian Churches seems to

---

7 The verb used here *(ψαλλέτω)* means, first, to twang the strings of a harp or some other musical instrument, then, to sing to the accompaniment of the harp, and then, simply to sing the praises of God in song.

have been developed out of the government of the synagogue. We read of Christian elders in Acts 11:30 (in Judaea), Acts 14:23 (in South Galatia), Acts 15:16 (in Jerusalem), Acts 20:17, where we have the same phrase as here, "the elders of the Church" of Ephesus, 1 Pet. 5:1 (of the Churches of Asia Minor). In one of Paul's earliest writings, written about the year 52, we read of those "who are over you in the Lord and admonish you," "presiding over you in the Lord and maintaining discipline," as Moffat has it (1 Thess. 5:12), and in Heb. 13:17 we read of them "that have the rule over you." We may regard the elders of the Church here as the spiritual leaders in the domestic life of any local congregation. Sick people are to *call for* these elders; in the second century Polycarp writes in his letter to the Church at Philippi: "Let the elders care for the sick." Some sick people neglect to do this, and then feel offended because nobody has come to visit them, though they have never sent any intimation of their illness to minister or elders. The elders are to pray *over* the sick man, perhaps stretching out their hands in earnest supplication for him.

The use of oil for medicinal purpose is referred to in Isa. 1:6, Mk. 6:13 and Lk. 10:34. We have here medicine and prayer. The anointing was to take place at the same time as the praying. In the early centuries we find references to the custom of anointing the sick in various parts of the Church. Before the end of the 8th century a change began to appear in the Western Church, whereby the medicinal use of oil began to merge into an anointing of those who were thought to be on the point of death — Extreme Unction — not as a means of recovery, but with a view to the remission of sins, and in connection with the giving of the *Viaticum* (the last Sacrament as provision for the *way*, for the last journey of the soul). In the 16th century, at the Council of Trent, the so-called Sacrament of Extreme Unction received authoritative definition in the Roman Church, that Council declaring that this manmade

Sacrament is "implied by Mark, and commended and promulgated by James the apostle and brother of the Lord." There never was a more glaring travesty of Scripture. The forthright words of Farrar cannot be challenged: "Neither for Extreme Unction, or for sacramental confession, nor for sacerdotal absolution, nor for fanatical extravagance, does this passage afford the slightest sanction."

15 It is the prayer of faith that heals, and the faith is not only the faith of the elder, but surely also that of the sick man, who ought to pray for himself, according to verse 13. The anointing with oil was in accordance with a popular custom and there was no element of superstition in it, because it was done "in the name of the Lord," and may sometimes have been a kind of help to faith. For the word "save" in the sense of recovery from bodily trouble, see Mk. 10:52, Jn. 11:12 (literally, "shall be saved"), Acts 4:9, etc. The Lord shall raise him up, from his bed of sickness. "I applied the remedies, the Lord was the healer," so runs an inscription in a French hospital. *If* he have committed sins...., — is there any doubt about that, in view of the fact that "in many things we stumble, all of us" (3:2). The special idea suggested here, quite likely, is that the sickness may have been directly caused by sin; at any rate, it may well bring the man's sins more vividly before him. If that lead to confession and forgiveness, then the deeper healing of the soul will have been brought about by Him who forgives all our iniquities and heals all our diseases (Ps. 103:3).[8]

16 There is certainly not the faintest shadow of justification here for the practice of secret confession to a priest, as candid Romanists have sometimes admitted. Luther has this comment, "A strange confessor! His name is 'One

---

[8] It may be interesting to recall what the great English physician, Sir Andrew Clark said, two days before his death, in answer to a question: "Not value prayers? Prayer is that which moves more than medicine; prayer is all-powerful: it is the basis of love. Pray for me always."

another'." The confession is to be made by any believer to
any other believer, the sick man here, for example, to the
elder, and sometimes, it may well be, by the elder to the
sick man or to others. The deeper meaning of the word
"heal" may well be intended here; it is used with reference
to the diseases of the soul in Mt. 13:15, Heb. 12:13 and
1 Pet. 2:24.

It is difficult to decide as to the precise translation that
should be adopted of the second part of this verse. It is
easy to see that we have there a very strong assertion of the
mighty power of prayer, but the difficulty is to decide how
the emphatic last word in the sentence (*energoumenos*)
should be construed. Is it middle or passive? Ropes says
that this participle means "when it is exercised," "exerted,"
"put forth," and actually asks us to adopt this flat, tautolo-
gical rendering: "A righteous man's praying has great effect
when he prays." He then adds the remark: "The participle
adds but little to the sense." That is surely a counsel of
despair. A word that is placed with such unmistakeable
emphasis at the end of this sentence must have some very
definite meaning. Moffat translates: "The prayers of the
righteous have a powerful effect." It seems that he has
simply shut his eyes to the presence of the word in the text.
Possibly, the participle should be regarded as passive. Mayor
argues at length for the passive significance, prayer *actuated
or inspired by the Spirit,* such prayer as Paul describes in
Rom. 8:26. Weymouth seems to take the same line. His
translation is: "The heartfelt supplication of a righteous
man exerts a mighty influence," and he adds a footnote:
"Or, 'inwardly prompted,' by the Holy Spirit." The word
rendered "prayer" is rendered "supplication" in Eph. 6:18
and Phil. 4:6, and stresses the *petitionary* aspect of prayer.

17-18 As James had appealed in his second chapter to
the stories of Abraham and Rahab, so now he appeals to
the example of Elijah. His prayers did indeed exert a
mighty influence, but let no one say: "Such power of prayer
is beyond my reach," for Elijah knew all the frailties of

101

COMMENTARY ON JAMES

human nature that harass us; he was a man of like passions with us, an expression which is found only once again in N. T., in Acts 14:15. Elijah prayed fervently, literally, "with prayer," a Hebraic idiom, like the expressions "with desire I have desired" (Lk. 22:15) and "rejoices with joy" (Jn. 3:29). Elijah really prayed. A man may pray with his lips and yet not pray with an intense desire of the soul. There is no specific mention in O. T. of the first prayer of Elijah mentioned here, unless we can regard it as implied in his first recorded words, "As the Lord God of Israel liveth," *"before whom I stand."* (1 Kings 17:1). The second prayer takes us to the summit of Mount Carmel. "He bowed himself down upon the earth, and put his face between his knees" (1 Kings 18:42). That was fervent prayer indeed.

19-20 James, addressing his readers as *my brethren,*[9] now concludes his message with a weighty word of good cheer for those whose hearts are set on bigger tasks than that of praying for sick folk, for those who are seeking to bring lost men and women back to the paths of righteousness. The people who are to be *turned back* to these paths are evidently Christians who have become backsliders, who have *strayed*[10] from the truth,[11] the people who have already been exhorted

---

[9] For the last time this loving form of address is used, introducing the final topic of the Epistle, the restoration of backsliders. He who would engage in that difficult form of Christian service must manifest a brotherly spirit; Paul says that he must manifest a spirit of gentleness (Gal. 6:1).

[10] *If any among you err (πλανηθῇ).* This word may mean that the person to be won back to the Church has gone astray of his own deliberate choice or that he has been led astray by evil influences, and that good influences must now be brought to bear upon him.

[11] This word seems to prove that it is a backsliding Christian that James has in mind here, one who has gone astray into sinful ways from that word of truth which brings new life when it operates in the soul (1:18). Such men, as Plummer puts it, "dishonour their Divine parentage and desert their Father's home." So this is James' last word to his readers—if you want to prove the reality of your faith by good

102

to confess their sins (vv. 15, 16). Dr. R. J. Knowling says that "no words reveal more fully the tenderness of James than this closing exhortation of the Epistle, and in them we may see an indication of his close following of the great Overseer and Shepherd of souls. James, we may also note, does not speak of the conversion of many but of one; with all his social teaching he thus never forgets to recognise, as the Gospel of Christ has always recognised, the infinite value of the individual soul." If only *one* soul be reclaimed, that will be to *save* a soul out of the realm of *death:* for "save" compare 1:21 and for "death" 1:15. Our Lord uses the same phrase "out of death" in Jn. 5:24. The deep seriousness of the situation into which sinners bring themselves is most impressively indicated — they are in the realm of *death* and they are burdened with a *multitude* of sins which cry for punishment.

In the very last words there seems to be an allusion to Prov. 10:12, "Love covereth all transgressions," words which are quoted in 1 Pet. 4:8. The verb is used of God covering sin in Ps. 32:1, 85:3, etc. God, indeed, alone can do that, but a man may be used of God to draw sinners back from the error of their ways and to bring them to Him who casts our sins into the deep places of the sea (Mic. 7:19). Dr. Andrew Bonar wrote these words in his Diary: "May we stand on the shore of that ocean into which our sins have been cast, and see them sink to the depths, out of sight, and the sea calm and peaceful, the sunshine playing on it, the sunshine of Thy love and Thy favour."

> Plenteous grace with Thee is found,
> Grace to cover all our sins.

James has had many severe things to say in this Epistle, but he ends it as he began it, with a message of strong

---

works, what finer and nobler work can be imagined than this, to bring such a wanderer back home again?

encouragement. Calvin says on these concluding words: "We must take heed lest souls perish through pure sloth whose salvation God puts in a manner in our hands. Not that we can bestow salvation on them, but that God by our ministry delivers and saves those who seem otherwise to be nigh destruction."

THE EPISTLES OF JOHN

INTRODUCTION TO FIRST JOHN

I

The Voice of Tradition

The external testimony here, or, in other words, the voice of Church tradition, is clear enough. The Epistle was used by Polycarp, who suffered martyrdom in the year 155, and by Papias, who was bishop of Hierapolis in Asia Minor in the early part of the second century, and who is described by Irenaeus in his treatise *Against Heresies* as "a hearer of John and a companion of Polycarp." Both Papias and Polycarp had been disciples of John the Apostle. Eusebius, the great Christian scholar of the fourth century, in his *History of the Church,* tells us that Papias "made use of testimonies from the First Epistle of John" (*History* III.39:16). In the only writing of Polycarp which has come down to us, his *Epistle to the Philippians,* he writes these words: "Everyone that confesseth not that Jesus Christ is come in the flesh is Antichrist; and whosoever confesseth not the witness of the Cross is of the devil," words in which we catch echoes of 1 Jn. 4:2, 3 and 3:8. When we remember that the word "Antichrist" in N. T. occurs only in John's Epistles, that it is not of frequent occurrence in the literature of the sub-Apostolic age, and that "confess," "witness," and "to be of the devil" are expressions which are characteristic of John's writing, the supposition that Polycarp knew and accepted our Epistle as Apostolic seems to be fairly well established.

Eusebius informs us that Irenaeus himself (c. 140—202) "mentions the First Epistle of John, citing very many testimonies from it" (*History:* V:8:7). In his treatise *Against Heresies* he quotes it twice, ascribing it to John. Irenaeus was a disciple of Polycarp of whom he has given a vivid

107

account in his Epistle to Florinus, of which a portion has been preserved by Eusebius (*History* V:20:4 and 5). If Polycarp was John's spiritual son, we may say that Irenaeus was his spiritual grandson. When Irenaeus ascribes this Epistle to John, he must have been echoing the teaching of his instructor in the faith. We can say that here the tradition of the Apostolic authorship goes back, through Irenaeus and Polycarp, to John himself.

Clement of Alexandria (who flourished A.D. 185—210) quotes this Epistle frequently and several times mentions it as John's. He writes thus, e.g.: "John too manifestly teaches the difference of sins in his larger Epistle in these words: if any man see his brother sin a sin that is not unto death, he shall ask, and He shall give him life" (1 Jn. 5:16). Tertullian (fl. 195—215) quotes the Epistle 40 or 50 times, repeatedly stating that the words he quotes are John's. Origen, too, (fl. 220—250) frequently cites the Epistle as John's. A review of this full and strong evidence shows that Eusebius was fully justified in including the Epistle in his list of those canonical books of the N. T. which had been universally received in the Church.

The Muratorian Canon, or the Muratorian Fragment, as it is sometimes called (c. 180), is a portion of the earliest attempt known to us to draw up a catalogue of those books of the N. T. which were recognised by the Church. In this Canon First John is not mentioned along with the other N. T. Epistles but in immediate connection with the Fourth Gospel. After recording a tradition with regard to the composition of the Gospel, which is ascribed to the Apostle John, this document continues: "What wonder is it then that John brings forward each detail with so much emphasis even in his Epistles, saying of himself, *what we have seen with our eyes and heard with our ears and our hands have handled, these things have we written to you?* For so he professes that he was not only an eye-witness, but also a hearer, and moreover a historian of all the wonderful works of the Lord in order." We have there an unmistakeable allusion to the opening words of First John. Bishop Light-foot made skilful use of the fact that First John is thus detached from the other two Johannine Epistles in confirmation of the theory, which has been advocated by Ebrard, Haupt, and others, that the Epistle was originally published with the Gospel as a kind of commendatory postscript, a theory which is probably correct.

II

Internal Evidence and Authorship

Dr. George Salmon, in his *Introduction to the N. T.*, writes: "I do not think it necessary to spend much time on the proofs that the First Epistle and the Gospel are the work of the same writer." Some of the phrases which are common to both writings are: "That your joy may be fulfilled" (1 Jn. 1:4; Jn. 16:24): "Walketh in darkness and knoweth not whither he goeth" (1 Jn. 2:11; Jn. 12:35): "To be of the truth" (1 Jn. 2:21; Jn. 18:37): "Have passed out of death into life" (1 Jn. 3:14; Jn. 5:24). In the Epistle (4:9) we have Our Lord's title "Only begotten," as in the Gospel (1:14 and 18; 3:16). In the Epistle (4:14) we have also His title "Savior of the world," as in the Gospel (4:42). The following words and phrases are common to both writings: *abide, advocate, believe on, children of God, darkness, do sin, do the truth, eternal life, keep His word, lay down one's life, life, light, love, murderer, new commandment, witness,* etc. Lists of such striking verbal resemblances are given in Alexander's commentary *(Speaker's Commentary)* and in Westcott's commentary. Plummer, to whose luminous commentary *(Cambridge Bible* and *Cambridge N. T.)* we acknowledge our deep indebtedness, points out no less than 29 coincidences of language in the first two chapters of the Epistle alone. It seems to us as clearly proved as anything in the realm of N. T. study can be proved that the writer of the Epistle was also the writer of the Gospel, whom in the light of the evidence in the Gospel, we may regard as being the Apostle John, the son of Zebedee. As Ramsay says, in his *Church in the Roman Empire,* "no two works in the whole range of literature show clearer signs of the genius of one writer, and no other pair of works are so completely in a class by themselves, apart from the work of their own and every other time."

This conclusion with regard to identity of authorship has been challenged, notably in recent times by Dr. C. H. Dodd, in the *Moffat Commentary* on the Epistle, published in 1946. His criticism of this conclusion is a laborious one, which is executed with what many will regard as much misplaced ingenuity. The mental acumen which he displays in his endeavor to find differences of style in the two writings yields a very meagre harvest. Such impressions of style, he admits, are apt to be subjective, and we can only affirm our own conviction that in his kind of special pleading we have failed to discover any argument that is really conclusive. "There is surely to be felt in the Fourth Gospel," Dr. Dodd writes, "a richness, a subtlety, a penetrating quality of style to which the Epistle cannot pretend. While the rhythm of both is slow and regular, in the Gospel it is subtly varied, within the limits imposed by its general character, but in the Epistle regularity often descends to monotony. The language of the Gospel has an intensity, a kind of inward glow, a controlled excitement, which the reader does not feel, or seldom feels, in the Epistle." Well, "so many men, so many opinions." We need only say that we have found, and that not seldom, this intensity, this inward glow, in the language of the Epistle, as in the language of the Gospel, and the fact that such a mental reaction is experienced at all in the reading of the Epistle tends to prove that we are all the time in contact with the same mind. And, if it be the case that in the Gospel we have a richness of language that is wanting in the Epistle, may the explanation not be that the Gospel was composed with greater care, as a book intended to bring home conviction of the truth of Christianity to enquiring minds, while the Epistle, written to believers, is composed with greater freedom and simplicity of language? Further, what looks like monotony often turns out, on closer inspection, to be something quite different, as is pointed out in the exposition, in what is written about such verses as 2:5 and 2:10.

Dr. Dodd, dealing with the theology of the Epistle, affirms that the statements made in it about the redemptive efficacy of the death of Christ "scarcely go beyond the terms of the primitive Apostolic preaching." Did that primitive Apostolic preaching not interpret the death of Christ in the light of the 53rd. chapter of Isaiah (Acts 3:13 and 26, 8:32—35 and 22:14) and therefore as an expiation for sin, though there may not be, in the addresses of Peter preserved in the early chapters of Acts, as explicit and as full a statemen of the meaning of that death as we have in the Epistles of Paul? In later years Peter quite explicitly interprets the death of Christ in the light of Isa. 53 (1 Pet. 2:22—25), and there is no valid reason for thinking that he was of a different mind at the time of the great Pentecost. Paul, in placing the death of Christ for our sins among the "first things" of Christianity (1 Cor. 15:3) was conscious of being in complete harmony with the teaching of the original disciples of Jesus. Dr. Dodd says that in this Epistle only one "technical term of theology" is used, the word "propitiation" (2:2 and 4:10), which he translates "expiation." That is a word that speaks of a profound estimate of the atoning value of the death of Jesus, whose blood cleanses from all sin (1:7), and it is a word that proves also that the man who used it was in entire harmony with Paul. It no doubt proves, too, that he was in entire harmony with the original disciples of Jesus, of whom indeed, according to the position defended by us, he was himself one.

According to Dr. Dodd, the writer of the Fourth Gospel, though he alludes to Isa. 53, "never develops the idea of expiation." If, like his brother-Apostles, he regarded Isa. 53

as being fulfilled in Jesus, he must have thought of the death of Jesus as an expiation for sin, though, for reasons clear to himself while they may not be clear to twentieth century critics, he may not have "developed" that idea. Does the writer of the Fourth Gospel not report the words of Jesus about the Son of Man being lifted up like the brazen serpent in the wilderness (3:14, 15), words which involve the idea that God's condemnation of sin was endured by Him in His "unknown sufferings"? Does he not report the words of John the Baptist about the sin-bearing Lamb of God (1:29, Isa. 53:7), because he is in hearty agreement with them? On Dr. Dodd's own showing, neither the writer of the Gospel nor the writer of the Epistle develops the idea of expiation: according to our position, each of them does evidence a belief in that idea. Thus, according to both Dr. Dodd and ourselves, there is no marked difference of standpoint or treatment discernible here between the two writings. The real truth is that laborious attempts like that of Dr. Dodd to ferret out points of difference between the two documents are doomed to failure and they involve a wasting of energy on a chasing of a will o' the wisp which might be devoted to more profitable studies.

There is no need to follow Dr. Dodd further in his microscopic search for points of difference. After a careful examination of the facts adduced by him we feel that their force is very slight and that they do not nullify the force of the admitted similarity of thought and vocabulary that characterises the two writings. It is no doubt true that there are expressions in the Epistle which are not found in the Gospel, expressions like *Antichrist, anointing, fellowship, lust of the flesh, lust of the eyes, presence* or *coming* (of the Second Advent), *propitiation, sin unto death,* etc. But what of that? Must an author maintain slavish uniformity of style and vocabulary in all circumstances, and no matter with what subject he may be dealing? Over against the list of expressions found in the Epistle but not in the Gospel stands the long list of words and phrases common to both writings, which seem to us to be absolutely convincing proof of common authorship.

We see no valid reason for seriously questioning the conclusion arrived at by Dr. George Salmon which he set forth in words that some might regard as rather sweeping. He said: "I am sure that any unprejudiced judge would decide that, while the minute points of difference that have been pointed out between the Gospel and the First Epistle are no more than must be expected in two productions of the same writer, the general resemblance is such, that a man must be devoid of all faculty of critical perception who cannot discern the proofs of common authorship." Alford pronounced just as emphatically on this question. He said: "To maintain a diversity of authorship would betray the very perverseness and exaggeration of that school of criticism which refuses to believe, be evidence never so strong." As Zahn says: "The unanimous traditon which attributed this writing to the author of the Fourth Gospel is corroborated by an affinity of thought, vocabulary, and style, such as can hardly ever be proved between a historical and a didactic writing of the same author, to say nothing of different authors." Peake says, in his *Introduction to the N. T.*, that "the links of connection are so numerous and unstudied, the peculiar Johannine style so inimitable, that it is hypercriticism to deny the identity of authorship."

There is one feature of the internal evidence that is of crucial importance. That is the fact that the writer claims quite definitely to have been an eye-witness of the events of the Gospel history, that, as Peake puts it, "the author appears to claim that he had known the Incarnate Christ during His earthly life." Such a claim is surely made beyond question in 1:1 and 4:14. In words like those written in these verses we hear the note of Apostolic authority. Who but one who had been an Apostle of Christ would have dared to write such words?

The vexed question of the "Elder John" is dealt with under Second John.

Purpose of the Epistle

The Fourth Gospel was written in order to lead men to faith in Jesus as the Son of God and so to the possession of eternal life in Him (Jn. 20:31). This Epistle was written to believers (5:13), in order to confirm them in their faith, in order that they may *know* that they have eternal life. As Plummer says: "The one is an historical, the other an ethical statement of the truth. The one sets forth the acts and words which prove that Jesus is the Christ, the Son of God; the other sets forth the acts and words which are obligatory upon those who believe this great truth." The Epistle was also written in order to warn believers against some dangerous errors that were threatening to lead astray unstable souls. The Epistle is thus more polemical in tone than the Gospel.

It seems likely that the heresy which John deals with is chiefly that of Cerinthus, as is pointed out at several points in the exposition: see what is written on 1:7, 2:22, 4:2 and 3, and 5:6. Cerinthus was a contemporary of John; and Polycarp, as Irenaeus informs us, said that Cerinthus and John had come into conflict at Ephesus. According to Polycarp, John on one occasion rushed out of a public bath at Ephesus, at the sight of Cerinthus, crying, "Let us fly, lest even the bath fall on us, because Cerinthus, the enemy of the truth, is within." Some passages in the Epistle read as though John were opposing docetic heresies. "Docetism" is defined in Chamber's *Twentieth Century Dictionary* as "a second Century heresy, which denied the human nature of Christ, affirming that His body was only a semblance." In the Epistles of Ignatius (c. 115 A.D.) such heresies are combated in their fullblown form, but in John's day, a little earlier, they were beginning to appear. His emphatic assertion of the reality of the Incarnation in 1:1, 4:2 and 3, and 5:6 may be regarded as having some kind of reference to such heresies, but the chief object of his attack seems to have been the more subtle and more dangerous heresy of Cerinthus.

Dr. W. D. Niven, in an article in Hastings' DAC, describes Cerinthus as "one of the earliest of the Gnostics. The world, he taught, was not made by the supreme God, but by a Power inferior to, and ignorant of Him. He denied the virgin birth of Jesus, who was, however, pre-eminent for righteousness, prudence and wisdom. He separated Jesus and Christ. Christ descended on Jesus after baptism, and left Him before the crucifixion. Jesus suffered and rose again, but Christ, a pure spirit, was impassible." Our chief authority for this is the treatise of Irenaeus *Against Heresies*. It can easily be seen that a knowledge of these facts helps us to understand John's meaning in 4:2 and 3, but especially his meaning in 5:6.

The Gnostic heretics were to become later on, in the second century, a prolific source of mischief to the Church, and Irenaeus and other Christian teachers waged against them a relentless warfare. In Gnosticism we see a strange mingling of Christian and heathen elements. It may be described as a welter, confused and often contradictory, of imaginative speculations regarding the universe and its relation to God. Remarkable indeed is the kaleidoscopic variety which marks Gnosticism, but two guiding principles may be seen running through all Gnostic thought.

(a). The first principle is that of the supremacy of the intellect and the superiority of mental enlightenment to faith and conduct. These heretics prided themselves on being the "knowing ones," as the word "Gnostic" implies, and they often ignored the ethical demands of Christianity. Dr. Dodd remarks that there is no reason to doubt that "some of the heretics believed themselves to be so far above good and evil that their conduct scandalised even the easy-going censors of Roman society. Yet it would certainly be unjust to tar all Gnostics with that brush." Many of them, however, if not most of them, were tarred with that brush, and John does not spare them. As Dr. A. T. Robertson says, he "uses plain terms for the leaders (liars, antichrists) in his effort to save the loyal followers of Christ from these plausible and perilous purveyors of speculative philosophy that sapped its victims of all spiritual life and energy." In opposition to such sadly mistaken and such dangerous teaching John insists very strongly that it is genuine Christians who are the true "knowing ones." He says that he writes to his readers, not because they do not know, but because they know (2:21). The knowledge which they possess as the result of the anointing from the Holy One (2:20) is a knowledge which involves holiness of life and conduct as well as intellectual enlightenment (2:3 and 4). Consider what John writes about Antinomianism in 1:8—10.

(b). The second guiding principle which ran through all Gnostic thought is the belief in the inherent evil of matter and everything material, an idea which is a persistent postulate of oriental thought, the influence of which is here apparent. If matter is inherently and radically evil, there can be no true Incarnation of the Son of God. It helps us to understand John's insistence on the reality of the Incarnation (1:2, 3; 4:2, 3; 5:20) to remember the kind of teaching that was in the air, in the intellectual atmosphere, around him as he writes.

The polemical element, however, forms, after all, only a small part of the Epistle. The greater part of it is of a more positive character. "It is probably true," Brooke writes, "that the writer never loses sight altogether of the views of his opponents in any part of the Epistle. But it is important to emphasise the fact that in spite of this the real aim of the Epistle is not exclusively, or even primarily, polemical. The edification of his 'children' in the true faith and life of Christians is the writer's chief purpose." As Westcott says, John's method is "to confute the error by the exposition of the truth realised in life. His object is polemical only so far as the clear unfolding of the essence of right teaching necessarily shows all error in its real character." Mere denunciation of error gets us nowhere, so John sets before him as his chief aim to lead his readers to a fuller understanding of all that is involved in what he and his fellow-Apostles had *heard* from the Incarnate Logos (1:5). The best way to become immune against infection by dangerous heresy is to *know* the truth (Jn. 8:32) and to be so firmly established in it that any teaching that is alien to the truth as it is in Jesus (Eph. 4:21) will at once be detected by us in its true character. John is here in agreement with Peter, who tells us that the way in which men of unstable mind can attain to spiritual stedfastness is to be in the grace and in the knowledge of our Lord and Savior Jesus Christ, and, in that blessed sphere, as in our abiding spiritual home, to *grow* (2 Pet. 3:17, 18).

IV

Time and Place of Composition

According to persistent and consistent Christian tradition (Justin Martyr, Irenaeus, etc.) the closing years of John's life were spent at Ephesus, from which as a center he went out on evangelistic or teaching missions to the region round about. "He would go away when invited," writes Clement of Alexandria, "to the neighbouring districts of the Gentiles, here to appoint presbyters, there to form new churches, and there to put into the office of the ministry some one of those that were indicated by the Spirit." It seems probable that the Epistle was a kind of circular letter sent out to the Christians in the many places in Asia Minor which John had often visited. Irenaeus, whose testimony, as indicated already, is invested with special weight and authority, says quite explicitly that "John, the disciple of the Lord, who also reclined on His bosom, published the Gospel while he was residing at Ephesus in Asia," and the testimony of the Muratorian Canon is to the same effect. If, as suggested above, the Epistle was a kind of "commendatory postscript" to the Gospel, then the date of both writings would be about the same, that is, towards the end of the first century. The whole tone of the Epistle would seem to indicate that it is the work of a man of mature years and of mellow Christian character, who, out of the depths of a profound experience through many years of the riches of the grace of Christ, addresses his frequent loving exhortations as to his "little children."

V

Analysis of Contents

It is extremely difficult to draw up any satisfactory analysis of the contents of the Epistle. An analysis which satisfies one reader may make no appeal to another. Most readers will agree with Westcott when he says that "it is extremely difficult to determine with certainty the structure of the Epistle. No single arrangement is able to take account of the complex development of thought which it offers, and of the many connexions which exist between its different parts." And yet, as Robertson says, "there is movement, progress, climax. All the threads are gathered together by the close. But meanwhile truth is presented, now from this angle, now from that, with a new focus, a fresh facet that like the diamond flashes light at every turn. The thought is not rambling, not disjointed, not disconcerting, but the author's quick intuitions of parallel lines of thought call for keen attention on the readers' part. The reward, however, is worth the trouble."

We follow here Plummer's analysis, with one or two slight modifications.

After the preface, which occupies the first four verses, the greater part of the Epistle may be divided into two sections, GOD IS LIGHT (1:5—2:29) and GOD IS LOVE (3:1—5:12).

The first section may be divided and sub-divided as follows:

1. WALKING IN THE LIGHT, ON THE POSITIVE SIDE, WILL MEAN CERTAIN THINGS IN THE LIFE AND CONDUCT OF THE BELIEVER (1:5—2:11).

   (a). *Fellowship with God and with the brethren (1:5—7).*

   (b). *Consciousness of sin and confession of sin, in the assurance that forgiveness wait for him in God, through the Advocate who is the Propitiation for our sins (1:8—2:2).*

   (c). *Walking as Christ walked and so obeying the commandments of God (2:3—6).*

   (d). *Love of the brethren (2:7—11).*

2. WALKING IN THE LIGHT, ON THE NEGATIVE SIDE, WILL MEAN THAT CERTAIN THINGS AND PERSONS MUST BE AVOIDED (2:12—29).

   (a). *John's threefold reason for writing (2:12—14).*

   (b). *The world and its ways will be shunned (2:15—17).*

   (c). *The persons to be shunned are the Antichrists (2:18—26).*

   (d). *The way to avoid all these perils is to abide in Christ, enjoying the blessings which come from the anointing of the Holy Spirit and looking forward to the coming of the Lord (2:27—29).*

The second section, GOD IS LOVE, may be divided and sub-divided as follows:

1. THE EVIDENCE OF SONSHIP: DEEDS OF RIGHTEOUSNESS BEFORE GOD (3:1—24).

   (a). *The present and future condition of the children of God (3:1—3).*

(b). *The children of God and the children of the devil* (3:4—12).

(c). *Love and Hate: Life and Death* (3:13—24).

2. THE SOURCE OF SONSHIP: POSSESSION OF THE SPIRIT AS PROVED BY CONFESSION OF THE INCARNATION OF THE ETERNAL SON OF GOD (4:1—5:20).

(4:1—6).

(a). *The Spirit of Truth and the Spirit of error* (4:1—6).

(b). *Love is the mark of the children of God, who is Love* (4:7—21).

(c). *This love makes the yoke of Christ an easy yoke* (5:1—5).

(d). *The threefold testimony to the reality of the incarnation* (5:6—8).

(e). *The acceptance of that testimony ensures the possession of eternal life* (5:9—12).

In the last nine verses of the Epistle we have

(a). *Intercessory prayer* (5:13—17).

(b). *Three great Christian certainties* (5:18—20).

(c). *A final warning* (5:21).

INTRODUCTION TO
SECOND AND THIRD JOHN

In these two short Epistles the author calls himself "The Elder," so that it may be convenient to consider them together here. It may be said that they stand or fall together. They are "twin-sisters," as Jerome said, and it seems impossible to assign them to different authors.

I

Historical Reception

The brevity of these two Epistles and the fact that they are addressed to private persons might lead us to expect few allusions to them in early Christian literature. Such references, however, we do find and that in fairly substantial quantity, at least so far as 2 John is concerned. What the Muratorian Canon has to say is somewhat ambiguous. As we have seen, 1 John is mentioned in this Canon in close association with the Fourth Gospel: later on, this document refers to "two Epistles of the John who has been mentioned before." This has sometimes been taken as referring to 1 John and 2 John, 3 John being omitted, and it has sometimes been taken as referring to 1 John and 2 John, regarded as one Epistle, and to 3 John, but, in view of the fact that 1 John is mentioned in connection with the Gospel, a more natural interpretation seems to be the interpretation which understands the reference to be to 2 and 3 John, If that be correct, we have these two Epistles regarded as canonical at Rome c. 180, and accepted also as the work of John the Apostle.

Irenaeus, the importance and weight of whose testimony we have repeatedly emphasised, says, in his treatise *Against Heretics,* "John, *the disciple of the Lord,* intensified their condemnation by desiring that not even a 'God-speed' should be bid to them by us; for, says he, *he that biddeth him God speed, partaketh in his evil works.*" Again, Irenaeus quotes I Jn. 2:18 and goes on to say: "These are they against whom the Lord warned us beforehand; and *His disciple,* in his Epistle already mentioned, commands us to avoid them, when he says: "*Many deceivers are gone forth into this world, who confess not that Jesus Christ is come in the flesh. This is the deceiver and the Antichrist. Look to them, that ye lose not that which ye have wrought.*" "In one or two respects, it will be observed, Irenaeus must have had a different text from ours," as Plummer points out, "but these quotations shew that he was well acquainted with the Second Epistle and believed it to be by the beloved Apostle. And though in the second passage he makes the slip of quoting the Second Epistle and calling it the First, yet this only shews all the more plainly how remote from his mind was the idea that the one Epistle might be by S. John and the other not."

Clement of Alexandria (fl. A. D. 185–210), as noted in connection with 1 John, quotes 1 Jn. 5:16 as from John's "longer Epistle," thus indicating that he was acquainted with at least another and smaller Epistle: elsewhere Clement quotes the tenth verse of the Epistle, definitely assigning it to John, describing it as "very simple" and as being addressed to "a Babylonian lady by name Electa." Dionysius of Alexandria (fl. A. D. 235–265), in his critical discussion of the authorship of the Apocalypse as cited by Eusebius (*History* VII.) refutes the idea that "the Elder" was an unlikely title for John to use by arguing that his not naming himself is like the Apostle's usual manner. Thus we have witnesses from two very different and widely separated centers, Irenaeus in Gaul and Clement and Dionysius in Alexandria.

Origen (fl. 220–250) knows of the existence of the two shorter letters, but says, as cited by Eusebius (*History* VI.xxv.10) that "not all admit that these are genuine." Eusebius himself, in his famous classification of Christian books (*History* III: xxv.3) includes these two Epistles among the "disputed books, which, however, are well known and recognised by most." Elsewhere he speaks of them without qualification as the Apostle John's. Jerome, about the end of the fourth century, says: "John wrote one Epistle, which is approved by all ecclesiastics and learned men; but the other two, at the beginning of which is 'the Elder,' are said to have been written by John the Presbyter, whose sepulchre is at this day shown at Ephesus." The canonicity of these two Epistles had, however, been recognised by the universal Church by the time of Jerome, as can be seen from the definite pronouncements of important Councils of the Church, like the third Council of Carthage (A.D. 397).

From the summary that has been given of the external evidence with regard to 2 John, "it is apparent," as Plummer says, "that precisely those witnesses who are nearest to S. John in time are favorable to the Apostolic authorship, and seem to know of no other view. Doubts are first indicated by Origen, although we need not suppose that they were first propounded by him. Probably the belief that there had been another John at Ephesus, and that he had been known as 'John the Presbyter' or 'the Elder,' first made people think that these two comparatively insignificant Epistles, written by someone who calls himself 'the Elder,' were not the work of the Apostle."

To 3 John there are far fewer allusions in early Christian literature than to 2 John. With the possible exception of 2 Peter, it is less frequently referred to than any other N. T. writing. The comparative want of external testimony in this case was only to be expected on account of the brevity of the Epistle, the nature of its contents and the fact that it is addressed to an unknown person. Dionysius, however, recognises it and it is mentioned, as we have seen, by Origen and Eusebius. After the time of Eusebius it was recognised by the universal Church, as is proved by the authoritative pronouncements of the Council of Hippo (A.D. 393) and the third Council of Carthage (A.D. 397). But, the chief argument in favor of the authenticity of this Epistle is to be found in the internal evidence, which seems to prove conclusively that it comes from the same hand as 2 John. Thus, the external evidence in support of 2 John is also evidence in favor of 3 John.

II

Internal Evidence and Authorship

It seems clear that these two Epistles come from the same hand: compare 2 Jn. 1 with 3 Jn. 1; 2 Jn. 4 with 3 Jn. 3, 4; 2 Jn. 10 with 3 Jn. 8; 2 Jn. 12 with 3 Jn. 13, 14. It seems just as clear that they come from the same hand as 1 Jn.: compare 1 Jn. 2:7 with 2 Jn. 5; 1 Jn. 2:18, 4:1—3 with 2 Jn. 7; 1 Jn. 2:23 with 2 Jn. 9; 1 Jn. 3:6, 9 with 3 Jn. 11. We seem to be shut up to this alternative, either the writer of these two short Epistles was the writer of 1 John, or he was someone who very successfully imitated his language and style. The first theory is distinctively preferable and far more reasonable.

The objection has been raised that it is difficult to imagine opposition like that of Diotrephes (3 Jn. 9) being offered to so exalted a person as the Apostle John. That seems to be a rather flimsy objection. There is no limit to the lengths to which the ambition of a self-important ecclesiastic like Diotrephes may carry them. Opposition as strong as that offered to John was offered to Paul by the Corinthian Church.

Jerome, as we have seen, informs us that in the fourth century the idea was ventilated that the writer of these two Epistles was not John the Apostle but the so-called "John the Elder." This theory was revived by Erasmus at the time of the Reformation and many moderns accept it. But, as Dr. David Smith says (in EGT), it can hardly be maintained in view of the self-revelation of the author in the Third Epistle. "He appears there as exercising authoritative supervision over a wide circle of churches, writing to them, visiting them, interfering in their dissensions and settling these by his personal and solitary arbitrament, sending deputies and receiving their reports. This is precisely the sort of ministry which, as we have seen, St. John exercised in Asia Minor, and it would have been impossible for any lesser personage than an Apostle. It may, moreover be questioned whether such slight compositions as these two little letters would have won recognition had they not been recommended by the name of the Apostle John." Besides, as Dr. Smith goes on to say, "it is very questionable whether this John the Presbyter ever existed." This vexed question must now be considered.

John the Elder

This "John the Elder" was described by Dr. George Salmon as "one of the most shadowy personages in ecclesiastical history." "A whole school of critics," Salmon wrote, "speak of him with an assured confidence as if he were a person concerning whose acts we had as much information as concerning those of Julius Caesar; but in truth his very existence seems to have been first discovered by Eusebius, and it is still a disputed matter whether the discovery be a real one." The truth seems to be that belief in the existence of a John the Elder at Ephesus, as distinct from John the Apostle, is based on some words written by Papias, and on those words *as interpreted in one particular way.*

Papias, in the preface to his *Exposition of the Oracles of the Lord,* as cited by Eusebius (*History* III.39) writes: "I shall not hesitate to incorporate for you with my interpretations as many things as I once learned well from the *elders* and remembered well, guaranteeing their truth. For I did not, like so many, take pleasure in those that have so much to say but in those that teach the truth, nor in those that remember alien commandments but in those that remember the commandments given by the Lord to the Faith and come from the Truth itself. Now if anywhere one came my way who had been a follower of the *elders,* I would inquire about the words of the *elders* — what Andrew or Peter had said, or what Thomas or James, or what John or Matthew, or any other of the Lord's disciples; and I would inquire about the things which Aristion and the *elder* John, the Lord's disciples, say."

This is what Eusebius makes of that passage in Papias: "Here it is worthy of observation how he twice enumerates the name of John. The former of these he reckons along with Peter and James and Matthew and the rest of the Apostles, plainly indicating the Evangelist; and the other John after an interval he ranks with others outside the number of the Apostles, having put Aristion before him, and he plainly names him an elder; so that the truth of their story is hereby demonstrated who have said that two persons in Asia had the same name, and there are two tombs in Ephesus and each is called John's to this day." The question is, Is that interpretation of the words of Papias the only possible one? We submit that it is not.

In the words quoted from Papias we have an explanation of the plan of his work. His method was (1) to quote a saying of Jesus, (2) to interpret it, (3) to illustrate it by any story which he had gleaned from oral tradition. There were two sources from which he derived such stories. He got some of them from the followers of "the Elders," i.e., quite plainly, as Papias uses that term, the Apostles. But he was not dependent altogether on hearsay. Two of the men who had been in close contact with Jesus were still alive in the early years of Papias, Aristion, an enigmatic person of whom we know nothing but who may have been a follower of Jesus, though not an Apostle, and the Elder John, and Papias had enjoyed the privilege of listening to their living voices. Dr. Smith says that "the transition from 'had said' to 'say,' though ignored by Eusebius, is significant and explains the double mention of St. John. Papias had derived his knowledge of St. John's teaching from two sources: (1) from the reports of men who had companied with him and

the other Apostles while they still tarried at Jerusalem, and
(2) from his own lips after his settlement at Ephesus, where,
Irenaeus says, Papias had been one of his 'hearers.' 'The
Elder John' must mean 'the Apostle John,' since the
Apostles have just been called 'the Elders,' and it is impossible that the term should bear different meanings within
the compass of a single sentence. In his phrase 'from the
Truth itself'," Dr. Smith also suggests, "Papias echoes
3 Jn. 12, and this renders it more than likely that he called
St. John an Elder because the latter had so styled himself
in each of the Epistles."

There may be difficulties in the way of accepting the
interpretation of words of Papias which is here advocated,
but we do not think that they are very serious. We are
inclined to agree with what Dr. George Salmon writes on
this subject in an article entitled "Johannes Presbyter" in
Smith's *Dictionary of Christian Biography*. He writes:
"While we own the Eusebian interpretation of Papias to
be a possible one, we are unable to see that it is the only
possible one; and therefore while we are willing to receive
the hypothesis of two Johns, if it will help to explain any
difficulty, we do not think the evidence for it enough to
make us regard it as a proved historical fact. And we frankly
own that, if it were not for deference to better judges, we
should unite with Keim in relegating, though in a different
way, this *Doppelgänger* of the Apostle to the region of
ghostland." Lightfoot, Westcott and others have admitted
the existence of a Presbyter John in Ephesus at the close
of the Apostolic Age, while Zahn, Plummer, Farrar, Salmon
and many others have regarded his existence as extremely
problematical.

Plummer has an appendix to his *Commentary on the
Johannine Epistle* in the *Cambridge Bible* series in which
he discusses with painstaking thoroughness this whole problem. He directs special attention to Irenaeus, "who made
much use of Papias's work, and independently of it knew a
great deal about Ephesus and St. John; and he makes no

mention of any second John. This fact at once throws the balance against the Eusebian interpretation of Papias." Plummer sums up his discussion of this problem in these words: "Does this hypothetical Presbyter explain a single difficulty? If so, let us retain him as a reasonable hypothesis. But if, as seems to be the case, he causes a great deal of difficulty and explains nothing that cannot be quite well explained without him, then let him be surrendered as a superfluous conjecture."

The curious tradition about the two tombs at Ephesus, originating one knows not how, need not cause us very deep concern. Polycrates was bishop of Ephesus towards the end of the second century. Writing within a hundred years of the Apostle John's death, he informs us that there were at Ephesus then the grave of "John who rested on the Lord's bosom" and the grave of the martyred Polycarp. He makes no mention of the grave of a second John, and, as Plummer asks, "would not the reputed author of two canonical Epistles and possibly of the Apocalypse have found a place in such a list, had such a person existed distinct from the Apostle?" Dionysius of Alexandria, writing a century and a half after the death of the Apostle John and far away from Ephesus, knows of two tombs, but he gives no indication that he or anybody else known to him believed that they were the graves of two Johns. Jerome, writing still later and still further away from Ephesus, as we have seen, says that a second tomb is shown at Ephesus as the tomb of John the Elder, but, in the same treatise as that in which he makes this statement (*Concerning Famous Men*) he says that "some think that they are two monuments of the same John, viz., the Evangelist." It is within the bounds of possibility that these people were quite right; there may have been two rival sites claiming to be the burial place of the Apostle.

Writing not a profound treatise on doctrine to a Christian Church but two simple notes to individual Christians, John prefers to designate himself, not by the lofty title of

"Apostle," but by the lowlier one of "Elder." He writes as one who is deeply concerned about the spiritual welfare of the flock over which the Holy Spirit has made him a "bishop," or an "overseer," to quote the words used by Paul in his farewell address to the *elders* of the Church of *Ephesus* (Acts. 20:28): the word "bishop" and the word "presbyter," or "elder" were, of course, in N. T. times interchangeable terms. If Peter could call himself an "elder," so also might John. See commentary on 2 Jn. 1.

III

The Persons Addressed

Second John is addressed to "the elect lady and her children." The first impression made on us by that form of address and by the whole tone of the letter is undoubtedly this, that it was written to an individual, to some outstanding Christian lady of Asia Minor. Many have followed Jerome in supposing that the letter was written to the Church universal, or to some particular Church. In Germany, Huther, Holtzmann and others have taken this view, and so have Lightfoot, Wordsworth and others in England; Salmon adopts the same theory. The list of names is impressive, and yet none of the arguments advanced in support of this theory are conclusive. We feel constrained to agree with Plummer when he says: "That 'the elect lady' *may* be a figurative name for a Church, or for *the* Church, must at once be admitted: and perhaps we may go further and say that such a figure would not be unlikely in the case of a writer so fond of symbolism as S. John. But is a sustained allegory of this kind likely in the case of so slight a letter?" To read into this simple little letter a mystic meaning seems quite unnecessary. The elect lady is spoken of throughout as a person; her children are mentioned and are described, some of them, as walking in the truth; the Apostle promises her a visit in the near future, when he will speak to her face to face; her elect sister and *her* children are mentioned. "It would be straining the letter," Dr. Paton J. Gloag writes in his *Introduction to the Catholic Epistles,* "and destroying its simplicity, to suppose that there is here a hidden meaning: that a Church and not an individual was the object of address.... And, on this supposition, the distinction between the elect lady and her children would vanish, as it is the children themselves, that is, believers, who constitute the Church; the two are identical."

Clement of Alexandria, as we have already noted, thought that the word "electa" was the lady's name, and that the letter was addressed to "the lady Electa." Others have thought that her name was "Kyria," the English transliteration of the Greek word here rendered as "lady," so that the letter was addressed to "the elect Kyria." This opinion is favored by Athanasius, who says: "John is writing to Kyria and her children," and it is adopted by Bengel, Neander, Alford and many others. Such speculations are, more or less, worthless, and it is better to retain the translation in our Version, "the elect lady." We do not know her name. Far more important for her than to have her name inscribed on this page of holy writ was it to have her name in the Book of Life (Phil. 4:3) and to have Christ's new name written on her (Rev. 3:12). These privileges were hers, for she was evidently a woman of the finest Christian character whom John esteemed very highly.

Third John is addressed to "Gaius the beloved." About him we know nothing whatever beyond what is suggested in the remarkable tribute which John pays to him in the second and third verses of the letter. The exposition seeks to bring out the significance of that tribute. If in the recipient of 2 John we have a noble example of Christian womanhood in the first century, in this letter we are introduced to a first century Christian gentleman of kindred spirit.

Elsewhere in the N. T. we meet with three men who bore the name Gaius: (1) Gaius of Corinth, who was baptized by Paul (1 Cor. 1:14), who is possibly the Gaius in whose house Paul was living in Corinth when he wrote the Epistle to the Romans (Rom. 16:23); (2) Gaius of Macedonia who was with Paul during the riot at Ephesus (Acts 19:29); and (3) Gaius of Derbe in Lycaonia, who is mentioned in the list of those who accompanied Paul on his last journey to Jerusalem (Acts 20:4). The attempts that have been made to identify John's friend with one or other of these men are futile: the name Gaius is the same as the Latin Caius, one of the most common names in the Greek and Roman world. The likelihood is that John's friend was somebody in Asia Minor distinct from the three men mentioned above.

IV

Time, Place and Occasion of Composition

These two little letters were probably written about the same time as 1 John, that is, towards the close of John's life. It may be, though such an idea may appear to be a rather precarious one, that the unwillingness to write a long letter expressed in both Epistles may indicate that the author is an old man who finds too much writing rather irksome. The place of writing was most likely Ephesus, where John spent the latter part of his life.

In both Epistles we seem to catch far-off echoes of the false teaching which is denounced in 1 John. While some of the elect lady's children were walking in the ways of true Christian doctrine and living, others of them may have been in danger of being led astray by the false teaching. Therefore, John writes a further warning about the deceivers and the "progressive" things of a wrong kind. Diotrephes the ambitious ecclesiastic (3 Jn. 9) may have been in sympathy with the false teaching, though that is by no means certain: it is his conduct that is censured, not his opinions. John warns Gaius against him and warmly commends Demetrius, who may have been the bearer of 3 John.

Analysis of Contents

The contents of 2 John may be analysed thus:

1. *A salutation* (1—3).
2. *A statement of the occasion of writing* (4).
3. *An exhortation to love and obedience* (5, 6).
4. *Warnings against false teachers* (7—11).
5. *A conclusion* (12, 13).

The contents of 3 John may be analysed thus:

1. *Gaius* (1—8).
2. *Diotrephes* (9, 10).
3. *Demetrius* (11, 12).
4. *A conclusion* (13, 14).

In these two Epistles we have precious specimens of the private correspondence of John, and they disclose the heart of the Apostle of love without restraint and with the utmost frankness. "They are eminently Christian letters," as Gloag says, "and by their high moral tone and spirituality are distinguished from the celebrated remains of antiquity, the letters of Cicero and Pliny." Some scholars, such as Moffat in his book *The Approach to the New Testament,* have ventured to say that we would not have suffered much loss if these two tiny notes had been excluded from the N. T. Canon. They seem at first sight to be very slight and almost insignificant, but closer inspection may lead us to revise such an idea. There is good reason for saying that we would have been spiritually poorer if we did not have the subtle rebuke of "advanced" thinkers in 2 Jn. 9 and the mordant pen-portrait of Diotrephes in 3 Jn. 9. And, further, the Epistles are interesting because of the glimpses which they give us of conditions in the Apostolic Churches — the threatened inroad of heretical teaching, the institution of travelling evangelists, and the occasional resistance even to Apostolic authority.

Archbishop Alexander, in the *Speaker's Commentary*, says that in these two short occasional letters John provided two safeguards for the Catholic Church. "Heresy and schism," he says, "are the dangers to which it is perpetually exposed. St. John's condemnation of the spirit of *heresy* is recorded in the Second Epistle; his condemnation of the spirit of *schism* in the Third Epistle. Every age of Christendom up to the present has rather exaggerated than dwarfed the significance of this condemnation."

Dr. Samuel Cox's interesting little book, *The Private Letters of St. Paul and St. John,* may be studied with profit.

CHAPTER I

THE PREFACE TO THE EPISTLE

1:1—4

1 That which was from the beginning, that which we have heard, that which we have seen with our eyes, that which we beheld, and our hands handled, concerning the Word of life

2 (and the life was manifested, and we have seen, and bear witness, and declare unto you the life, the eternal life, which was with the Father, and was manifested unto us);

3 that which we have seen and heard declare we unto you also, that ye also may have fellowship with us: yea, and our fellowship is with the Father, and with his Son Jesus Christ:

4 and these things we write, that our joy may be made full.

1 The opening words remind us inevitably of the opening words of the Fourth Gospel and provide the first clear piece of evidence that the two books had the same author. The *beginning* here takes us back into the infinite reaches of the past eternity. From that beginning the Throne of the Eternal stood firmly established (Jer. 12, Ps. 93:2) and the Eternal Word was with the Eternal Fathei then. He did not come into existence at some point in time; He *was* from all eternity.

In his opening words John strikes his first blow at the heresy which he has in view throughout the Epistle, the heresy of the Gnostics who said that the body of Jesus was no true human body. We heard Him speak, John says, we saw with these eyes of ours, some sixty years ago, and what we saw and heard has left on us an impression which lasts until this day: such seems to be the force of the perfect tenses used here. "His readers," says Dr. David Smith, "might doubt it, since they belonged to a later generation and had never seen Jesus; but St. John had seen Him, and he assures them, with elaborate iteration, that it is no dream."

We not only saw Him, John proceeds, we *beheld* Him, and this word, as in Jn. 1:14, suggests a steady and deliberate gazing upon. Here we have an aorist tense, followed by another, "handled," and they suggest that there John is thinking of some special occasion when he and his fellow-Apostles had the experience here described. The word *handled*[1] occurs in Lk. 24:39, the verse to which Ignatius refers thus, using the same word, in his letter to the Church at Smyrna: "I know and believe that He was in the flesh after the resurrection: and when He came to Peter and his company, He said to them, Take, *handle* Me, and see that I am not a bodiless demon." Westcott thinks that there is a clear reference to the Risen Christ in *handled*, and he asserts that this "makes it probable that the special manifestation indicated by the two aorists is that given to the Apostles by the Lord after the resurrection, which is in fact the revelation of Himself as He remains with the Church." He adds the remark that "the tacit reference is the more worthy of notice because St. John does not mention the fact of the resurrection in his Epistle." Thus John asserts in the most emphatic language the reality of our Lord's body before the Resurrection and after it.

The One who was thus manifested in the reality and fulness of human nature is the Word of Life, the Logos of life.[2] Out of about 20 instances of the use of the preposition

---

[1] ἐψηλάφησαν. In addition to Lk. 24:39, the Greek verb here used occurs in N. T. in Acts 17:27 (*feel after*) and in Heb. 12:18 (*touched*). It occurs in Deut. 28:29, Job 5:14 and 12:25 (LXX) of the act of groping in the dark. Plato uses it in his *Phaedo* of vague guesses after truth. Now that the Eternal Logos has been manifested, we no longer fumble in the dark, feeling after God; in Christ we have grasped hold of Reality.

[2] ὁ λόγος τῆς ζωῆς. Whence did John derive this term, which he evidently assumes that his readers will understand? There can be little doubt that the roots of the ideas conveyed by this term are to be sought in the O. T. In the Book of Psalms the Word of God is spoken of as

concerning in the Fourth Gospel all except two refer to witness concerning *persons,* so that the reference here is probably to the *personal* Logos of the opening words of the Gospel, the personal Logos, in whom, as Plummer says,

---

the instrument or agent of God in creation (33:6; 107:20; 147:15). In chapter eight of Proverbs the Wisdom of God is personified in a striking way. In such O. T. passages we have a preparation for the revelation in the N. T. of the personal Logos (Jn. 1:1), the personal Wisdom of God (1 Cor. 1:24), the One through whom all things came to be (Jn. 1:3) and in whom all things cohere (Col. 1:17).

Philo, the famous Jewish philosopher who flourished in Alexandria between the year 40 and the year 50 of our Era, has much to say about the Logos. His teaching here is confused and indeterminate, but by the Logos he means, we may say, some kind of intermediate agency, by means of which God created the material universe and communicates with it. But, as Plummer says in a note on Jn. 1:1 in the *Cambridge Bible,* "whether this Logos is one Being or more, whether it is personal or not, we cannot be sure; and perhaps Philo himself was undecided." His misty, vague philosophising is worlds away from John's concrete, historical outlook on the personal Logos, who from times eternal was with God and who became flesh in Jesus Christ. The theory that John derived the term *Logos* from Philo is very wide of the mark; there is indeed no real evidence that John had ever heard of Philo.

It is just as wide of the mark to regard John as having derived this term from Greek philosophy. It is true that the Stoics had much to say about the Logos as the principle of reason diffused throughout the universe, and similar ideas occur elsewhere in Greek philosophy. It is conceivable that the term may have been, so to speak, in the air, in the intellectual atmosphere, around John in Ephesus when he wrote his Gospel. He *may* have used the term right at the beginning of the Gospel to catch the ear of the thinkers of Ephesus. "Here," he may have intended to say to them, "is what you have been vainly fumbling after in your philosophical speculations, here is the solution of the 'Riddle of the Universe.'" "Human thought," says Plummer, "had been searching in vain for some means of connecting the finite with the Infinite, of making God intelligible to man and leading man up to God. John knew that he possessed the key to this enigma. He therefore took the phrase which human reason had lighted on in its gropings, stripped it of its misleading associations, fixed it by identifying it with the Christ, and filled it with that fulness of meaning which he himself had derived from Christ's own teaching."

"had been hidden from all eternity all that God had to say to man, and who was the living expression of the Nature and Will of God." He is the Logos who is the Life (Jn. 14:6) and who communicates to all believers the fulness of the life eternal."

2 "Because," says Calvin, "the greatness of the thing demanded that its truth should be certain and proved, he insists much at this point." The Life was manifested, in the Word made flesh, as John had said in his Gospel (1:14). He repeats the words, "we have seen," but he does not merely repeat himself. He has the added idea of the witness of himself and his fellow-Apostles to the great fact of the Incarnation and their announcement of it to men. When men believe in the Incarnate Logos they have life in Him (1 Jn. 5:12). The Apostles declared to men "the Life, the eternal (Life)," the repetition of the definite article emphasising the two ideas of "life" and "eternal."

3 Our purpose, John now says, in announcing the great fact of the Incarnation is that "you also," who have not seen and heard what we have been privileged to see and hear may share in the spiritual blessings which we enjoy, as you have fellowship with the Father and the Son. That great word *fellowship*,[3] as used in Acts 2:42, may have some kind

---

[3] In connection with this great N. T. word κοινωνία chapter 26 of the *Westminster Confession of Faith*, "Of Communion of Saints," might be studied with considerable profit. The first two paragraphs read: "I. All saints that are united to Jesus Christ their Head by His Spirit and by faith, have fellowship with Him in His graces, sufferings, death, resurrection and glory. And being united to one another in love, they have communion in each other's gifts and graces; and are obliged to the performance of such duties, public and private, as do conduce to their mutual good, both in the inward and outward man. II. Saints, by profession, are bound to maintain an holy fellowship and communion in the worship of God, and in performing such other spiritual services as tend to their mutual edification; as also in relieving each other in outward things, according to their several abilities and necessities. Which communion, as God offereth opportunity, is to be ex-

of reference to the sharing in worldly goods which marked the Church of the early days. In the Apostolic Benediction (2 Cor. 13:14) we have mention made of "the fellowship of the Holy Spirit." The Three-one God shares all the good things of His grace with those who are His through vital union with Christ. They have been called into the fellowship of the Son of God (1 Cor. 1:9) and through the Son they come to the Father and have the Holy Spirit dwelling in them in order to lead them to personal possession of all that the Three-one God means them to have and to enjoy.

4 In Jn. 20:31 John states his reason for writing his Gospel. Here he states one of his reasons for writing this Epistle; he gives other reasons in 2:1, 2:12—14 and 5:13. He desires that "our joy[4] may be made full and remain full." That may mean that he desires that the joy of himself and his fellow-Apostles may be made full, as they see their converts growing in grace continually and possessing their possessions: "fill up the cup of my joy," Paul writes to his Philippian converts (Phil. 2:2). Perhaps, the reference is to the joy in which the recipients of the letter may share — "yours as well as ours." Christians should long for fulness of joy, so that they, so to speak, may have not just a drop or two in the bottom of the cup but may have a cup that

---

tended unto all those in every place who call upon the Name of the Lord Jesus."

It is fellowship with the Father and the Son that John emphasises, and the exposition seeks to bring out something of the meaning of such fellowship. It is a fellowship which commits the child of God to a life of holiness, as John proceeds to say, and as Paul says in 2 Cor. 6:14. But, the idea of having fellowship with the saints in the supply of their bodily needs, so strongly emphasised in the Confession, is a N. T. idea. John touches upon it in this Epistle (3:17). In the exposition reference is made in this connection to Acts 2:42. Paul writes of the fellowship of the churches of Macedonia in the ministering to the Jerusalem saints (2 Cor. 8:4). The Greek word is translated "contribution" in Rom. 15:26 and 2 Cor. 9:13. In Heb. 13:16 we have the words, "Do not forget beneficence and *koinonia*."

4 *Our joy.* This is the better attested reading. The English A. V., following some of the later MSS, has "your joy."

runs over (Ps. 23:5). In the Upper Room Our Lord told His disciples that this was His purpose with regard to them (Jn. 15:11, 16:24, 17:13). The note of joy is heard everywhere in the N. T. Think of Paul (Rom. 5:11, 2 Cor. 6:9, etc.). Think of what Peter writes about people who, amid manifold trials, have joy unspeakable and full of glory, joy that is *glorified,* joy that has in it a foretaste of the joy of heaven (1 Pet. 1:8). Think of what James writes about the same kind of people (Jas. 1:2). These early Christians assurdely did receive that fulness of joy which their Lord had promised to give them.

Plummer sums up the teaching of these four opening verses in this way: "There is a Being who has existed with God the Father from all eternity: He is the Father's son: He is also the expression of the Father's Nature and Will. He has been manifested in space and time; and of that manifestation I and others have had personal knowledge: by the united evidence of our senses we have been convinced of its reality. In revealing to us the Divine Nature He becomes to us life, eternal life. With the declaration of all this in our hands as the Gospel, we come to you in this Epistle, that you may unite with us in our great possession, and that our joy in the Lord may be made complete."

PART I: GOD IS LIGHT — 1:5—2:29

We come now to the first main division of the Epistle; it extends, with some digressions here and there, to the end of the second chapter and the theme is GOD IS LIGHT. Two sections can be distinguished here: (1) Walking in the light will have positive meaning for the life and conduct of the believer (1:5—2:11). (2). Walking in the light, on the negative side, will mean that certain things and persons must be shunned (2:12—29).

1. WALKING IN THE LIGHT — 1:5—2:11

Walking in the light, on the positive side, will mean certain things in the life and conduct of the believer.

"This section," as Plummer says, "is largely directed against the Gnostic doctrine that to the man of enlightment all conduct is morally indifferent. Against every form of this doctrine, which sapped the very foundations of Christian Ethics, the Apostle never wearies of inveighing. So far from its being true that all conduct is alike to the enlightened man, it is the character of his conduct that will shew whether he is enlightened or not." If he is walking in the light these things will be found in his life and conduct: (a). *Fellowship with God and with the Brethren* (1:5—7); (b). *Consciousness of sin and confession of sin, in the assurance that forgiveness waits for him in God, through the Advocate who is the Propitiation for our sins* (1:8—2:2); (c). *Walking as Christ walked and so obeying the commandments of God* (2:3—6); (d). *Love of the Brethren* (2:7—11).

5 And this is the message which we have heard from him and announce unto you, that God is light, and in him is no darkness at all.

6 If we say that we have fellowship with him and walk in the darkness, we lie, and do not the truth:

7 but if we walk in the light, as he is in the light, we have fellowship one with another, and the blood of Jesus his Son cleanseth us from all sin.

5 John's message he has received from Christ; it is no invention of his, evolved out of the depths of his own inner consciousness. In that message this great truth emerges which is stated by John in most emphatic terms, "God is light and darkness in Him there is none at all." There may be suggested here the idea that in God dwells the light of perfect knowledge: those upon whom His light shines *know* Him that is from the beginning (2:13, 14), they *know* the Father (2:13), they *know* all things, they all *know* (2:20). But, in the light of the context, the supreme idea suggested seems to be that of the *holiness* of God. In 4:8 John says that God is love, in Jn. 4:24 we have the words of Our Lord "God is Spirit." These three declarations suggest to us profound thoughts regarding God; spirit, light, love are His very Nature. God *is* light; such a statement goes beyond such O. T. declarations as Ps. 27:1 or Isa. 60:19, 20. God is in the light (v. 7), He dwells in the light (1 Tim. 6:16), but, more than that, He *is* light. So, when the Eternal Son was manifested, that meant the breaking of a great light into the darkness of a sinful world (Mt. 4:16, Lk. 1:78, 79). The figurative use of "darkness" to describe moral and spiritual evil is frequent in John; in the Gospel see 1:5, 8:12, 12:35, 46; in this Epistle see 2:8, 9, 11. The figurative use of "light" to describe the blessings of the Gospel is found in Paul as well as in John: see 2 Cor. 4:6 and Eph. 5:8.

6 Here the "son of thunder" speaks and he hurls a shattering thunderbolt against the deadly heresy of Antinomianism. Note the thrice-repeated phrase, "if we say," indicating three false claims (vv. 6, 8, 10); cf. "he that saith" (2:4 and 9). God is light and sin is darkness. It is impossible to be living in sin or to compromise with it and to have fellowship with the holy God. We lie — our whole life is a lie. For the thought of "doing the truth" cf. Jn. 3:21. Not merely must we know the truth, or understand the truth, or speak the truth; we must *do* the truth. "The truth," says Brookes (ICC), "has no exclusive reference to the sphere of the intellect. It expresses that which is highest, most completely in conformity with the nature and will of God, in any sphere of being. 'Speaking' the truth is only one part of 'doing' the truth, and not the most important part. To 'do the truth' is to give expression to the highest of which he is capable in every sphere of his being. It relates to action and conduct and feeling, as well as to word and thought." The life of practical godliness is expected of us. We may *say* that we have fellowship with God, but no amount of fair speech will make up for the want of such practical godliness.

7 We are called to walk in the light, to make steady progress in the life of conformity to the revealed will of God, who is light. As we walk on in the light, it ought to increase and widen ever more and more around us, even unto the perfect day (Prov. 4:18): God, on the other hand, *is* in the light, eternally, unchangeably. If we walk in the light, two blessed results will follow.

(1). *Fellowship with one another.* This possibly means principally the mutual fellowship of Christians *among themselves,* such fellowship as is enjoined in 3:23, 4:7 and 11 and 2 Jn. 5. Sin tolerated in the life of any Christian mars the fellowship of the Church. Plummer refers in a deeply suggestive way to the description given in Ex. 10:22 and 23 of the thick darkness which prevailed "in all the land of Egypt three days; *they saw not one another, neither rose any from his place* for three days." That means that there was an absolute cessation of fellowship. "Society could not continue in the dark: but when the light returned, society was restored. So also in the spiritual world: when the light comes, individuals have that communion with one another which in darkness is impossible." Augustine and Calvin understood the reference here to be to fellowship *with God,* and it is possible to argue that this idea is more in harmony with the context. We can have true fellowship with God only as we walk in the light and have no fellowship with the unfruitful works of darkness (Eph. 5:11). In some ancient texts, some as old as the Second Century, we have "with God" or "with Him," but that looks like an attempt at simplification. The real truth is that the two fellowships go together, that they ought to go together. The fellowship of Christians with one another is based on fellowship with God, and it is the active realisation of that fellowship and the evidence of it. We recall John Wesley's well-known saying. "The Bible knows nothing of a solitary religion."

(2). *Cleansing in the blood of Jesus.*[5] If we are really walking in the light, the stains and defilement of our life will be more and more clearly revealed to us and thus the keener will be our sense of our need of the Atonement wrought by Jesus. As the sense of sin arises again and again in the soul, the soul betakes itself again to the cleansing fountain (Zech. 13:1) and so fellowship is maintained. The blood means the life freely given, freely sacrificed as an atonement for sin. Elsewhere John speaks of the death of Jesus as removing a burden from the guilty conscience (3:5), or he speaks of the blood as washing us, or loosing us from our sins (Rev. 1:5). He has the figure of the washing of robes in Rev. 7:14 and 22:14. The blood cleanses, he says here, and, as we shall see presently, it does so because

---

[5] This is the reading in ℵ B, C and several of the ancient Versions. The reading "the blood of Jesus Christ" has inferior attestation.

Jesus is the Propitiation. The *present* tense is deeply significant. It speaks of something which goes on constantly, that constant cleansing which the holiest Christians need. Calvin says that "this passage shews that the gratuitous pardon of sins is given us not once only, but that it is a benefit perpetually residing in the Church, and daily offered to the faithful." This verse, no doubt, speaks to us of both Justification and progressive Sanctification.

The blood cleanses from *all* sin, from *every* sin; there is no limit to its efficacy when it is sprinkled on the believing soul. In his *Passion for Souls.* Dr. J. H. Jowett quotes some words of C. H. Spurgeon which he describes as "quite Pauline". "The blood of Christ can wash out blasphemy, adultery, fornication, lying, slander, perjury, theft, murder. Though thou hast raked in the very kennels of hell, yet if thou wilt come to Christ and ask mercy, He will absolve thee." If that be Pauline, it is also Johanine. The blood has such power because it is the blood of the Son of God, of Him who through the Eternal Spirit offered himself without spot to God (Heb. 9:14). In the phrase "His Son" we may say that we have a contradiction in passing of the teaching of the heretic Cerinthus, who according to Church tradition encountered John at Ephesus, who taught that Jesus was a mere man when His blood was shed, because the Divine element in His being left Him when He was arrested in the garden.

PROPITIATION FOR OUR SINS

8 If we say that we have no sin, we deceive ourselves, and the truth is not in us.

9 If we confess our sins, he is faithful and righteous to forgive us our sins, and to cleanse us from all unrighteousness.

10 If we say that we have not sinned, we make him a liar, and his word is not in us.

1 My little children, these things write I unto you that ye may not sin. And if any man sin, we have an Advocate with the Father, Jesus Christ the righteous:

2 and he is the propitiation for our sins; and not for ours only, but also for the whole world.

Consciousness of sin and confession of sin in the assurance that forgiveness waits for him in God, through the Advocate who is the Propitiation for our sins.

8 John now proceeds to deal with a second heresy, that of perfectionism. In v. 8 he deals with indwelling or original sin, in v. 10 with actual transgressions. Later on we will come to some teaching (3:9, 10) which some may have misunderstood. Whatever be the meaning of that somewhat difficult passage in the third chapter, it does *not* teach perfectionism. No one who really understands the exacting requirements of God's law can ever think of himself as sinless. Dealing with perfectionism in his *Systematic Theology* Dr. A. H. Strong says: "This view reduces the debt to the debtor's ability to pay — a short and easy method of discharging obligations. I can leap over a church steeple, if I am only permitted to make the church steeple low enough; and I can touch the stars, if the stars will only come down to my hand.... So I can obey God's law, if I may only make God's law what I want it to be. The fundamental error of Perfectionism is its low view of God's law;

145

its second is its narrow conception of sin." To think of ourselves as sinless is not merely to err or to be deceived, but to *lead ourselves astray*. We are wilfully blind to what is in us. The light is shining, but we are like a man who pulls down the blinds and sits in a self-made darkness. The truth which is Christ Himself (Jn. 14:6), who is also the light, is not in us and so we are blind to our sin.

9 The existence of sin is a patent fact, but it does not make fellowship with God impossible. To those who confess their sins forgiveness comes. In Prov. 28:13 we read about confessing and *forsaking* sin. Here we have simply "confess." Genuine, wholehearted confession implies forsaking. "He who confesses and condemns his sins," says Augustine, "already acts with God. God condemns thy sins: if thou also dost condemn them, thou art linked on to God." The confession, of course, is confession to *God*. The idea of confession to a human priest is absolutely foreign to the N. T. In forgiving sin God is *faithful* to His promises (Heb. 10:23), and His promises of mercy to the penitent are scattered all over His Word, both in the O. T. and in the New. In forgiving sin God is also *righteous:* there is no abating of the demands of His holy law. The Cross of Christ tells us how that is possible: cf. Rom. 3:26. If Christ has made full atonement, "God will not payment twice demand, once from my bleeding Surety's hand and then again at mine". He forgives sins, absolving us from the punishment they deserve, delivering us from guilt. The verb suggests the idea of the *dismissal* of sins, so that they no longer hold us in thrall and we are set free to serve God. The corresponding noun occurs in Acts 5:31, Eph. 1:7, etc. The righteous God cleanses us from all unrighteousness, removing the pollution of sin, so that the new life of holiness is begun in the soul which is to issue in complete conformation to the image of God's Son (Rom. 8:29), who is called in 2:1 "the Righteous One."

10 We may deny that we personally have committed sinful acts. John uses here a perfect tense and it has its full

146

force — present result of past action: we may claim that we are in the condition of having avoided acts of sin. But, if we dare to make such a claim, we make God a liar. That is very strong language, and we ought to observe how John's language increases in strength and intensity in this paragraph. "We lie" (v. 6) and that is bad; "we lead ourselves astray" (v. 8) and that is worse; but to make God a liar is worst of all and indicates a tragic spiritual condition. As Plummer says: "God's promise to forgive sin to the penitent would be a lie if there were no sin to be repented of. And more than this; God's whole scheme of salvation assumes that all men are sinful and need to be redeemed: therefore those who deny their sinfulness charge God with deliberately framing a vast libel on human nature. Whereas St. Paul says, 'Let God be found true, but every man a liar' (Rom. 3:3)."

To say that we have not sinned is to turn a deaf ear to the voice of conscience, which is the voice of God, in the soul. It means that the Word of God is not in us, that the revelation which He has given us of Himself, and especially the revelation given in the Gospel of Christ, has never really entered into us and exercised any influence over us. The delusion against which John is here warning us would be impossible if we steeped our minds in Scripture. Think of how the Scriptures tell us of the sins of great men of God, David in the O. T., Peter in the New.

1 A tender note comes into John's voice as he proceeds to address another warning to his readers: he designates them as his "little children," as he does repeatedly in this Epistle. John had heard Jesus use this form of address once (Jn. 13:33). A tenderness like that of Jesus Himself here fills his soul and this old man of 90 or more addresses his readers of all ages as his little children. "John learned the name from Christ at the first Communion Table," says Dr. Andrew Bonar. "Christ only said it once and John, leaning on His bosom, caught up and repeated it." John, as Dr.

David Smith points out, foresees the possibility of a twofold perversion of his teaching.

(1). "If we can never in this world be done with sin, why strive after holiness? It is useless; sin is an abiding necessity." (2). "If escape be so easy, why dread falling into sin? We may sin with light hearts, since we have the blood of Jesus to cleanse us." "No," he answers, "I am not writing these things to you either to discourage you in the pursuit of holiness or to embolden you in sinning, but, on the contrary, in order that you may not sin."

If, however, we fall into sin, a Paraclete we have with the Father. We *have* sin (1:8 and we *have sinned* 1:10) but also we *have* a Paraclete. Paraclete is the English transliteration of the Greek word. It is passive in form and means "one summoned to the side of another," to aid him, especially to aid him in a court of justice, and "advocate," a "pleader." It was applied by the Greeks especially to "the counsel for the defence," one who undertakes and champions the cause of another when he is arraigned in a court of justice. It occurs four times in the Fourth Gospel, translated "Comforter," with "Advocate, or Helper, or Paraclete" in the margin (Jn. 14:16; 14:26; 15:26; 16:7). Westcott in his *Commentary on John* has a long note in which he gives good reasons for believing that in the Gospel "Advocate" is the most suitable rendering.[6] In the Gospel, he says, "the sense of

---

6 The double rendering "Comforter" in John's Gospel and "Advocate" in his Epistle dates from Wycliffe. Many of the early Versions, the Syriac, Memphitic, Arabic and Ethiopic, keep the original word παράκλητος. Westcott points out, in the note referred to above that Philo uses the word several times in the sense of *Advocate*, or *Intercessor*. Westcott's note seems to make it quite clear that, in all the passages where this word is found, it ought to be translated "Advocate." He says: "Christ as the Advocate pleads the believer's cause against the accuser Satan (1 Jn. 2:1; compare Rom. 8:26, and also Rev. 12:10 and Zech. 3:1). The Holy Spirit pleads the believer's cause against the world (Jn. 16:8—11); and also Christ's cause with the believer, Jn. 14:26; 15:26; 16:14." The Holy Spirit, of course, does *comfort* the believer, in the old sense of that English word; he infuses strength,

Advocate, counsel, one who pleads, convinces, convicts, in a great controversy, who strengthens on the one hand and defends on the other, meeting formidable attacks, is alone adequate." Lightfoot, in his book *On a Fresh Revision of the N. T.* has an interesting discussion of the word and he comes to the same conclusion. Here certainly "Advocate" is the only translation that suits the argument.

God is not merely Judge, He is the Father, and our Advocate is with the Father, always at home with Him. He is the Eternal Son of God, who from times eternal was with God (Jn. 1:1 and 1 Jn. 1:1). Brookes says that "as true man (Jesus) He can state the case for men with absolute knowledge and real sympathy. As God's anointed messenger (Christ) He is naturally fitted for the task and acceptable to Him before whom He pleads. As righteous He can enter the Presence from which all sin excludes." And the position of the word *righteous* at the end of the sentence emphasises very strongly the thought that we have as an Advocate One who is in His own nature righteous. Thus He can well plead with the "righteous Father" (Jn. 17:25; 1 Jn. 1:9) for those who are unrighteous. "Such an highpriest became us, holy, guileless, undefiled, separated from sinners" (Heb. 7:26).

It may be suggested that it is instructive to place John 16:10 alongside John's words here. The Holy Spirit, the Advocate, Our Lord says there, will convict the world in respect of righteousness, "Because I go *to the Father.*" The world which condemned Christ will come to see in the Resurrection and Ascension of Christ proof that Christ is righteous and that God has accepted Him and highly exalted Him to His right hand. And, further, in Christ's atoning sacrifice a righteousness of God, to use Pauline language, has been provided for sinful men, so that they are made

---

fortitude, into his soul when he faces the unbelieving world or when he is oppressed by a sense of loneliness and desolation (Jn. 14:16), so that he no longer feels that he is a friendless orphan (Jn. 14:18).

the righteousness of God in Him (2 Cor. 5:21) and stand accepted in the Beloved, who is the Lord their righteousness (Jer. 23:6 and 33:16). John Bunyan tells us in *Grace Abounding* how this message from God was spoken to his soul, "Thy righteousness is in heaven." "And me thought I saw, with the eyes of my soul, Jesus Christ at God's right hand; there, I say, was my righteousness; so that wherever I was, or whatever I was doing, God could not say of me, he wants my righteousness, for that was just before Him. I saw also, moreover, that it was not my good frame of heart that made my righteousness better, nor yet my bad frame of that made my righteousness worse; for my righteousness was Jesus Christ Himself, 'the same yesterday, and to-day and for ever.' Now did the chains fall off my legs indeed."

Christina Rossetti says:

> Day and night the Accuser makes no pause,
> Day and night protest the Righteous Laws,
> Good and Evil witness to man's flaws;
> Man the culprit, man's the desperate cause,
> Man midway to death's devouring jaws
> And the worm that gnaws.

But, over against that we have this:

> Day and night our Jesus makes no pause,
> Pleads His own fulfilment of all laws,
> Veils with His perfections mortal flaws,
> Clears the culprit, pleads the desperate cause,
> Plucks the dead from death's devouring jaws
> And the worm that gnaws.

2 Our Advocate does not plead our innocence; He acknowledges our guilt and presents His vicarious sacrifice as the ground of our acquittal. It is for sinners that He intercedes, and John includes himself among their number —

we have an Advocate.... He is a propitiation[7] for *our* sins. This word "propitiation" occurs in N. T. only here and in 4:10. Paul uses a very similar word in Rom. 3:25 and the cognate verb occurs in Lk. 18:13 and Heb. 2:17. In Ps. 130:4 the LXX has for "there is forgiveness with Thee" "before Thee is the propitiation" (the word that John has here). Jesus Christ is ever present before the Father as the propitiation. A study of the N. T. passages mentioned, especially Rom. 3:25 and Heb. 2:17, shows that the idea in the word is that of expiation which is based on

---

[7] We must always, when we think of this word ἱλασμός, remember that it is God Himself who provides the propitiation, that it is God who has in Christ reconciled the world to Himself (2 Cor. 5:18, 19). John's word ἱλασμός should be studied in connection with Paul's word ἱλαστήριον (Rom. 3:25), which comes from the same root and conveys a similar meaning. The only other place in N. T. where Paul's word occurs is in Heb. 9:5, where it means the lid of the Ark, the Mercy Seat, which was sprinkled with the atoning blood, a meaning which the word often has in LXX. Farrar says that "the Mercy Seat, sprinkled with the blood of atonement and dimly seen in the darkness through the clouds of incense, was a type of the means whereby man may stand redeemed and accepted in the presence of God. The emblem and the expression belonged to the Jewish ritual; but, as John here adds, Christ's atonement was not only for Jews, but for the whole world. 'Wide as was the sin, so wide was the Propitiation.' "

It is doubtful exegesis to take Paul's meaning to be, "God hath set forth Christ as a Mercy Seat," though Smeaton and others favor that idea. As Charles Hodge remarks, "the sacred writers are not accustomed to compare the Savior to the cover of the ark, nor to illustrate His work by such a reference. This passage, if thus interpreted, would stand alone in this respect." At the same time, ideas which center around the mercy Seat are in place here. Paul's word should possibly be construed as an adjective—God has set forth Christ *in propitiatory power*, and this propitiatory power resides in His blood. As Denney says on Rom. 3:25 (EGT): "It is in His blood that Christ is endued with propitiatory power; and there is no propitiatory power of blood known to Scripture unless the blood be that of sacrifice." When Paul says that God set forth Christ as a propitiation *in His blood* his meaning is exactly the same as his meaning in that other profound statement of his, God *made Him to be sin* for us (2 Cor. 5:21). The Death of Christ makes it plain that God treats sin seriously. His condemnation

sacrifice or *offering.* There is wrath in God, holy indignation against sin, and Christ is the propitiation. It is not
that the propitiation wins God's love for us; it is the other
way about, as John tells us later on (4:10); God in His love
provides the propitiation.

---

of sin was endured to the uttermost in the unfathomable and unknown
sufferings of Christ.

> Bearing shame and scoffing rude,
> *In my place condemned* He stood.
> The Holy One did hide His face,
> O Christ, 'twas hid from Thee;
> Dumb darkness wrapt Thy soul a space,
> *The darkness due to me;*
> But now that face of radiant grace
> Shines out in love on me.

That blessed result follows in the case of every one who has faith in
Jesus (Rom. 3:26), every one, to quote Denney again (EGT) "who is
properly and sufficiently characterised as a believer in Jesus," the Jesus
who shed His precious blood for our redemption.

Denney says on 2 Cor. 5:21, in his *Death of Christ,* "We ought to
feel that moralising objections here are beside the mark, and that it is
not for sinful men, who do not know what love is, to tell beforehand
whether, or how far, the love of God can take upon itself the burden
and the responsibility of the world's sin; or, if it does so, in what way
its reality shall be made good. The premise of the Gospel is that we
cannot bear that responsibility ourselves; if we are left alone with it, it
will crush us to perdition. The message of the Gospel, as it is here
presented, is that Christ has borne it *for* us; if we deny that He *can* do
so, is it not tantamount to denying the very possibility of a Gospel?
Mysterious and awful as the thought is, it is the key to the whole of
the N. T., that Christ bore our sins. Of this, God made Him to be sin
for us is merely another equivalent; it means neither more nor less.
The end contemplated—that we might be made the righteousness of
God in Him—is here stated religiously or theologically. Christ takes
our place in death, and in so doing is identified with the world's sin;
the end in view in this is that we should take His place in life, and in
so doing stand justified in God's sight."

Van Oosterzee, in his *Christian Dogmatics,* in the section which deals
with the High-Priestly Office of Christ, lays down these propositions
and expounds them with his accustomed clarity and fulness of instruction: Reconciliation with God is the first need of humanity. The

It is a remarkable thought that we have here, not, Christ has provided the propitiation, or has offered it, but He *is* the propitiation. He is high-priest, altar and sacrifice all in one; He offered Himself (Heb. 9:14). A propitiation was necessary, Dr. A. H. Strong says, "to satisfy an inner demand of the Divine holiness," and that propitiation is the Son of God himself. Shedd says: "The offended party (1) permits a substitution; (2) provides a substitute: (3) substitutes Himself." The propitiation is *with reference to our sins*. Compare two other passages where the same preposition is used: the Son of God came into the world *with reference to sin* (Rom. 8:3); He suffered, or died, once for all *with reference to sins* (1 Pet. 3:18). The benefits of the Atonement extend to all nations; cf. Jn. 1:29. "As widely as sin had reached, so widely does the propitiation reach," says Bengel. "There is plenteous redemption in the blood that has been shed, there is joy for all the members in the sorrows of the Head," joy for all the great multitude that no man can number (Rev. 7:9).

---

reconciliation of the sinner with God (*katallage*, the word which Paul uses in Rom. 5:11 and 2 Cor. 5:18 and 19) is inconceivable without an atonement for sin in the sight of God (*hilasmos*): true reconciliation can only be the fruit of expiation. God Himself can bring about this atonement in no other way than one in perfect harmony with the majesty of His character. God has in reality accomplished this atonement, by the intervention of His once abased and now exalted Son. The true nature of this atonement we can learn only from the Gospel of the Old Testament and the New, viewed in the light of conscience, and of the Christian life-experience.

CHAPTER II

WALKING AS HE WALKED

2:3—6

3 And hereby we know that we know him, if we keep his commandments.

4 He that saith, I know him, and keepeth not his commandments, is a liar, and the truth is not in him;

5 but whoso keepeth his word, in him verily hath the love of God been perfected. Hereby we know that we are in him:

6 he that saith he abideth in him ought himself also to walk even as he walked.

3 Peter tells us that, since Christ has died for our sins, we ought to die unto sin and to live unto righteousness (1 Pet. 2:24), and John says here that we do not really *know* the Christ of the Cross and the Throne unless we live our lives in practical conformity to His will. "Keeping His commandments" is what is meant by "walking in the light" (1:7). *Keeping* the commandments means being vigilant and watchful to discover them and to observe them strictly — such is the force of the word.

4 The previous statement is enforced by a strong statement of the opposite of it. Hammer stroke after hammer stroke is directed against the men of inconsistent lives.

5 John may seem, as elsewhere, to be repeating himself here, but in every case of apparent repetition we can discover an advance in his thought. We may say of him what Dr. A. B. Bruce says on the writer of the Epistle to the Hebrews, commenting on Heb. 4:13: "The movement of his thought is like that of the flowing tide, which falls back upon itself, yet in each successive wave advances to a point beyond that reached by any previous one." "Word" is a more comprehensive expression than "commandments," describing the sum-total of God's self-revelation and His revelation of the duty which He requires of man. In the man who is vigilant in the keeping of all the requirements of that "Word" verily, or truly, or in deep reality the love of God has been made perfect, or, as Moffat has it, "love to God is really complete."

It is probable that "the love of God" should be understood as meaning our love to God, as it seems to mean in 2:15, 3:17, 4:12 and 5:3; only once does it mean clearly God's love to us, as the context shows (4:9). Of course, our love to God springs from and is inspired by His love to us. "We love because He first loved us (4:19). If we take the phrase as meaning God's love to us, then the idea will be that the redeeming love of God has reached its end, has attained to the goal that love had in view in the man here described, not in the Gnostic heretics whom John has in view who stopped short at mere intellectual knowledge, claiming indeed to be the truly "knowing ones," as their designation suggests. Their brand of knowledge was utterly different from the only true knowledge of God, described by John in vv. 3 and 4. "Some of these Gnostics with slick tongues," says Dr. A. T. Robertson, "were notoriously immoral or nonmoral, as some would say to-day. The test for them and for true Christians is the same 'if we go on keeping His commandments' ". Of course, absolute perfection in love is impossible in this life, but, as we go on keeping the Word of God, we shall advance steadily toward that goal. If we are like the man described here, we are in Him who is righteous; we not merely know Him, we are in Him, in closest union with Him.

6 This union is one that lasts: we *abide* in Him, as in our eternal home. Our Lord's teaching about abiding in Him as the True Vine (Jn. 15:4—7) should be remembered here. The man who makes this high claim for himself should feel *bound,* by an inward obligation springing out of a sense of his infinite debt to Christ, to walk even as *that One* walked, that great One whose Name is above every name. That same expression occurs again in 3:3, 5, 7 and 16 and 4:17, always with reference to Christ. Here we have a further definition of what it means to walk in the light, for Jesus Himself is the Light of the world (Jn. 8:12). For the thought of imitating Christ by walking in His steps, compare Paul in Eph. 5:2 and Peter in 1 Peter 2:21.

7 Beloved, no new commandment write I unto you, but an old commandment which ye had from the beginning: the old commandment is the word which ye heard.

8 Again, a new commandment write I unto you, which thing is true in him and in you; because the darkness is passing away, and the true light already shineth.

9 He that saith he is in the light and hateth his brother, is in the darkness even until now.

10 He that loveth his brother abideth in the light, and there is no occasion of stumbling in him.

11 But he that hateth his brother is in the darkness, and walketh in the darkness, and knoweth not whither he goeth, because the darkness hath blinded his eyes.

7 John now proceeds to say what Paul says in Eph. 5:2, that walking in the steps of Christ means walking in love. "About to enjoin love," says Dr. David Smith, "he begins by loving," using the affectionate form of address which he has also in the third chapter, in verses 2 and 21 and in the fourth chapter, in verses 1, 7 and 11.

The phrase "from the beginning" has been understood in various ways. Augustine and others have taken it as meaning "from the beginning of creation," so that John has been understood to mean that the law of love was imprinted on the mind of man as God made him. Others have understood the phrase to mean "from the beginning of the Law" and point to the commandment in Lev. 19:18. A third idea is perhaps a more likely one, "from the beginning of your life as Christians." John says that his readers had *heard* this commandment, in the oral teaching which they had received, when they were first seeking the Lord.

8 Again, in another sense, from another standpoint, the commandment is new. The commandment "Love one another," according to Church tradition, was continually repeated by John in his teaching at Ephesus. He seems to feel that it cannot be too often repeated, and that we can always find new and deeper meanings in it. Christ has deepened the meaning of such an old commandment as Lev. 19:18, has given us a higher standard to guide and to inspire us — *"as I have loved you...."* (Jn. 13:34). The law of love is exemplified *in* Him and *in* you, the repetition of the preposition suggesting that the law is exemplified in Christ in a different sense and in a deeper degree than is the case with Christians. "He reissued the commandment and was the living embodiment and example of it," says Plummer; "they accepted it and endeavoured to follow it; both illustrated its truth and soundness." The darkness is passing, it is on the wane, the true light is showing more and more of its power; therefore, I bid you walk as children of light, that is, in love. The darkness is not past, far from it; shadows remain here, there and everywhere, but it is passing, for the light is certain to conquer it ultimately. Christianity is the *genuine* light, as opposed to the heresies John has in view. This adjective is very common in John's writings, occurring four times in this Epistle, nine times in the Gospel and ten times in the Apocalypse, and elsewhere in N. T. only five times. Instances of its use are "the true Bread" (Jn. 6:32) and "the true Vine" (Jn. 15:1).

9 Again John dwells on the thought that *saying* is not enough; profession must be tested by conduct. He that *saith* he is in the light and hateth his brother (believer) is in reality in the darkness *up to this very moment,* though the light is shining all around him.

10 He that loveth his brother has his *abode,* his *home* in the light, and not merely *is* in the light. Thus, again, John is not merely repeating himself; there is an advance in his thought. The word *skandalon,* translated "occasion of stumbling," occurs only in Biblical Greek and is found 15 times in N. T. and some 25 times in O. T. Strictly, it means a trap or a snare; then, any impediment placed in

158

the way and causing a stumble or fall. In most places it is used of offence caused to others, as in Rom. 14:13, etc., and so some take John's words to mean that in the case of the man described there is nothing likely to cause others to stumble. Yet, in view of the following verse, the meaning perhaps is, "he has in him nothing to ensare *him* or cause *him* to stumble. We have a close parallel in our Lord's words recorded in Jn. 11:9, 10. It may be that John had before his mind the words of Ps. 119:165 (LXX): "Great peace have they that love Thy law: and they have no occasion of stumbling," there is not to them *skandalon*.

11 The man who hates his brother has his home and his sphere of activity in the darkness; cf. Prov. 4:19. We have here a very graphic description of his condition and his peril. He who walks about in the darkness can have no idea of whither he is going and is at every moment in danger of falling. Dropping the figure we may say that this means that hatred perverts a man's whole action and prevents conscious progress toward any satisfactory goal: cf. Jn. 12:35.

2. Shunning the Darkness — 2:12—29

Walking in the light, on the negative side, will mean that certain things and persons must be shunned.

"Hitherto," says Westcott, "St. John has stated briefly the main scope of his Epistle, He has shewn what is the great problem of life, and how the Gospel meets it with an answer and a law complete and progressive, old and new. He now passes, as it were, to contemplate those whom he is addressing more distinctly and directly, and to gather up in a more definite form the charge which is at once the foundation and the end of all he writes."

We may sub-divide this section of the Epistle as follows: (a). *John's threefold reason for writing (2:12—14)*; (b). *The world and its ways will be shunned (2:15—17)*; (c). *The persons to be shunned are the Antichrists (2:18—26)*; (d). *The way to avoid all these perils is to abide in Christ, enjoying the blessings which come from the anointing of the Holy Spirit and looking forward to the Coming of the Lord (2:27—29)*.

12 I write unto you, my little children, because your sins are forgiven you for his name's sake.

13 I write unto you, fathers, because ye know him who is from the beginning. I write unto you, young men, because ye have overcome the evil one.

14 I have written unto you, fathers, because ye know him who is from the beginning. I have written unto you, young men, because ye are strong, and the word of God abideth in you, and ye have overcome the evil one.

12 A study of the Epistle seems to show that *little children,* whether expressed by the Greek word *paidia,* as in verses 14 and 18 of this chapter, or by the Greek word *teknia,* as in verses 1, 12 and 28 of this chapter, in 3:7 and 18, in 4:4 and in 5:21, means all John's readers and has nothing to do with age or standing in the Christian community. Then, "fathers" and "young men" are two classes among his readers, his older and younger readers. This old man of 90 or more addresses all his readers, first of all, as his *little children,* and he reminds them again of the fundamental blessing of the Gospel, of which he had written already in 1:7, 1:9 and 2:2. Their sins have been forgiven and remain forgiven — such is the force of the perfect tense used. They have been forgiven for the sake of the *Name* of Christ. The Westminster *Shorter Catechism,* dealing with the Third Commandment, says that the *Name* of God is "anything whereby God maketh Himself known." It was by believing on the Name of Christ, that is, by believing on Christ Himself as revealed in His Gospel, that Christians have been given the right to be called children of God (Jn. 1:12). John now reminds his readers again that, because of what Christ is and because of what He has done, their sins are forgiven and they have fellowship with God. The fundamental blessing of the New Covenant from which all

161

the other blessings of that Covenant flow is the forgiveness of sins (Jer. 31:31—34).

13 John now addresses the older men among his readers. Ministers of the Gospel ought to study their people and think of the spiritual needs of all classes among them. They will then *handle aright,* or "rightly divide" the Word of truth, as the English A. V. has it, allocating to each person the portion of spiritual food suited to his need (2 Tim. 2:15). In Eph. 6:4 and Col. 3:21 fathers of *families* are addressed, but here it is older Christians who are meant. Compare our phrase "Fathers and brethren." These "fathers" have had long mature experience in the Christian life, but He whom they know (Christ) is from the beginning (1:1). They know Him with the right kind of knowledge, the knowledge which means keeping His commandments and walking as He walked (vv. 3—6), and that knowledge has grown and deepened with the passing years.

John next addresses the younger men among his readers, some of them perhaps youths, some perhaps in the prime of life. For them life is a conflict, and John reminds them of the strength that has been given them to overcome the evil one: for that designation of Satan cf. 3:12, 5:18 and 19, Mt. 6:13, Mt. 13:19 and 38, Jn. 17:15 and Eph. 6:16.

John next addresses again all his readers, but now he has a change of tense, "I have written," or, "I wrote," instead of the present tense, "I write." Various reasons have been suggested for this change of tense. Some have suggested that "I write" is written from the writer's point of view, "I wrote" from the reader's point of view: that is to say, we have in the latter an example of what is called the epistolary aorist, as in Phil. 2:25 and 28 and Philem. 12. That seems rather a bizarre idea. Why should John make three statements from his own standpoint and then repeat them from his readers' standpoint? And if so, why make any change in them? The most reasonable theory is perhaps this, that "I write" refers to the Epistle, "I wrote" to the Gospel, to which, as many have supposed, the Epistle was a kind of postscript. John first gives reasons why he *is writing* the Epistle, and then gives reasons partly the same and partly not, why he *wrote* the Gospel to which it makes frequent allusions.

John has already reminded all his readers that their sins are forgiven; he now reminds them that they know the Father, such knowledge being possible only when our sins are forgiven.

14 To the "fathers" the same words as before are written. Their spiritual experience cannot be better summed up than as consisting in knowledge of the Incarnate Word. Change and decay they see all around them, but they know Him who changes not (Heb. 13:8). To the younger readers two additional things are said. To overcome the evil one, who is called "the strong man" by our Lord (Mt. 12:29) we need to be strong and Paul tells us where we are to find that strength (Eph. 6:10) and then proceeds to describe the different parts of the panoply of God. The one weapon of *offence* mentioned by Paul is "the sword of the Spirit which is the Word of God" (Eph. 6:17). John says here that the young men are strong, and that they are strong because the Word of God is an *abiding* power at work in them; *contrast* 1:10. Bunyan's description of the conflict between Christian and Apollyon is a fine commentary on Paul and John here. John's next paragraph suggests surely one way in which we may be robbed of spiritual strength.

2:15—17

15 Love not the world, neither the things that are in the world. If any man love the world, the love of the Father is not in him.

16 For all that is in the world, the lust of the flesh and the lust of the eyes and the vainglory of life, is not of the Father, but is of the world.

17 And the world passeth away, and the lust thereof: but he that doeth the will of God abideth for ever.

15 The *world* here is not the world of nature around us, and *the things that are in the world* are not material objects which can be possessed and enjoyed quite innocently, though, of course, they may sometimes be occasions of sin. The natural world is full of wonder and beauty, and ought to lift our minds to thoughts of the "uncreated loveliness," whose dwelling is "the light of setting suns, and the round ocean, and the living air and the blue sky." Scripture, of course, encourages us to entertain such thoughts (Ps. 19:1—6; Ps. 104, etc.). But, there is another world which Christians are to conquer (5:4). They are to fight successfully, as Liddon says in his Bampton Lectures on *The Divinity of our Lord,* "against that view of life which ignores God, against that complex system of attractive moral evil and specuous intellectual falsehood, which is marshalled and organised by the great enemy of God and which permeates and inspires non-Christianized society." Or, to put it otherwise, "world" here means all that is alienated from and opposed to God, the world which lies in the evil one (5:19).

"The things that are in the world," Plummer says, are "those elements in the world which are necessarily evil, its lusts and ambitions and jealousies, which stamp it as the kingdom of 'the ruler of this world' (Jn. 12:31) and not the

kingdom of God." These things are summed up in the three
deadly enemies of the soul mentioned in the next verse.
He who delights in them is a foe of God and has no love
to the Father in him: we have a similar thought in Jas. 4:4.

16 The desire for unlawful pleasures of the senses and
the longing to behold unlawful sights because of the sinful
pleasure to be derived from the sight, idle diseased
curiosity about such evil things — these are two of the dead-
liest foes of the soul. The Greek word translated *vain-glory*[1]
occurs in Greek philosophers from Aristotle onwards; it
occurs in N. T. only here and in Jas. 4:16, in the plural,
"vauntings." Moffat translates here "proud glory of life"
and Weymouth "show and pride of life," someone has suggested, "the braggadocio of life." The cognate adjective
occurs in Rom. 1:30 and 2 Tim. 3:2, translated "boastful."
The person who is described by this adjective, says Dr. C.
H. Dodd, is "a conceited, pretentious humbug." The
radical meaning of the noun is pretentious ostentation as
of a wandering mountebank. What John condemns,

---

[1] In his Tyndale New Testament Lecture for 1944 on *Words
Worth Weighing in the Greek New Testament*, Mr. E. K. Simpson
gives us some interesting information about the word ἀλαζονεία which
John here uses. "Bogus assumption," he says, lies at the base of the
word. Plutarch applies the cognate adjective, which, as indicated in
the exposition, occurs twice in N. T., to a quack doctor—"healer
alazon," boastful and presumptuous. The Greek writer Theophrastus,
in his *Characters*, uses John's word to describe the braggart, "with his
gross exaggeration and gasconading airs," to quote one of Mr. Simpson's
resounding phrases. Mr. Simpson thinks that, while the translation
"vain-glory of life" is a real improvement on the A. V. translation
"pride of life," it is not quite adequate. "When the apostle John,"
Mr. Simpson writes, "abandons, as here, his spare vocabulary for a
polysyllabic noun, there must be cogent reasons for his procedure. He
is contemplating the unregenerate world as a Vanity Fair, and the full
strength of his expression can be brought out only by some such translation as the *charlatanry* or *make-believe* of life. In Plato's *Definitions*
(if they are his) ἀλαζονεία is explained as a state of mind pretentious
of what does not belong to it. James so employs it (4:16) of those who
boast of to-morrow, which is not theirs to boast of at all."

Plummer says, is ostentatious pride in the possession of worldly resources, and he adds these remarks: "These three evil elements or tendencies 'in the world' are co-ordinate: no one of them includes the other two. The first two are wrongful desires of what is not possessed; the third is a wrongful behavior with regard to what is possessed. The first two may be the vices of a solitary; the third requires society. We can have sinful desires when we are alone, but we cannot be ostentatious without company."

These evil things, John says, did not originate with the Father. They sprang from the corrupt heart of man, after man had been seduced by "the ruler of the world." According to Gen. 3:6, Eve was confronted with a threefold temptation which forms a remarkable parallel to the three evil things mentioned here.

17 It is supremely foolish to set our heart's desires on what is already in *process of passing away:* the same verb is used here as in 1 Cor. 7:31. It is only the man who does the will of God who possesses in himself the secret of endurance, because he has, in fact, eternal life in Christ. He has love to the Father in his heart, that love revealing itself in practical obedience to the Father's will.

18 Little children, it is the last hour: and as ye heard that antichrist cometh, even now have there arisen many antichrists; whereby we know that it is the last hour.

19 They went out from us, but they were not of us; for if they had been of us, they would have continued with us; but they went out, that they might be made manifest that they all are not of us.

20 And ye have an anointing from the Holy One, and ye know all things.

21 I have not written unto you because ye know not the truth, but because ye know it, and because no lie is of the truth.

22 Who is the liar but he that denieth that Jesus is the Christ? This is the antichrist, even he that denieth the Father and the Son.

23 Whosoever denieth the Son, the same hath not the Father: he that confesseth the Son hath the Father also.

24 As for you, let that abide in you which ye heard from the beginning. If that which ye heard from the beginning abide in you, ye also shall abide in the Son, and in the Father.

25 And this is the promise which he promised us, even the life eternal.

26 These things have I written unto you concerning them that would lead you astray.

18 Again John addresses his readers as his "little children," as he proceeds to warn them against some deadly errors that were being taught by certain teachers in their vicinity. The phrase "the last hour" presents some difficulties. It is quite literally "a last hour," and some, like Westcott, suggest as a feasible interpretation, "a time of extremity, a very grievous time," but that is doubtful exegesis. The phrase does seem to be an eschatological one. It is only in John's writings that we find mention made of "the last day" (4 times in Jn. 6; Jn. 11:24 and 12:48). The phrase used here is unique. Most modern commentators take John's meaning to be that the end of the world and the coming of the Lord was near at hand, just as they take Paul's words in 2 Tim. 3:1 in a similar sense. The older commentators looked at John's words from another angle, which we ought to consider very carefully.

It is important to remember that, according to the N. T., with the coming of Christ, with His Death and Resurrection and Ascension, the last period of the world's history has begun. God has spoken His final message in His Son (Heb. 1:2). No event in the world's history can ever equal in epoch-making importance the coming of Christ till He comes again. The Christian era, as it has been put, is "the last on the Divine program; the next will be the coming of the Lord." That period has lasted more than 1900 years since John wrote the words before us and it may last some time yet, but, apart from its duration, it can be thought of as being, in a very real sense, the last hour. It is "the last time," as Calvin says, "in which all things are so completed that nothing remains except the final revelation of Christ." That kind of exegesis may not appeal to everybody, but there is something to be said for it. The only real difficulty in the way of accepting it fully is that it is difficult, on this theory, to give a satisfactory meaning to the last clause of this verse, but John may simply mean there that the appearance of the antichrists on the scene is a sign of the beginning of the end, which may or may not be in the immediate future. Dr. G. G. Findlay understands the words in this way: "A last hour it certainly was; and it might be (who could tell?) the last hour of all. Many great and notable days of the Lord there have been, and perhaps will be — many last hours before the last hour of all." Christians should live as though the day of judgment, of which John will write presently, is to be to-morrow, or to-day. The world is on the wane already, John wrote in his day: with mightier emphasis we can say that to-day, and, therefore, with all the more earnestness should we listen to John's loving exhortation to a good life.

John refers to *Antichrist*[2] and to many *anti-Christs*. You *heard* of him, John says: this was a favorite topic in early Christian teaching. Our Lord had prophesied that *false*

---

2   This word ἀντίχριστος is found in the N. T. only in the writings of John (1 Jn. 2:18 and 22, 4:3; 2 Jn. 7). The first of these passages seems to mean that Antichrist is a *person*; the other passages, if they stood alone, might be taken as indicating that Antichrist is a spirit or a tendency, but they ought to be interpreted in the light of the first passage. If, as is suggested above and as is almost certainly the case, John's Antichrist is to be identified with Paul's "man of lawlessness" (2 Thes. 2:3), then the *personality* of Antichrist is clearly proved. Paul's meaning seems to be that there will arise some yet future opponent of Christ who will, at the close of the world's history, gather together into a gigantic confederacy of hell all the forces of ungodliness. "Then the Lawless one will be revealed, whom the Lord Jesus will sweep away with the tempest of His anger, and utterly overwhelm by the awful splendour of His Coming" (2 Thes. 2:8, Wey). The language of this "Little Apocalypse," as it has been called (2 Thes. 2:3—8) is to us obscure, but it was, no doubt, not quite so obscure to Paul's first readers, who had received from him oral instruction on such matters (2 Thes. 2:5), just as John's readers were familiar with *his* teaching on such matters (1 Jn. 2:18). The subject of Antichrist, indeed, must have been a favorite one in early Christian teaching. Outside the N. T., we find writers like Justin Martyr, Irenæus, Tertullian and Jerome dealing frequently with the subject of Antichrist, and all of these take Antichrist to be a person.

In an Appendix to his excellent commentary on the Thessalonian Epistles in the *Cambridge Bible*, Dr. G. G. Findlay says, with reference to 2 Thes. 2:3—8, "like other great prophecies of Scripture, the word of the Apostle Paul has, it appears to us, a progressive fulfilment. It is carried into effect, under the action of Divine laws operating throughout human history, in partial and transitional forms, which prefigure and may contribute to its final realisation." Some of the tendencies of Antichrist had already been manifested, John says, and the "mystery of lawlessness" was already at work, Paul says, in the Apostolic Age. There are some who will agree with Warfield when he says (English *Expositor* for 1886) that it was Nero, the first persecutor of the Church —and Vespasian, the miracle-worker—and Titus, who introduced his divine-self and his idolatrous insignia into the Holy Place, perhaps with

Christs would arise (Mt. 24:24) and that they would be many in number, (Mt. 24:5), but the word which we have here does not mean a *mock Christ,* but an *opponent of Christ,* or a *rival Christ.* It denotes one great enemy of and rival to Christ, probably to be identified with the "man of sin" of 2 Thes. 2:3, who has yet to be revealed but who has many fore-runners. The fore-runners of John's day were heretics like Cerinthus and others who had wrong views of the Person of Christ, which is always the worst kind of heresy. They denied that He had come in the flesh (4:3).

19 John now describes the relation of these anti-Christian teachers to the Church. They did not arise in the heathen world; they were apostate Christians. They had at one time been members of the Church, but only nominal members. They are now not members in any sense. Note the fivehold repetition of "us," as indicating the Christian Church. It was God's will and purpose that these spurious members should be known as such, that it should be made clear that they are *not, any of them,* of us.

20 You *have* an Advocate, John has already told his readers; now he tells them of another precious spiritual possession — ye *have* an anointing.... Over against the Antichrist and his follower he places the Anointed One and His anointed ones. In both O. T. and N. T., oil is a symbol

a directly anti-Christian intent—and Domitian—and the whole line of human monsters whom the world was worshipping as gods that Paul had in mind in his "Little Apocalypse," though they may hesitate to go so far as to assert, with Warfield, that every item in Paul's prophecy was fulfilled in the terrible story of the emperors of Rome. A *partial* fulfilment may be found there, but not a *final* fulfilment. A partial manifestation of the spirit and tendency of Antichrist John found in the heresies of his own day, and we find a partial manifestation of the same spirit and tendencies in the heresies of our own day, but there may be worse outbreaks of heresy yet before the final Consummation.

For further study of the subject of "Antichrist," reference may be made to Findlay's Appendix, referred to above, to an Appendix on "Antichrist" in Plummer's commentary on the Johannine Epistles (*Cambridge Bible* and CGT) and to an article "Antichrist" in Hastings' DAC, which, with some reservation, may be read to considerable profit.

of the Holy Spirit (Ps. 45:7, Isa. 61:1, Acts 10:38, 2 Cor. 1:21). "The Holy One" is, almost certainly Christ, who is so designated elsewhere (Mk. 1:24; Jn. 6:69; Acts 3:14; Rev. 3:7). In this Epistle He is described as "righteous" 2:1 and 29) and "pure" (3:3). In the Upper Room Our Lord promised to send the Spirit of truth to His Church to guide it into the truth (Jn. 16:13) and at the great Pentecost that promise was fulfilled (Acts 2:33).

There is uncertainty with regard to the text here — should we read "ye know all things" or "ye all know"?[3] If we adopt the first reading, the meaning will be, "it is you, not these anti-Christian heretics with their proud claim to superior insight, who possess the true knowledge and that in its fulness, *all the* truth, in accordance with the Lord's promise recorded in Jn. 16:13, the truth in all the width and depth and range of its scope." If the other reading is adopted, there is no great difference in meaning. Spiritual knowledge is not the privilege of any favoured clique in the Church, it is the privilege of the whole Church. Moffat translates: "You all possess knowledge." Christians to-day under the guidance of the Spirit of truth, remain indifferent to any fancy religion that may spring up with a claim to superior knowledge. They are under the New Covenent, so that they are not dependent for knowledge of God and His truth on any *neighbour*, however enlightened (Jer. 31:34); they have independent personal knowledge, as the result of the anointing from the Holy One.

21 "I have not written unto you, or, I did not write to you," John proceeds, "because ye know not the truth...." This is probably an example of the epistolary aorist. John's meaning is, "Do not think that I am warning you against lying teachers because I have any doubts about the reality

---

3   The reading of our ASV text is adopted also by the English A. V. and R. V. It is found in some of the later MSS, in the Vulgate and other Versions. The reading "Ye all know" is found in ℵ and B, so that it has strong attestation. It is adopted by Moffat and others.

of your faith or the soundness of your knowledge. You *know* quite well what I mean and the seriousness of the dangers against which I warn you. You know the truth, you know also that no lie has its origin in the truth, and this poisonous system of thought to which I refer has its origin in the Father of lies. John is writing to them, says Dr. A. T. Robertson, "because they understand what he is saying and know no lie comes out of the truth, which is more than some people see to-day. The gullibility of apparently reasonable people is amazing, when they listen to lies claiming to come out of God's Word." Liddon says that John "does not treat Christianity as a religion containing elements of truth, or even more truth than any religion which had preceded it. John presents Christianity to the soul as a religion which must be everything to it, if it is not really to be worse than nothing."

22 John describes the denial of Jesus as the Christ as "the master-falsehood," as Westcott puts it. "There is no liar if he who denies that Jesus is the Christ is not one." Weymouth translates: "Who is a liar compared with him who denies that Jesus is the Christ?" We have here, Brooke says, "the liar *par excellence,* in whom falsehood finds its complete expression." John is aiming another blow at teaching like that of Cerinthus, who held that "the Christ" was an *aeon,* an emanation from the Deity, that came on the man Jesus at His baptism and left Him on the Cross, or even earlier, in the garden. (See notes on 1:7). Such teaching really denied the full deity and the full humanity of Jesus. Jesus was the Anointed One from His birth to His death; He was the Son of God (1:7) through all His human history. John proceeds to say that the denial of Jesus as the Christ involves the denial of the Father and the Son. That it means the denial of the Son is evident, but that it means the denial of the Father ought to be just as clear. The Son is the revelation of the Father and the only way to the Father (Mt. 11:27; Jn. 14:6). This kind of teaching is indeed one of the manifestations of Antichrist. The reference here does not seem to be to the sinister personal rival of Christ yet to be revealed, but to teachers like Cerinthus, who is the mouthpiece of the rival yet to be and one of his fore-runners.

23 The previous statement is emphasised by an expansion of it, expressed first in a negative proposition and then in a positive one. The man who denies the Son not merely denies the Father, but is cut off from fellowship with the Father: he is an orphan, a fatherless child in the vast loneliness of the universe. "The God of those who deny the Son," Meyer says, "is not the true God, but a false image of their own thoughts, an idol (5:21)." Over against the denial of the Son is placed the confession of the Son — as Lord (Rom. 10:9).[4] The sentences in the preceding verse, the German scholar Haupt says, "fall on the readers' soul like notes of a trumpet," and that can be said also about this verse and the following verse.

24 "*As for you,* whatever others may say and whatever others may teach," let the truths which were taught you in the early days of your Christian experience have a home in your hearts; if these truths have a home in your hearts, you also shall have a home in the Son and in the Father." The Son, we note, is here placed first, the Son through whom alone we can come to the Father. As *abiding* in the Son is the secret of fruitfulness (Jn. 15:4, 5), so it is only by *abiding* in the Son that we can enjoy real fellowship with the Father.

25 It is worth while abiding in this spiritual home, because there we have that eternal life which *He,* that is the Eternal Son, promised to give (Jn. 3:15; 4:14; 6:40; 6:47, etc.).

---

[4] This second clause of this verse is printed in A. V. in italics, as though there were nothing to represent it in the Greek. The words, however, are undoubtedly part of the true text, being found in ℵ ABC and many other authorities. A few authorities omit it accidentally, owing to the fact that the two halves of the verse in the Greek end with the same three words (*hath the Father*).

26 John cannot remain silent while his "little children" are being led astray, for to stray from the truth is a serious thing (Jas. 5:21). He is writing concerning them who *are leading you astray;* they are trying to do so, but they have not succeeded and there is no reason why they should succeed.

27 And as for you, the anointing which ye received of him
abideth in you, and ye need not that any one teach you;
but as his anointing teacheth you concerning all things,
and is true, and is no lie, and even as it taught you, ye
abide in him.

28 And now, my little children, abide in him; that, if he shall
be manifested, we may have boldness, and not be ashamed
before him at his coming.

29 If ye know that he is righteous, ye know that every one
also that doeth righteousness is begotten of him.

*The way to avoid all these perils is to abide in Christ,
enjoying all the blessings which come from the anointing of
the Holy Spirit, and looking forward to the coming of the
Lord.*

27 We have here a somewhat involved sentence, but
the meaning is clear enough. *First,* John says that his
readers have no need that one keep on teaching them. Here
he goes back to what he has already said is vv. 20 and 21.
They had received the anointing from Him, that is, from
Christ, who, as Huther says, "in this whole passage forms
the centre round which all the statements of the Apostle
move"; thus, we have a confirmation of the view that "the
Holy One" in v. 20 means Christ. That anointing *abides*
in them; the Holy Spirit given at Pentecost has never been
withdrawn. Therefore, they are not dependent on any
human teacher. There are many human teachers to whom
we shall be for ever grateful but we should not be slavishly
dependent on any one of them. *Second,* John reiterates his
exhortation to his readers to stay where they are, in the
place of safety, in Christ; it is possibly a command that we
have at the close of the verse, "abide in Him." We might
compare Paul's words directed against false teachers in
Colosse (Col. 2:3, 9 and 10).

28 *And now* — this is the practical conclusion of this whole passage of warning — abide in Him. The words "if He shall be manifested" may be understood with the sense, "If, as is the case. . . ." The verb "to manifest" is used by John of the first coming of Christ in 1:1, 3:5 and 8, as it is by Paul in 1 Tim. 3:16. It is used here and in 3:3 of His second coming in glory as it is by Paul in Col. 3:4. The Greek word translated "boldness" conveys often the idea of "freedom of speech." Such an idea is clearly suitable in Acts 4:13, 29 and 31. As used in this Epistle (5:14) and in Hebrews (4:16 and 10:19), in connection with prayer, it may indicate that holy boldness with which the child of God pours out his heart at the Throne of Grace, telling God everything (Ps. 62:8). Plummer says that, in this Epistle and in Hebrews, "it means especially the fearless trust with which the faithful soul meets God." Here, and in the third passage where it occurs in this Epistle, (4:17), the word is used with reference to meeting the Son of God when He comes in His glory. Some will be "ashamed from Him"; that is the literal translation of John's language here: they will turn with shame, shrink with shame from Him. Plummer remarks on the "graphic terseness" of John's words, and says that "we see the averted face and shrinking form, which are the result of the shame, clearly indicated in the Greek." For the word *Parousia*, which occurs nowhere else in John's writings, see commentary on Jas. 5:7.

29 "To be born of God" is a common Johannine phrase (Jn. 1:13; I Jn. 3:9; 4:7; 5:1, 4, 18). We are also born of the Spirit (Jn. 3:6 and 8). We are nowhere said to be born of Christ, unless the reference in this verse be to Him, and certainly, as Dr. A. T. Robertson says, "to be born of Christ is a possible idea." The proof that we are begotten from on high and remain God's children (perfect tense) is to be found in the *habitual doing* of righteousness. Other signs of the new birth are *love* of the brethren (4:7) and *faith* in Jesus as the Christ (5:1). John proceeds in his next words to describe some of the wonderful results of the new birth.

CHAPTER III

PART II: GOD IS LOVE — 3:1—5:12

We come now to the second main division of the Epistle which may be regarded as extending as far as the 12th. verse of the 5th. chapter, the remaining 9 verses forming a kind of summary of the teaching of the Epistle. The main theme in this second division, with some digressions here and there, may be regarded as being GOD IS LOVE. We may further sub-divide this section into two parts: (1). The evidence of sonship: deeds of righteousness before God (3:1—24). (2). The source of sonship: possession of the Spirit as proved by confession of the incarnation of the eternal Son of God (4:1—5:12).

1.   THE EVIDENCE OF SONSHIP — 3:1—24

We have here (a). *The present and future condition of the children of God* (3:1—3). (b). *The children of God and the children of the devil* (3:4—12). (c). *Love and Hate: Life and Death* (3:13—24).

3:1—3

1 Behold what manner of love the Father hath bestowed upon us, that we should be called children of God; and such we are. For this cause the world knoweth us not, because it knew him not.

2 Beloved, now are we children of God, and it is not yet made manifest what we shall be. We know that, if he shall be manifested, we shall be like him; for we shall see him even as he is.

3 And every one that hath this hope set on him purifieth himself, even as he is pure.

1 The Greek adjective translated *what manner of* occurs again in Mt. 8:27, Mk. 13:1, Lk. 1:29, Lk. 7:39 and 2 Pet. 3:11. It sometimes expresses astonishment and sometimes admiration. In Classical Greek it bore the sense "of what country." It is usually thought that this sense has faded from it in N. T. Greek, though one cannot help wondering whether it may not have retained in some places something of its proper and original meaning. Here, for example, is it too fanciful to discern at least a suggestion of this idea, that the love of God in Christ is foreign to this world; it is no flower that has blossomed in the cold climate of this world? Again, in 2 Pet. 3:11, is it permissible to translate, "What other-worldly people ought we to be"?

Sonship to God is not something to be taken for granted. It is ours through the grace of God and it ought to fill our souls with wonder like the wonder to which John here gives expression. As the Scottish Paraphrase of this passage puts it:

Behold the amazing gift of love
The Father hath bestowed
On us, the sinful sons of men,
To call us sons of God.

178

The idea of God *bestowing,* or *giving* love occurs only here. John calls believers children of God, as he does also in Jn. 1:12. Paul calls them sons of God in Rom. 8:14, Gal. 3:26, Gal. 4:6, 7, but he also calls them children of God in Rom. 8:16. In using the word "son" Paul has at the back of his mind the idea of adoption in Roman law, so that the word emphasises the thoughts of legal right and privilege. In the word "children" the idea emphasised is that of the actual communication of the *life* of God to the soul.

Because of the overwhelming evidence in favor of it, modern critical texts add to the Received Text as represented in the English A.V. the words "and such we are."[1] We have been *called* children of God, and that is not the empty bestowal of a high sounding title; we really *are* children of God, though the enemy of our souls may sometimes have whispered doubts about our standing and though "blind unbelief" may sometimes have listened to these whisperings. *For this cause,* because we belong to the family of God of whose joys and privileges the unbelieving world knows nothing, that world knows us not.

> Concealed as yet this honour lies,
> By this dark world unknown,
> A world that knew not when He came,
> Even God's Eternal Son.

---

[1] *And such we are.* The words "and we are" have overwhelming support in the MSS; they are found in ℵ ABC and many Versions. They are not found in English A. V.; when they appeared in R. V., Charles Haddon Spurgeon was moved to preach a sermon on this verse, with the title, "A Jewel from the Revised Version." Luther was once asked, "Do you feel that you are a child of God this morning," and he answered, "I cannot say that I do, but I know that I am." In Justin Martyr's *Dialogue with Trypho the Jew* we have the words: "And true children of God we are called, and we are." That seems to be a clear reference to this verse, and it bears witness to the fact that, in the text which Justin had before him, about the middle of the second century, these words had a place. *Purifieth.* For this verb see commentary on Jas. 4:8.

If the world did not recognise Him for what He really was (Jn. 1:10), we need not be surprised if it passes us by without remark.

2 *Beloved.* That form of address occurs only once up to this point in the Epistle (2:7), at a point where the subject of love appears for a few verses; in the section of the Epistle on which we have now entered where the main theme is love, this form of address occurs repeatedly, twice in this chapter and three times in the following chapter. The Scottish Paraphrase again brings out beautifully John's thought here.

> High is the rank we now possess,
> But higher we shall rise;
> Though what we shall hereafter be
> Is hid from mortal eyes.

Some hints are given us as to what we shall be, as in Mt. 13:43, Jn. 17:24, Rom. 8:17, Rev. 22:4, etc., but all that is waiting for us has not been manifested to us. One thing we do know, John says, that we shall be like Him, because we shall see Him as He is, not as He was in His state of humiliation, but as He is now in His glory. The manifestation of the Son of God in the flesh raised us to the position of children of God. How much greater transforming power must there be in the vision of Him as He is, when "all His glory, full disclosed, shall open to our sight."

3 The child of God has this hope that rests on Him (Christ), that is based on Him and that is, therefore well-grounded. *Everyone* who has this hope, every one without exception, is pledged to a life of growing holiness. Paul says that in this life the vision of Christ, mirrored in the Word, leads to progressive sanctification (2 Cor. 3:18). John says that every one who has this hope of being like Christ purifies himself, with the unsullied standard of the purity of Christ ever before him. He does so by resorting continually to the cleansing blood (1:7). Though it is only the blood that can cleanse, on each of us rests the responsibility of seeking that cleansing with all our heart; cf. Paul's words in 2 Cor. 7:1. Of the adjective *pure* Westcott says that it suggests "the notion of shrinking from contamination, of a delicate sensibility to pollution of any kind." It will be noted that John does not write, "even as He (That One, as in 2:6, etc.) purified Himself." Christ *is* pure, eternally, unchangeably.

3:4—12

4 Every one that doeth sin doeth also lawlessness; and sin is lawlessness.

5 And ye know that he was manifested to take away sins; and in him is no sin.

6 Whosoever abideth in him sinneth not: whosoever sinneth hath not seen him, neither knoweth him.

7 My little children, let no man lead you astray: he that doeth righteousness is righteous, even as he is righteous:

8 he that doeth sin is of the devil; for the devil sinneth from the beginning. To this end was the Son of God manifested, that he might destroy the works of the devil.

9 Whosoever is begotten of God doeth no sin, because his seed abideth in him: and he cannot sin, because he is begotten of God.

10 In this the children of God are manifest, and the children of the devil: whosoever doeth not righteousness is not of God, neither he that loveth not his brother.

11 For this is the message which ye heard from the beginning, that we should love one another:

12 not as Cain was of the evil one, and slew his brother. And wherefore slew he him? Because his works were evil, and his brother's righteous.

In these verses the thought is more emphatically expressed that our dignity as children of God demands righteousness of life, that righteousness revealing itself supremely in love.

4 In contrast with those who seek to purify themselves are set those who *go on doing* sin, the sin which clouds the vision of God and which separates from God. Sin and lawlessness are interchangeable terms. Sin means living as though there were no God and no law of God which we are bound to obey. We notice how frequently John uses in this chapter the emphatic expression *every* one that...., translated "whosoever" in vv. 6, 9, 10 and 15. Westcott suggests that "in each case where this characteristic form of language occurs there is apparently a reference to some who had questioned the application of a general principle in particular cases." Here John says with decided emphasis that there is no special class of specially illuminated men who are superior to the obligation to keep the law of God.

5 Not only does the man who habitually sins throw off the yoke of God's law but he stultifies the whole purpose of the coming of the Son of God in the flesh. That purpose was to *lift away* our sins: the same verb is used as in Jn. 1:29. This He did by bearing them Himself (1 Pet. 2:24).

> O Christ, what burdens bowed Thy head!
> Our load was laid on Thee.

He who did this was Himself sinless: *sin in Him does not exist.* Compare other N. T. declarations of the sinlessness of Christ (2 Cor. 5:21; Heb. 7:26; 1 Pet. 2:22). See then, says John, how utterly incompatible sin is with sonship.

6 This strong statement seems to contradict what John has already written (1:8—2:2), but the contradiction is only in appearance. Grammar has been enlisted here in the service of exegesis and of sound doctrine, and justifiably so. John has recognised the fact that a child of God may commit an act of sin (2:1). Here he uses present tenses. *Every* one who abideth in Him sinneth not, does not sin habitually and deliberately: *every* one who *goes on sinning*, sinning habitually and deliberately, has not seen Christ in His sinlessness and purity and has never really known Him with the knowledge of those who are in spiritual kinship with Him. "Denial of a sinful nature (1:8) or of any sinful act (1:10) is a lie," Robertson says. "But there is a world of difference between one sin in a struggle against sin (2:1) and the habit of sin (3:6 and 9), which is what John is seeking to prevent." Sin is not in the believer the ruling principle, as it is in the case of the defiant, persistent sinner.[2]

---

2   Ebrard says that John's meaning is that the man so described cannot sin deliberately and intentionally. Augustine says that, so far as

7 The loving form of address, *My little children,* is again repeated, and it prefaces another solemn word of warning. John deals in a short and sharp way with the idea that it does not matter how one lives. He who *habitually does* righteousness is righteous, as that One is righteous, not he who claims to be righteous. Any one can say that he possesses a superior knowledge of divine truth, but does he act accordingly? Let no one lead you astray, John says, with regard to matters of such vital importance.

8 Here we have the two families into which the human race is divided. He who makes sin his business, who daily, continuously sins is of the devil, in the sense that the devil is the source of the evil which masters and dominates him. "The devil made no man." Augustine says, "begat no man, created no man: but whoso imitates the devil, becomes a child of the devil, as if begotten of him." *From the beginning* the *devil sinneth:* the order of the words is emphatic: the activity of the devil is not an affair of yesterday, nor of the day before. The meaning, probably, is "from the beginning of the world," or, better, "from the beginning of sin." The devil was the first to sin and he has never ceased to sin. Note the present tense: not "he has sinned," but "he is sinning," his whole existence is sin. The personality of the devil is clearly recognised, as it is by our Lord in Jn. 8:44, where the devil is said to be a fallen being: "he did not stand firm in the truth." In v. 5 John had given one reason for the manifestation of the Son of God: here he gives another reason. The two verses should be studied together. It is by making atonement for sin that Jesus destroys the works of the devil. The word *destroy* occurs

---

this man is true to himself, he does not sin. Grotius says that it is alien to the nature of such a man to sin. Various writers say that this man does not wish to sin, or ought not to sin. Farrar says that "the only possible escape from some such modification is by asserting the possibility of sinlessness in this life (which contradicts 1:8), or else by asserting that *none* of us have seen God, and none of us are children of God (which contradicts the whole Epistle)."

very frequently in N. T., with the sense of undo, pull to pieces, destroy. The works of the devil are the sins which he causes men to commit: they are the opposite of the works of God (Jn. 9:3) and the same as the works of darkness (Rom. 13:12; Eph. 5:11). The action of the man who makes sin his practice is in direct opposition to *this* purpose of the Incarnation of the Son of God.

9 *Every one* who has been made a child of God and remains so does not *go on sinning,* because His seed abideth in him: and he cannot *go on sinning,* because he has been made a child of God and remains so." That is a very strong and an utterly uncompromising statement, to be understood, however, in the light of the interpretation already given of v. 6. The germ of the new life has been implanted in the soul of the child of God and it grows, is certain to grow — a gradual process and subject to declensions from time to time, but it assuredly grows from more to more. The incorruptible seed of the Word of God, implanted in the soul by the Holy Spirit, has brought to the soul the new life of the children of God (1 Pet. 1:23). The man to whom that has happened cannot live habitually in sin, though there may be lapses into acts of sin, he cannot revel in sin, because he has been born of God and remains a child of God. He can say with Paul: "It is not I (the real 'I', in whom the seed of God abides) who do the deed, but sin that dwells within me" (Rom. 7:17, Moffat), for sin is still there in his soul, though not now dominant. "The believer's lapses into sin," says Dr. David Smith, "are like the mischances of the weather which hinder the seed's growth. The growth of a living seed may be checked temporarily," but, after that temporary check, it begins again, and it goes on until the time of harvest arrives.

10 *In this,* by applying this practical test, we can distinguish clearly between the members of the two families into which the human race is divided. The phrase "children of the devil" occurs nowhere else in N. T., but we have "son of the devil" in Acts 13:10 and "sons of the evil one" in Mt. 13:38; cf. Our Lord's words in Jn. 8:44. Plummer reminds us that, as Irenaeus in his treatise *Against Heretics* informs us, it was for pressing the doctrine that a tree is known by its fruits to an extreme, and maintaining that a world in which evil exists cannot be the work of a good God, that the heretic Marcion was rebuked by John's disciple Polycarp, in words which sound like a reminiscence of this verse, "I know thee for the *firstborn of Satan.*" John wants to emphasise now for a little one special aspect of righteousness, love of the brethren, for love is *righteousness in relation to others:* cf. Gal. 5:14.

11 One of the first lessons you learned in your first days in the school of Christ, John says, was the command to love one another; cf. 2:7. In 1:5 he wrote about the message received from Christ which tells us of the nature of God; he now refers to another message which tells us of our duty to the other children of the Father. Jerome informs us that during John's last years, "Little children love one another" was the one exhortation which, after he had become too old and feeble to preach, he never ceased to give. "It is the Lord's command," he would say; "and if this is done, it is enough." The old commandment which is ever new (2:7—11) is here reiterated by John, not merely as being a duty to which believers are bound, but as being one of the most decisive proofs of their Divine sonship.

12 Love of a brother suggests its opposite, hatred of a brother. The first death which took place in the human race was a murder. Cain allowed his smouldering hatred of Abel to burst forth into a devouring flame; his hands became stained with a crime of specially crimson hue, the murder of a brother. The verb "slew" is a link between this Epistle and the Apocalypse; it occurs only here and 8 times in the Apocalypse (Rev. 5:6, 9 and 12; 6:9, etc.). Cain proved himself to be a child of the evil one. Christians have overcome the evil one (2:13): hatred in the heart shows that the evil one is master there, and that hatred may easily, but for the grace of God, develop into murder (v. 15). The devil is a murderer *par excellence*, as our Lord said (Jn. 8:44). The diabolical nature of Cain's crime came out in this, that it was his brother's righteousness and his acceptance with God that excited his murderous hate (Gen. 4:4, 5). It is interesting to observe that, in 3 out of the 5 places in which Abel is mentioned in the N. T., he is described as "righteous" (Mt. 23:35; Heb. 11:4 and here). In the two parallel passages, Mt. 23:35 and Lk. 11:51, the "blood of Abel" is mentioned as denoting the first transgression which called for special judgment from God. In the remaining passage, Heb. 12:24, there is another deeply significant reference to the "blood of Abel."

The word "righteous" and the word "righteousness" do not occur again in the Epistle. Righteousness is now, as Plummer puts it, "merged in the warmer and more definite aspect of it, love."

3:13—24

13 Marvel not, brethren, if the world hateth you.

14 We know that we have passed out of death into life, because we love the brethren. He that loveth not abideth in death.

15 Whosoever hateth his brother is a murderer: and ye know that no murderer hath eternal life abiding in him.

16 Hereby know we love, because he laid down his life for us: and we ought to lay down our lives for the brethren.

17 But whoso hath the world's goods, and beholdeth his brother in need, and shutteth up his compassion from him, how doth the love of God abide in him?

18 My little children, let us not love in word, neither with the tongue; but in deed and truth.

19 Hereby shall we know that we are of the truth, and shall assure our heart before him:

20 because if our heart condemn us, God is greater than our heart, and knoweth all things.

21 Beloved, if our heart condemn us not, we have boldness toward God;

22 and whatsoever we ask we receive of him, because we keep his commandments and do the things that are pleasing in his sight.

23 And this is his commandment, that we should believe in the name of his Son Jesus Christ, and love one another, even as he gave us commandment.

24 And he that keepeth his commandments abideth in him, and he in him. And hereby we know that he abideth in us, by the Spirit which he gave us.

13 We have here a form of address, *brothers,* which occurs nowhere else in the Epistle, and it is very appropriate here, where the subject of *brotherly* love is being treated. We have here an echo of Our Lord's words in Jn. 15:18. Christians ought not be surprised or perplexed if the world,

the unbelieving world which is mastered and dominated by
the things that do not originate with the Father (2:16) hates
them. The family of the devil still hates the family of God,
and if hatred be meted out to us, we should remember that:
above all, we should remember the experience of Jesus
Himself (Jn. 15:18).

14 Love is life and hatred is death. *We* know — that
"we" is very emphatic — *we* know, in contrast with the
world which is blind to spiritual realities, *we* know that
we have left the abode of death for the abode of life, another
echo of words of Jesus recorded in the Fourth Gospel (5:24).
The verb "passed" is used in Jn. 7:3 and 13:1 of transition
from one place to another. Plato used it in his *Republic* of
changing from one form of government to another. The
Christian has passed over from one spiritual climate to
another. He proves that he is now living in the realm of
life by the fact that love is now the master-principle in him.
Why worry overmuch about the hatred of the world — it
only shows that *we,* by the grace of God, have passed over
out of its baleful atmosphere into a purer air. He who loves
not is still living in the realm of death, which, it is implied,
is the original spiritual home of all.

15 *Every one,* no matter what his religious professions
may be, who hates his brother is a manslayer. Our Lord
had spoken words which conveyed the same truth (Mt. 5:22,
23). The man who is mastered by hate is a child of the
devil, who, according to our Lord's words in Jn. 8:44, is a
murderer, a manslayer — the only other place in N. T.
where the Greek word used here occurs. The child of God
has eternal life as a present possession (Jn. 3:36; 1 Jn. 5:12,
13, etc.), but no murderer has eternal life abiding in him:
cf. Rev. 21:8 and 22:15. This does not mean that there cannot
be forgiveness for those who are guilty of hate and murder,
but John does mean, most definitely, that, so long as such
sins are unrepented, there can be no fellowship with God.

16 The supreme revelation of love, of what love really
is, of the uttermost limit to which love can go, is in the

Cross, where *that One* laid down His life for us. The verb used here is used of the laying aside of garments in Jn. 13:4. As applied to the death of Christ, it is peculiar to John's writings, occurring in Jn. 10:11, 15 and 17 and here. It is used of men laying down their lives in Jn. 13:37, 38 and 15:13. The Son of God laid down His life, divested Himself on our behalf of His life, so that wonderful benefits result to us. Paul says that the love of God is commended to us, is decisively proved to us in this, that Christ died for us (Rom. 5:8) and to sinners rich and vast benefits have come from that death. The N. T. is full of that thought (Eph. 1:7, 1 Pet. 2:24 and 3:18, etc.). John has already in this Epistle referred to such blessed results of the Atonement of Jesus (1:7; 2:2 and 12). Here, however, he writes of the death of Christ as a death that calls if need be, to self-sacrifice to the uttermost on behalf of others, though, of course, there can never be in anything we do, even should we make the supreme sacrifice of ourselves, the infinite value that resides in the death of Jesus.

17 We may never have to make that supreme sacrifice, in the less exacting duties of life we may fail. The inconsistent man whom John here pictures *has* the world's goods and he beholds his brother who *has* need, as his sole possession; he *beholds* him, surveys him, considers him, so that it is not a careless, passing glance he gives, and then he shuts up his heart *from* him — the same kind of picture being suggested here as in 2:28, that of one turning away from, turning his back on another. How can a heartless man like that dare to claim that the love of God, real love to God, has its home in him? The word translated *goods* is the word which is translated "life" in 2:16, the means of maintaining life; it is translated "living" in the Parable of the Prodigal Son (Lk. 15:12). The word translated *compassion* is, quite literally, "bowels." The ancients thought of the bowels as the seat of the affections (Gen. 43:30; 1 Kings 3:26; Jer. 31:20; Phil. 1:8, etc.). Coverdale's Bible here alters Tyndale's "shutteth up his compassion" into "shutteth up his heart." The cognate verb is used several times of Jesus (Mt. 9:36; Mk. 6:34, etc.). As Isaac Watts says,

His heart was filled with tenderness,
His bowels yearn with love.

18 John now asks his *little children,* again using that tender form of address, to remember that fine professions of love and tall talk about love are not enough, Moffat translates: "My dear children, let us put our love not into words or into talk but into deeds, and make it real." Bunyan says: "Practical love is best. Many love Christ with nothing but the lick of the tongue." In connection with this verse and the preceding one we should study Jas. 2:15—17.

19 John writes here some wonderful words about *the security and serenity of conscience which genuine and active love is able to produce,* to quote Plummer's summary of the teaching of this verse and the next. Hereby, or, *in this,* that is, by loving in deed and truth, we shall know that we are of the Truth, that we are the children of the God of Truth, not the children of the devil, who is the Father of lies. Further, we shall assure our heart before God: John uses the singular *heart,* because, as Westcott says, he directs attention to "the personal trial in each case." The usual meaning of the verb translated *assure* is "persuade". Possibly, "assure" brings out John's meaning clearly; we shall persuade our heart *that it need not condemn us;* cf. "We will *persuade* him and rid you of care" (Mt. 28:14). We shall persuade our hearts, in spite of much sin still remaining in us, that we are God's children; we shall quiet our hearts with that assurance. The important point is that we can so quiet our heart *in the sight of God.* The persistent evildoer, or the hypocrite, may often quiet his conscience, by drugging it with various opiates, but such pernicious activities are not done *in the sight of God.*

20 The fact that "God is greater than our heart and knoweth all things" is evidently not considered by John to be one that should frighten us or discourage us. Neither

191

did Peter so regard it when he said to Jesus on the shore
of the Galilean Lake: "Lord, thou knowest all things, Thou
knowest that I love Thee." (Jn. 21:17).

> Jesus! Why dost Thou love me so?
> What hast Thou seen in me
> To make my happiness so great,
> So dear a joy to Thee?

> Wert Thou not God, I then might think
> Thou hadst no eye to read
> The badness of that selfish heart
> For which Thine own did bleed.

> But Thou art God and knowest all;
> Dear Lord, Thou knowest me,
> And yet Thy knowledge hinders not
> Thy love's sweet liberty.

The all-seeing eyes see the deepest things in the children
of God and these are the real things. Our heart condemns
us often, as our black sin rises up before us, but, by the grace
of God, we have also in our heart love revealed in deeds,
and that is something to encourage us. Peter, as Dr. A. T.
Robertson reminds us, made his appeal "in the full glare of
his own terrible sin. It is true that we dread for man, let
alone God, to read the inner secrets of our hearts (Rothe),
but the Christian looks on God as all-loving as well as all-
knowing (Brooke), and that makes all the difference. The
full grasp of God's love for us silences the condemnation
of our own hearts, for His love is a love that knows all and
still loves, a love that gave the highest for us (Jn. 3:16) and
that cannot be made to cease loving us (Rom. 8:31—39)."[3]

---

[3] *Because if our heart condemn us...* Strong MSS evidence
(א BC etc.) seems to show that we ought to read the Greek conjunction
ὅτι which may mean either "because" or "that" after these words and
before the words, "God is greater..." If we understand the conjunction as meaning "because," John's words in vv. 19, 20 may be translated

21 There are blessed seasons of peace when our heart does not condemn us, and if, when our heart *does* condemn us, we nevertheless find rest in the thought that God knows all things, much more, this more blessed state of mind should mean closer communion. For *boldness* see on 2:28. We come with boldness to the Throne of Grace (Heb. 4:16), as children to a Father. We have boldness *toward* God; cf. "peace *toward* God" (Rom. 5:1).

22 This verse runs on without any real break between it and the preceding one. Children who come so confidently to their Heavenly Father cannot ask anything that He will refuse. As Augustine says: "He who gave us love cannot close His ears against the groans and prayers of love." We receive what we ask for in the moment of asking — a *present* tense —, though it may be a long time before the fulness of the boon desired is enjoyed by us. *"Every one* that asketh receiveth"* (Mt. 7:8). Our Lord also said: "All things whatsoever ye pray and ask for, believe that ye did receive them and it shall be so unto you." (Mk. 11:24). This is the blessed result of prayer in the case of those who do the commandments of God, who, therefore, do not regard iniquity in their hearts (Ps. 66:18) and do not practice all kinds of cruelty and injustice in their lives (Isa. 1:11—17). We do what is *pleasing* in the sight of God when the grace of the risen and exalted Redeemer is at work within us (Heb. 13:21).

---

as in the English R. V.: "Hereby shall we know that we are of the truth, and shall assure our heart before Him, whereinsoever our heart condemn us; because God is greater..." We have a similar translation in the American RSV. It seems fairly clear, however, that *if our heart condemn us* at the beginning of v. 20 must be right, as standing in natural apposition to "if our heart condemn us not" in the following verse, which is unquestionably right. In that case, we must understand the conjunction as meaning *that*, and we should, possibly, assume an ellipse of some kind—"if our heart condemn us, (it is plain) or (it is evident) that God is greater..." We have perhaps a similar ellipse in 1 Tim. 6:7—"we brought nothing into the world, and (it is plain) that we can carry nothing out."

23 In the preceding verse we had *commandments,* here we have the singular, *commandment.* This is a summary of the requirements of God, *faith* in His Son and *love* to one another. It is often said that it does not matter what a man *believes* so long as he *does* what is right. That is utterly wrong, John says. *Faith* is the first essential, for without faith there can be no right doing. The commandment is that we should *believe the Name* of Christ — so the Greek reads here. Elsewhere we have the phrase, "believe *into,* or *on,*" as in Jn. 1:12, 3:18, 1 Jn. 5:13, etc., and that is a somewhat stronger expression, describing permanent trust and repose. To believe the Name of Christ is to believe all that His Name, which is here given with solemn fulness, contains and implies; His Deity, His Eternal Sonship and His saving work as the Anointed of the Father. Such belief ought to lead to permanent trust and repose in Him who bears the Name. Such faith will always reveal itself in love, because as James says, "faith apart from works is barren" (Jas. 2:17), and, as Paul says, faith always works *through* love (Gal. 5:6). John recalls again the scene in the Upper Room when Jesus gave the commandment of love (Jn. 13:34).

24 Keeping the commandments of God is vitally important, because that alone is the final proof that we abide in Him and that He abides in us. "Let God be a home to thee, and be thou a home of God," says the Venerable Bede. We *come to know,* in our experience, the blessed fact of the Divine indwelling, *from* the Spirit, as the source of our knowledge. God *gave* us the Spirit, at a definite moment, the initial moment of believing in Jesus; cf. Acts 19:2, "Did ye receive the Holy Spirit when ye believed?" and Eph. 1:13, "having also believed, ye were sealed with the Holy Spirit of promise." This is the first mention of the Spirit in the Epistle, though there is an allusion to His working in 2:20.

CHAPTER IV

2. THE SOURCE OF SONSHIP — 4:1—5:12

Possession of the Spirit as proved by confession of the incarnation of the eternal Son of God.

We have here (a) *The Spirit of Truth and the Spirit of error* (4:1—6); (b) *Love is the mark of the children of God, who is Love* (4:7—21); (c) *This love makes the yoke of Christ an easy yoke* (5:1—5); (d) *The threefold testimony to the reality of the Incarnation* (5:6—8); (e) *The acceptance of that testimony assures the possession of eternal life* (5:9—12).

Plummer says that "like the doublings of the Maeander near which he lived, the progress of the Apostle at times looks more like retrogression than advance: but the progress is unmistakeable when the whole field is surveyed. Here we seem to be simply going back to the subject of the Antichrists (2:18—28); but whereas there the opposition between the Holy Spirit in true believers and the lying spirit in the antichrists is only suggested (2:20, 22, 27), here it is the dominant idea."

4:1—6

1 Beloved, believe not every spirit, but prove the spirits, whether they are of God; because many false prophets are gone out into the world.

2 Hereby know ye the Spirit of God: every spirit that confesseth that Jesus Christ is come in the flesh is of God:

3 and every spirit that confesseth not Jesus is not of God: and this is the spirit of the antichrist, whereof ye have heard that it cometh; and now it is in the world already.

4 Ye are of God, my little children, and have overcome them: because greater is he that is in you than he that is in the world.

5 They are of the world: therefore speak they as of the world, and the world heareth them.

6 We are of God; he that knoweth God heareth us; he who is not of God heareth us not. By this we know the spirit of truth, and the spirit of error.

The mention of the Spirit (3:24) leads John to write a warning about false teachers who claim to have deep spiritual insight, who indeed often claim to have the Holy Spirit, but who are really animated and inspired from another source. *Test the spirits,*[1] John says to his *beloved children.* The verb he uses was used of the testing of metals; Paul uses it in 1 Thess. 5:21, "Test all things; hold fast that which is good." The Spirit of God is the source of your sonship and the Spirit of God can give you spiritual insight, so that you can distinguish between the fine gold

---

[1] Plummer says that a precept like this "cuts at the root of such pretensions as the Infallibility of the Pope. What room is left for Christians to 'prove the spirits,' if all they have to do is to ask the opinion of an official? The Apostle's charge, 'prove *ye* the spirits,' may be addressed to Christians singly or to the Church collectively; it cannot be addressed to an individual."

of heaven and base metal, between true teaching and false. Such a warning is needed, because many false prophets have gone out into the world, some of them apostate Christians (2:19). Think of Our Lord's words in Mt. 24:24, Paul's words in Acts 20:30 and Peter's words in 2 Pet. 2:1. Paul's words were addressed to the elders of the Church of Ephesus, and now John, whose sphere of activity was largely at Ephesus, warns the Christians of that city and the surrounding neighbourhood. A. T. Robertson says that "it is absolutely essential, in the medley of conflicting voices which we have to-day — such as atheism and materialism and pantheism and humanism and Unitarianism and Christian Science — that the disciples of Jesus be able to 'recognise the Spirit of God.'" In order to do that they do not need any Pope; they have the infallible guide to religion and morals in themselves.

2 John now tells us how we can recognise the Spirit of God. "Every spirit that confesseth Jesus Christ *as come in the flesh* is of God." It should be carefully noted that John does not say "come *into* the flesh," but "*in* the flesh." Christ did not descend into an already existing man, as Cerinthus and others were teaching, but He came in human nature; He *became* flesh (Jn. 1:14). Further, John does not say that the confession is to be of a Christ who *came,* but of a Christ who *is come, who came and who abides in the flesh* — a perfect tense being used. As the Westminster *Shorter Catechism* says, Our Lord "was and continueth to be God and man, in two distinct natures and One Person, for ever."

3 Every spirit that confesseth not Jesus, that is, in the sense explained, is not of God. A very interesting reading, which is at least as old as the 2nd. century has here: "Every spirit which *severs* Jesus (or, as in the margin, which *annuls*) Jesus." This reading can scarcely be genuine, because it is not found in a single Greek MS., nor in any version except the Vulgate, but it certainly describes in quite a felicitous way the heresy of Cerinthus and those who thought like him. Westcott explains it as meaning, "separates the divine from

197

the human, divides the one divine-human Person."[2] The dangerous teaching which John is refuting is an expression of that spirit of Antichrist to which he had already referred (2:18).

4 *You*, in emphatic contrast with the false teachers, are born of God and have overcome them, with a victory the results of which abide — another perfect tense. You have been able to prevent their pernicious teaching from corrupting the Church, and that not in any strength of your own, but in the strength of Him whose Word abides in you (2:14). The ultimate source of the false teaching is "he that is in the world," "the ruler of the world," (Jn. 12:31), "the ruler of the powers of the air" (Eph. 2:2). On that verse in Ephesians G. G. Findlay *(Expositor's Bible)* quotes these words of Beck: "The Power of the air is a fitting designation for the prevailing spirit of the times, whose influence spreads itself like a miasma through the whole atmosphere of the world." Great is the subtle power of the enemy of God over the human soul, but God is mightier, and He is in you.

5 The source of the inspiration of the false teachers does not rise higher than this world, and, therefore, it is not at all surprising that men of worldly mind should rest quite content with the feeble light which such teachers are able to throw on the things of God and man. Cf. Jn. 15:19.

6 At the beginning of v. 4 John had placed his readers in marked contrast with the false teachers: he now places

---

2   The reading "every spirit which *severs* Jesus," seems to have been known to Tertullian, about the beginning of the third century, who, in his treatise *Against Marcion*, quotes John as speaking of "the forerunners of Antichrist denying that Christ has come in the flesh and severing Jesus." About the year 180 Irenæus in his treatise *Against Heretics*, seems to furnish proof that he also knew this reading. The fact, however that it is not found in a single Greek MS nor in any version except the Vulgate weighs very heavily against it, though it is one of the most interesting variants that we encounter in the realm of textual criticism, and though Zahn describes it as "the evidently original reading."

himself and his fellow-Apostles in as marked contrast with them. *We* are of God. This whole Epistle impresses us as being the work of a man who writes with Apostolic authority. At some points, as in the opening verses and here, that note of authority sounds out with special clearness. Because we Apostles are of God, because we have been specially commissioned by the Lord to teach His truth, he who knows God, he who *goes on knowing* the Lord, who wants to *follow on* to know the Lord (Hos. 6:3), listens to us. He who is not of God, and who therefore does not know God and has no desire to know God with the right kind of knowledge, does not listen to us. He thinks that he has sufficient light on life's problems elsewhere. He prefers his poor, feeble, flickering taper to the Light of the world.

By this, that is, by their listening or not listening, we recognise those who are under the guidance of the Spirit of truth and those who are under the guidance of the spirit of error. The phrase *the spirit of error* occurs only here. In "the Spirit of Truth" we have another link with the Fourth Gospel. The Spirit of truth was promised by the Lord to His Church (Jn. 14:17; 15:26; 16:13). His sphere of operation is the truth. He is the Truth (5:7). He proceeds from Him who is the Truth (Jn. 14:6, 26), and His peculiar office is to guide into all the truth (Jn. 16:13). Those who refuse that guidance are under the control of the spirit of *wandering,* of mental wandering, and they know not on what dark mountains (Jer. 13:15) they may yet stumble. It might be profitable to study some other N. T. passages in which that word "error" is found, such passages as Eph. 4:14, 1 Thes. 2:3, 2 Thes. 2:11 and 2 Pet. 3:17. The last mentioned passage leads on to a verse which tells us that the best safeguard against error is to grow in the grace and in the knowledge of Christ.

LOVE AND GOD'S CHILDREN

7 Beloved, let us love one another: for love is of God; and every one that loveth is begotten of God, and knoweth God.

8 He that loveth not knoweth not God; for God is love.

9 Herein was the love of God manifested in us, that God hath sent his only begotten Son into the world that we might live through him.

10 Herein is love, not that we loved God, but that he loved us, and sent his Son to be the propitiation for our sins.

11 Beloved, if God so loved us, we also ought to love one another.

12 No man hath beheld God at any time: if we love one another, God abideth in us, and his love is perfected in us:

13 hereby we know that we abide in him and he in us, because he hath given us of his Spirit.

14 And we have beheld and bear witness that the Father hath sent the Son to be the Saviour of the world.

15 Whosoever shall confess that Jesus is the Son of God, God abideth in him, and he in God.

16 And we know and have believed the love which God hath in us. God is love; and he that abideth in love abideth in God, and God abideth in him.

17 Herein is love made perfect with us, that we may have boldness in the day of judgment; because as he is, even so are we in this world.

18 There is no fear in love: but perfect love casteth out fear, because fear hath punishment; and he that feareth is not made perfect in love.

19 We love, because he first loved us.

20 If a man say, I love God, and hateth his brother, he is a liar: for he that loveth not his brother whom he hath seen, cannot love God whom he hath not seen.

21 And this commandment have we from him, that he who loveth God love his brother also.

John refers for the last time to the subject of brotherly love and he writes great words about it which, as A. T. Robertson truly says, are only equalled by Paul's Hymn on Love in 1 Cor. 13. "Paul's chapter is a perfect prose poem, while John's is like a diamond turned round and round for different angles of light to flash upon it." We may follow the lines of Westcott's analysis of this passage. (1). *The ground of love* (7—10); (2). *The inspiration of love* (11—16); (3). *The activity of love* (17—21).

(1). *The ground of love* (7—10).

7-8 John evidently never tires of the subject of love; see on 3:11. Orthodoxy in belief is not enough. Unless orthodoxy be inspired and warmed by love, it can sometimes be a very unlovely and a very unattractive thing. John has already written of brotherly love as a sign and evidence of our walking in the light and walking as Christ walked (2:7—11). He has also written of brotherly love as one of the most vital aspects of righteousness (3:10—18). He now writes of it as a fruit of the Spirit in our lives and a reflection of the love of God. Here is the ground of love, in that profound truth, so simply and succinctly stated, "God is Love." That means that those who are truly His children will reflect in their lives something of that love with which He has loved them. If those who know that "God is light" (1:5) are under obligation to walk in the light, those who know that "God is Love" are under obligation to walk in love. It is only the man who loves who can claim to be a child of God, it is only he who knows God with that intimate spiritual knowledge which means eternal life (Jn. 17:3).

Plummer points out that teachers like Cerinthus "knew a good deal about God, but they did not know Him, for instead of loving those brethren who did not share their intellectual attainments, they had an arrogant contempt for them. They had recognised that 'God is spirit,' and to some extent that 'God is light'; for they knew Him to be an immaterial Being and the highest Intelligence; but they had wholly failed to appreciate that 'God is love' and yet of the three great truths this is the chief." Dr. W. N. Clarke, in his *Outline of Christian Theology,* says that "from Christ we learn that 'God is love': that is, God has boundless impulse to impart Himself and all good to other beings, and equally boundless desire to possess other beings as His own, in spiritual fellowship." "We learn at the same time," he continues, "that love in Him is always holy love; that is, His love is always in complete harmony with that perfect goodness of character which is eternally His guiding principle." That seems to be another way of stating the vital truth that the love of God will never operate in any way that is inconsistent with the stern demands of His law. That is possible only because of the propitiation to which John will presently refer for a second time.

9 The love of God was manifested, it was made clear as noonday to us, when He sent, with abiding results, His son into the world; the love of God, as Paul says, is in Christ Jesus our Lord (Rom. 8:39). For that verb sent, see Jn. 3:17; 6:29; 6:39, 40; 8:29; 10:36; 20:21. Jesus is the Father's Apostle (Heb. 3:1), His Sent One, sent on a mission of mercy, not to condemn but to save (Jn. 3:17). The Messenger was God's Son, His *only begotten.* We are children of God by grace, through the miracle of the new birth; Jesus is God's Eternal Son, of one essence with the Father (Jn. 10:30). The adjective *only begotten,* as applied to Jesus, is peculiar to John; it occurs four times in his Gospel (1:14 and 18, 3:16 and 18) and here. We should compare "His own Son" in Rom. 8:3 and 32.

The purpose of the sending of the Son was that we should not die in our sins, as we deserved, but that we should live through Him, with the only life that is worth calling life: cf. 3:14; 5:11, 12; Jn. 3:16; 17:36 and Rom. 6:23. All the wealth and glory of the life eternal have been brought to us through the propitiatory sacrifice of the Son of God.

The love of God has been manifested *in* us, John says,

so that it is a fact of personal experience. We should compare what Paul writes about the revelation of the Son of God *in* him (Gal. 1:16).

10 *Herein is love* — not, to quote some words from Denney's *Studies in Theology*, "not that we loved God, not that the world has had the passion of parents, of patriots, of martyrs, but that God loved us, and sent His son as a propitiation for our sins. The other loves do not explain this; it is here and here only — in the Cross, where the sinless Son of God died for the sins of men — that we see what love itself is, and find a scale for the measurement of all these lesser loves." In the N. T., that God is *love* is a *conclusion* from the fact He has provided in Christ, and supremely in His death, a propitiation for sins. We are justified in bringing that significant fact to the notice of the shallow theologians who tell us that, because God is love, He does not need any propitiation. "Propitiation," Denney says again, "in the sense of an absolutely serious dealing with God's condemnation of sin for its removal, is essential to forgiveness, as long as we regard God's condemnation of sin as an absolutely real thing. Of course we cannot provide the propitiation — that is the assumption on which the Gospel proceeds — but God provides it; and the fact that He does so, in the sin-bearing death of the sinless One, is the final demonstration of His love. Apart from this, His love is at best meaningless, and ethically indifferent. The Cross, with His condemnation in it, reveals at once the immensity and the sanctity of His love."

God is love eternally, Christ is eternally the Son of His love, the Cross is the supreme, the unique manifestation in time of God's eternal love — such is the burden of John's message in this passage. For the word *propitiation* see on 2:2.

(2) *The inspiration of love* (11—16).

11 John never ceases to wonder, as Dr. G. G. Findlay puts it, at "the thought of the Eternal Father's love, that flows through Christ into human souls and draws them into blissful union with itself and with each other." The command to love one another is "too tough," as Uncle Tom said, unless we are constrained by the motive and the incentive supplied by the love of God in Christ. *If* God *so* loved us, we ought to feel under obligation — the same phrase as in 2:6 and 3:16 — to love one another. The phrase "so loved" is exactly the same as in Jn. 3:16.

12 No amount of beholding, of contemplation, has ever enabled mortal man at any time to behold God, but, if we love one another, and are thus in true spiritual accord with Him, we have God not only with us but *in* us, and, not only that we have God *abiding* in us. He does not come to us to tarry for a night (Jer. 14:8) but to abide with us for ever, the promise of Jesus recorded in Jn. 14:23 being thus fulfilled. As the result of the Divine indwelling, the love of God, that is, our love to God (as in 2:5, 3:17 and 5:3) grows from more to more until it is perfected.

13 John touches again on the witness of the Holy Spirit in the soul. "The witness of the Spirit," says Dr. A. H. Strong, "is not a new revelation from God, but a strengthening of faith so that it becomes conscious and indubitable." When we are enabled to keep the commandments of God, John had said in 3:24, the Spirit bears witness to our spirits that God does indeed abide in us, that we are the children of God, as Paul says (Rom. 8:16). John now says here that, when we love one another, the Spirit bears that same witness within us. Sometimes Christians are said to have received the Spirit (Gal. 3:2, 4:6, etc.), sometimes they are said (as in 3:24 and here) to have received *of* the Spirit. Of Christ alone can it be said that He received the Spirit "not by measure" (Jn. 3:34).

14 No man has ever beheld God (v. 12), but, says John, we Apostles beheld the Incarnate Son (same verb as in Jn. 1:14 and the opening verse of this Epistle, indicating a close and long-continued contemplation), and the impression then made on us remains to this day — such is the force of the perfect tense used. The result is that we witness

continually (present tense) to the fact that the Father hath
sent the Son, with abiding results, (another perfect tense),
as Savior of the world. That designation of Jesus occurs
only once again, in Jn. 4:42, on the lips of Samaritans. The
word *Savior* occurs in the Synoptic Gospels only in Lk. 1:47
(of God) and in Lk. 2:11 (of Jesus). In Paul, outside the
Pastoral Epistles, it occurs only in Eph. 5:23 and Phil. 3:20.
In the Pastoral Epistles it occurs 10 times and in 2 Peter 5
times. The cognate verb, "to save," of course, is of far more
frequent occurrence.

15 Genuine confession of Jesus is far more than the
recital of a creed with our lips; it involves a movement of
the soul towards Him who is confessed (Rom. 10:9, 10).
Wherever there is a man who makes that genuine confession, the kind of confession already defined in 4:2, 3, God
has His home in that man and that man has his home
in God.

16 We have *come to know* the love of God for us, John
now says, and we have believed it, with a faith that lasts.
"Sound faith is intelligent," Plummer says: "sound knowledge is believing." John writes of the love that God hath
in us, conveying the same idea as in v. 9; in Pauline language,
"the love of God hath been shed abroad in our hearts
through the Holy Spirit which was given unto us" (Rom.
5:5). John then repeats the great words *God is love,* but in
the words that follow he does not merely repeat himself,
for, instead of writing "he that loveth," he writes "he that
has his home in the blessed domain of love has his home
in God and God has His home in him."

(3)   *The activity of love* (17—21).

17 That mutual indwelling, also described in v. 12 and
in 3:24, ensures that love will more and more advance to
perfection with us, and that with this end in view that we
may have boldness in the day of judgment. A comparison
of this verse with 2:28 seems to show that the day of
judgment coincides with the Coming of the Lord; the N. T

writers seem to think of the future as containing only one
Coming of the Lord in glory which will be to the ungodly
a day of wrath but will mean for the people of God rest
(2 Thes. 1:7—10). The true child of God, with Christ as
Advocate and Propitiation (2:2), has nothing to fear in that
day. "The day of judgment" is, quite literally, "*the* day
of *the* judgment"; elsewhere we have "day of judgment"
(Mt. 10:15; 11:20, 24; 12:36; 2 Pet. 2:9 and 3:7); we have
also "the last day" (see on 2:18), "the day" (1 Cor. 3:13),
"that day" (2 Tim. 1:12; 1:18, 4:8) and "the great day of
wrath" (Rev. 6:17). In that day, which is described in so
many impressive ways, the child of God will have boldness.
That word occurs for the third time here in the Epistle; see
on 2:28.

This attitude of boldness is not presumption, because
"as He (*That One,* as in 2:6; 3:3, 5, 7, and 16) is, even so
are we in this world." We "share alike Christ's attitude
towards the world of evil, His separation from its corruption, and the hatred of the world towards Him."
(*Century Bible*). By the grace of God we have attained to
something of Christ's spirit of love. Our hope is that we
shall yet be perfectly like Him (3:2), and, as our sanctification progresses, we grow more like Him every day
(2 Cor. 3:18). We are one with Him, so that, "when Christ,
who is our life, shall be manifested, then shall we also with
Him be manifested in glory" (Col. 3:4).

18 The opposite of love and this attitude of boldness
which it inspires is the fear which is slavish and cringing,
the servile fear which Paul condemns in Rom. 8:15. We
recall the words of Robert Burns: "I backward cast my e'e
on prospects drear! An' forward, tho I can see, I guess
an' fear!" *Contrast* with such gloomy words Paul's
triumphant "I know" in prospect of "that day" (2 Tim.
1:12) and John's words here about the perfect love which
casts fear out of the heart. There is a right kind of fear,
that reverential awe in the presence of God which is the
beginning of knowledge (Prov. 1:7) and also the beginning

of love. "The sinner must begin by fearing the God against whom he has sinned," Plummer says. And, he quotes the description which Bengel gives of the various stages through which the soul of the believer passes: "Neither love nor fear; fear without love; both fear and love; love without fear." "Fear is the child of bondage, love of freedom," Plummer continues. "In this case also the bondwoman and her son must be cast out" (Gal. 4:30). The portion of slaves is punishment, the portion of sons is chastisement (Heb. 12:5—11).

The wrong kind of fear *hath punishment;* as it gazes forward, it can think only of that punishment which is to be meted out to the finally impenitent (Mt. 25:46, the only other place in N. T. where the noun here used occurs); this kind of fear has in it a foretaste of that future punishment. He who is mastered by it is very far indeed from being made perfect in love. The child of God ought to be delivered from *all his fears* (Ps. 34:4).

19 The Received Text, as represented in the English A.V., reads here: "We love Him," but "Him" seems to be addition to the true text. What John writes is: *We love, because He first loved us.*[3] Christian love of every kind is meant. *First* is the important word here. The eternal, sovereign love of God is the fountain of all that is good in us. He loved us when we were utterly unlovely (Tit. 3:3—7). He loved us and washed us, according to one reading in Rev. 1:5, not He washed us and then loved us, as D. L. Moody used to say. As Dora Greenwell sings: "He did not wait till I loved Him, but He loved me at my worst: He needn't ever have loved me at all, if I could have loved Him first." *Such* love ought to move us to love the utterly unlovely (Mt. 5:43—48).

20 Earlier in the Epistle John had dealt in summary fashion with those who make false claims for themselves

---

3   "Him" is omitted in A and B. In ℵ, the Vulgate and several other versions we have "we love God."

(1:6, 8 and 10; 2:4 and 9). He uses similar language here, branding again the inconsistent professor as a "liar," as he had done in 2:4. Plummer points out that John does not describe the "brother" as one whom he "can see," but as one "whom he has continually before his eyes." "The perfect tense, as so often, expresses a permanent state continuing from the past. His brother has been and remains in sight, God has been and remains out of sight. . . . If a man fails in duties which are ever before his eyes and are easy, how can we credit him with performing duties which require an effort to bear in mind and are difficult? And in this case the seen would necessarily suggest the unseen: for the *brother* on earth implies the *Father* in heaven. If therefore the seen is not loved, what must we infer as to the unseen?"

21 John again emphasises the fact that we have God's express command to love one another given us with new and deeper meaning in His Son (Jn. 13:34). See on 2:7, 8. Love is not an emotion to which we may give expression now and then, as we feel inclined; it is a *duty* required of us at all times by God, and the children of God ought surely to obey their Heavenly Father.

CHAPTER V

LOVE AND CHRIST'S EASY YOKE

5:1—5

1 Whosoever believeth that Jesus is the Christ is begotten of God: and whosoever loveth him that begat loveth him also that is begotten of him.

2 Hereby we know that we love the children of God, when we love God and do his commandments.

3 For this is the love of God, that we keep his commandments: and his commandments are not grievous.

4 For whatsoever is begotten of God overcometh the world: and this is the victory that hath overcome the world, even our faith.

5 And who is he that overcometh the world, but he that believeth that Jesus is the Son of God?

1 To believe that Jesus is the Christ is to believe that He is the centre and focus of revelation, that He was the One to whom the whole of the O. T. looked forward, that He is the Eternal Son of God, as various O. T. passages hinted (Ps. 2:7; Prov. 8:25—31; Micah 5:2, etc.) and as He was clearly revealed to be in His historical manifestation. The possession of this faith proves that the new life has been implanted in the soul by God, and the soul in which that new life is must needs love the Heavenly Father and all His children. "Since God regenerates us by faith," Calvin says, "He must be loved by us as a Father; and this love embraces all His children." Or, as Dr. C. H. Dodd puts it, "to be born of God is to be born into a family with obligation, not only towards the Father of the family but also (as part of our obligation to Him) towards all His children." There is no exception to this obligation — *every one,* John declares, who has this faith will manifest such love.

2 In the last 2 verses of chapter 4 we were told that love and obedience to God involve love of His children: here it is strongly emphasised that love to God and love to the brethren confirm and prove each other. If either is found alone, there is something wrong with us. John again lays stress on the truth that our love to God is decisively proved by the *doing* of His commandments. That phrase *do His commandments* occurs nowhere else: it seems to be the true reading here, being supported by the great Vatican Ms (B), all ancient Versions and several Fathers.

3 In the *keeping* of the commandments of God true love to God always issues: see on 2:3. Compare Jn. 14:15, 21, 23; Jn. 15:10; 2 Jn. 6. And the commandments of God are not *irksome* (Moffat and Weymouth), they do not press on us as an intolerable burden. The American RSV has "burdensome". The yoke of Christ is easy and His burden is light (Mt. 11:30), as opposed to the rigorous legal code of the Pharisees who lay *heavy* burdens on men's shoulders (same word as John uses) (Mt. 23:4; cf. Acts 15:10). Love to Christ makes His yoke easy and His burden light.

4 Here is another reason why the commandments of God are not irksome — we have supernatural strength given us to enable us to keep them. The statement that these commandments are not burdensome does not mean that they are less exacting than men supposed, but that the grace of God at work in the soul enables us to keep them gladly. In our endeavours to live according to the will of God we have against us the power of the world, of paganism, or of human society organised without God, the world in which the desire of the flesh, etc. (2:16) is at work, but He who is within us is greater (4:4).

*What*soever is begotten of God overcomes. The negative participle emphasises the *power* that is at work in the child of God and diverts attention from the child of God himself. It is not the child of God himself, but the new life that is in him, that conquers. And, it is not the mere fact of the new birth from God that is emphasised, but the abiding results of that birth — whatsoever is begotten of God and abides as the soul's permanent possession. At the same time, man's faith must be in lively exercise, laying hold on the power of God. You can look back to many occasions, John says, when your faith overcame the world. The word "faith" occurs nowhere else in John's Epistles and nowhere in his Gospel, though the cognate verb "to believe" occurs often in his writings. The word *victory* occurs nowhere else in N. T., though a somewhat similar word is found in 1 Cor. 15:54, 55 and 57 and Mt. 12:20. The cognate verb "to overcome" occurs often in John's writings (Jn. 16:33; 1 Jn. 2:14, 4:4; Rev. 2 and 3, in the promises contained in the Messages to the Seven Churches, Rev. 5:5, 12:11, 21:7, etc.).

5 Here John uses the present tense, *he that overcometh,* because the fight is still in progress. Christ is the supreme Victor (Jn. 16:33), and, if victory is to be ours, it must be through Him (1 Cor. 15:57). It is no mere vague belief in God that conquers, but belief in the Incarnation, belief in that glorious victory won by the Son of God against all the forces of sin and darkness.

5:6—8

6 This is he that came by water and blood, even Jesus
Christ; not with the water only, but with the water and
with the blood.

7 And it is the Spirit that beareth witness, because the Spirit
is the truth.

8 For there are three who bear witness, the Spirit, and the
water, and the blood: and the three agree in one.

6 How can we be sure that the Incarnation is a fact?
There are three witnesses to it. The identity of the historical person, Jesus of Nazareth, with the Eternal Son of
God is again strongly insisted upon. Faith in this is the
only faith that can give victory over the forces which are
antagonistic to the spiritual life. And the threefold witness
to the fact of the Incarnation has extraordinary force.

This is one of the most perplexing verses in the N. T.
We begin to understand it, or at least to get a hint of its
meaning, when we remember that John still has the heresy
of Cerinthus before his mind; see on 1:7 and 2:22. Various
explanations of the water and the blood have been given.[1]

---

[1] The two principal interpretations that have been given of the
water and the blood are (1) The baptism by means of water in the
Jordan and the death by means of blood on the Cross and (2) The
water and blood which flowed from Christ's pierced side. Other interpretations such as purification and redemption, and the sacraments of
Baptism and the Lord's Supper may be safely disregarded, as they
seem to be rather farfetched. It seems fairly clear that the reference is
to facts in the earthly life of the Son of God. The participle *He who
came* shows that the reference is to facts in the life of the Messiah;
"The Coming One" was a title of the Messiah (Mt. 11:1); now He is
He who came. The first interpretation seems the more likely one, in
view of the fact that John seems to be attacking here once more the
heresy of Cerinthus. The second is Augustine's interpretation, and it is
defended in *The Speaker's Commentary* and in Farrar's *Early Days of*

The Son of God came *through,* or *by means of* water and blood; not *with the* water only, but *with the* water and *with the* blood. His Baptism in the Jordan and His death on Calvary with the shedding of blood were, both of them, essential parts of His self-manifestation. "Christ's Baptism,

---

Christianity. An article in the *British and Foreign Evangelical Review* for 1887 defends the theory that the reference is chiefly to John 19:34. But, it ought to be noted that the order there is "blood and water," and attention seems to be drawn to *water* as the wonderful thing. As Plummer remarks, "the difficult passage in Jn. 19:34 and the difficult passage before us do not really explain one another."

The first interpretation is adopted by Plummer, Brooke (ICC), Smith (EGT), and many others. Westcott adopts it, though not to the entire exclusion of Jn. 19:34. He thinks that the additional reference to Jn. 19:34 "beyond question," the mysterious happening recorded there being symbolic. C. H. Dodd (*Moffat Commentary*) is inclined also to accept the first interpretation, though suggesting also a possible additional allusion to the two sacraments of Baptism and the Lord's Supper, which "attest and confirm to believers the abiding effect of the life and death of Christ."

The first interpretation, as Plummer points out, explains the *order,* "water and blood," not "blood and water"; it explains the *first preposition,* "by, by means of" (cf. the remarkable parallel Heb. 9:12); it explains the *second preposition* "in, or with," indicating the element *in* which Christ's work was done (cf. the remarkable parallel Heb. 9:25, "with blood not his own." Christ's Baptism and Death were in one sense the *means by which,* in another sense the *spheres in which* His work was accomplished. Above all, this interpretation explains the emphatic addition, "not in the water only, but in the water and in the blood." That implies that somebody had taught that Christ came in water, but not in blood. Such an affirmation seems to describe accurately enough the teaching of men like Cerinthus and others who taught that through His baptism Jesus, by union with the divine Christ, was fitted for His public ministry of teaching and healing, but that, the divine Christ having left Him, He suffered as a mere man, the consequence being that His Death had no atoning and redeeming efficacy. The Gospel affirms, upon the testimony of those who saw and heard, as Dodd says, that "Jesus Christ was both baptized and crucified, and both these facts are essential to our faith in Him, because both taken together bear the meaning that Jesus is the Christ or Son of God incarnate (4:2), and that as such He is the Savior of the world (4:14), and not merely its Enlightener."

213

with the Divine proclamation of Him as the Son of God and the Divine outpouring of the Spirit upon Him," as Plummer says, "is not merely the opening but the explanation of the whole of His Ministry. The bloody death upon the Cross is not merely the close but the explanation of His Passion." In His Baptism we see Him numbering Himself with transgressors, submitting to be baptised alongside sinful men, identifying Himself in their relation to God as sinners. It was "a great act of loving communion with our misery," and, as Denney says in his *Death of Christ,* "in that hour, in the will and act of Jesus, the work of atonement was begun." On the Cross the work of atonement was consummated, through the shedding of the blood of the Son of God, which brings to all believing souls forgiveness and cleansing (1:7; 2:2; 2:12; 4:10).

7 The third witness is the Holy Spirit, whom each believer has in himself (v. 10). The Spirit brings the truth of the Incarnation and of the Atonement home to the souls of men. He witnesses continually in the Church — a *present* tense is used. In John's Gospel we have seven witnesses to Christ: *the Scriptures* (5:39—47), *the Baptist* (1:7), *the Disciples* (15:27, 16:30), *Christ's words* (8:14 and 18, 18:37), *Christ's works* (5:36, 10:25 and 38), *the Father* (5:37, 8:18), *the Spirit* (15:26). In the Epistle three of these seven are mentioned, *the Disciples* in 1:2, *the Father* in 5:9 and 10, and *the Spirit* here; but to these two more are added, the *water* and the *blood*. We see how full and how varied and how strong the witness is.

The special and peculiar office of the Holy Spirit is to glorify Christ, by taking of His and declaring it unto the Church (Jn. 16:14). He is "The Spirit of Truth" (Jn. 14:17; 15:26; 16:13); indeed, as John says here, He *is* Truth and can speak only Truth. His witness, therefore, can be relied on, when He testifies to the fact that Jesus was not only the Son of God at His Baptism but also when he shed His precious blood amid the agonies and the dereliction of the Cross.

8 "The witnesses are three, the Spirit and the water and the blood, and the three of them are in accord" (Moffat), literally, they *are* (united) *into the one;* they cooperate for the one object of establishing the truth.

The Three Heavenly Witnesses

In v. 8, after the words "bear witness," the English A.V. has the words, *"in heaven, the Father, the Word, and the Holy Ghost; and these three are one. And there are three that bear witness on earth.* It is practically certain that these words are not part of the true text, because the MS. evidence in support of them is hopelessly weak. Out of between 200 and 300 known Greek cursive MSS. they are found only in *two* (No. 162 of the 15th century and No. 34 of the 16th century). In these two MSS., as Plummer says, the passage is *a manifest translation from a late recension of the Latin Vulgate.* Not one Greek uncial MS. contains the words. Every ancient Version of the first four centuries omits them. Every Version earlier than the 14th century, except the Latin, omits them. No Greek Father quotes them in the numerous controversies on the doctrine of the Trinity, though such a quotation might well have been decisive sometimes in their arguments with the deniers of the doctrine. No Latin Father earlier than the fifth century quotes the words. The MS. evidence seems to be decisive against the genuineness of the passage.

When we examine the *internal* evidence, we find that there is good reason for asserting that the words in question break the sense. In vv. 6 and 7 we have the water, the blood, and the Spirit mentioned, and they are recapitulated in John's manner in v. 8. We cannot help feeling that the words in question make an awkward parenthesis.

Haupt says that "no one can deny that in the whole compass of Holy Writ there is no passage even approaching the dogmatic precision with which, in a manner approximating to the later ecclesiastical definitions, this one asserts the immanent Trinity." It would appear that we cannot quote this passage in defence of the doctrine of the Trinity. That doctrine, however, finds a firm and unassailable basis elsewhere in the N. T. For a defence of the genuineness of the Baptismal Formula (Mt. 28:19), as against the objections of Harnack and others, reference may be made to J. C. Lambert's book, *The Sacraments in the New Testament.* Dr. C. F. D'Arcy, in an article "Trinity" in Hastings DCG., referring to Mt. 28:19, says that "we have to note that there is no textual evidence against the passage, that 2 Cor. 13:14 contains the threefold Divine Name in a way which shows that the combination was familiar in the mind of the Christian Church at a time which was certainly less than thirty years after the Ascension, and that there is a continuous stream of testimony from the earliest times as to baptism in the threefold Name, the *Didache* providing the connecting link between the Apostolic Age and Justin Martyr. . . . It is surely somewhat hard to suppose that the Christian doctrine of God could have so rapidly assumed the form in which we find it in St. Paul's Epistles, if our Lord Himself had not brought together the various strands in His teaching; and when was this so likely to happen as when He manifested Himself to His disciples after His Resurrection?"

Outstanding N. T. passages in which we have Trinitarian language are 2 Cor. 13:14 and 1 Pet. 1:2; above all; we have our Lord's teaching, as recorded in Jn. 14—16. There is abundant justification in N. T. for Van Oosterzee's assertion, "Christianity is monotheistic, but it is not Unitarian."

The evidence bearing on the Three Heavenly Witnesses is set forth exhaustively in an Appendix to Plummer's commentary in the *Cambridge Bible* and CGT.

9 If we receive the witness of men, the witness of God is greater: for the witness of God is this, that he hath borne witness concerning his Son.

10 He that believeth on the Son of God hath the witness in him: he that believeth not God hath made him a liar; because he hath not believed in the witness that God hath borne concerning his Son.

11 And the witness is this, that God gave unto us eternal life, and this life is in his Son.

12 He that hath the Son hath the life; he that hath not the Son of God hath not the life.

9 If, as we do, we accept the witness of men who companied with the Son of God in the days of His flesh, the witness of God is greater. That witness centres on His Son, saluted by the Father as His beloved Son at His Baptism (Mt. 3:17), the Son of God who loved us and gave Himself for us (Gal. 2:20), who was declared to be the Son of God with power by His Resurrection (Rom. 1:4).

10 For the first time in the Epistle we have that phrase which occurs nearly 40 times in John's Gospel and elsewhere in N. T. only about 10 times, "to believe *on,* or *into.*" It describes the faith which moves *towards* and *rests* on its object, that saving faith by which, as the *Shorter Catechism* has it, "we receive Christ, and rest on Him alone, for salvation, as He is offered to us in the Gospel." See on 3:23. This faith must be always in exercise — "he that *believeth*": we have a present tense with similar significance in Jn. 1:12. Such a believer as is here described has the witness in him, as an abiding possession. The external testimony, in the words, works, etc. of Christ, accepted with the whole heart, becomes inward certainty.

There are some people, however, who very far indeed

from attaining to such faith. They have not even got the length of *believing God,* of believing what He says about His Son. Of .such people John uses again the strong expression which he had used in 1:10. There are two perfect tenses used here, the force of which Plummer brings out thus: "The perfect tense in both cases indicates a permanent result: He has been and remains an unbeliever in the witness which God has given and continually supplies concerning His Son."

11 This witness of God, accepted with saving faith, means that eternal life is the present possession of the believer (Jn. 3:16 and 36, etc.). All life is *in* the Son (Jn. 1:4), but especially that eternal life which consists in saving knowledge of God (Jn. 17:3). This life has its infinite source and fountain in the Son, whom Peter calls the Prince, or Author, of life (Acts 3:15).

12 The true believer *has* the Son, in the arms of his faith, and he who has the Son has *the* life, the only life that is worth calling life, the life that is life indeed (1 Tim. 6:19). In describing the unbeliever John varies his language in a significant way: he describes the unbeliever not merely as one who has not the Son, but as one who has not the Son *of God.* The unbeliever needs to be reminded whose Son He is whom he spurns. Compare the last words of the Baptist (Jn. 3:36).

CONCLUSION TO THE EPISTLE

13 These things have I written unto you, that ye may know that ye have eternal life, even unto you that believe on the name of the Son of God.

14 And this is the boldness which we have toward him, that, if we ask anything according to his will, he heareth us:

15 and if we know that he heareth us whatsoever we ask, we know that we have the petitions which we have asked of him.

16 If any man see his brother sinning a sin not unto death, he shall ask, and God will give him life for them that sin not unto death. There is a sin unto death: not concerning this do I say that he should make request.

17 All unrighteousness is sin: and there is a sin not unto death.

18 We know that whosoever is begotten of God sinneth not; but he that was begotten of God keepeth himself, and the evil one toucheth him not.

19 We know that we are of God, and the whole world lieth in the evil one.

20 And we know that the Son of God is come, and hath given us an understanding, that we know him that is true, and we are in him that is true, even in his Son Jesus Christ. This is the true God, and eternal life.

21 My little children, guard yourselves from idols.

(1). *Intercessory prayer* (13—17). (2). *Three great Christian certainties* (18—20). (3). *A final warning* (21).

(1). *Intercessory prayer* (5:13—17).

13 John has given us already several reasons for his writing of the Epistle (1:4; 2:1 and 12, 13). He wants his readers to be a joyful people (1:4), he wants them to be a holy people (2:1), and now he tells them that he wants them to be a sure people. He wrote his Gospel in order to lead men to exercise faith in the Son of God and so to have life in Him (Jn. 20:31); he now writes his Epistle in order that believers may *know* that they have eternal life. The Westminster *Confession of Faith* says that "although hypocrites, and other unregenerate men, may vainly deceive themselves with false hopes and carnal presumptions of being in the favor of God and estate of Salvation; which hope of theirs shall perish; yet such as truly believe in the Lord Jesus, and love Him in sincerity, endeavouring to walk in all good conscience before Him, may in this life be certainly assured that they are in the state of grace, and may rejoice in the hope of the glory of God; which hope shall never make them ashamed." The inward witness of the Holy Spirit may give them this assurance (Rom. 8:16).

14 For the fourth and last time we have the word *boldness*. See on 2:28. The word occurs twice with reference to the day of Judgment (2:28 and 4:17). Here, in 3:21, Heb. 4:16 and Eph. 3:12, it is used of the spirit in which believers come to God in prayer. Prayer must be for things that are in accordance with the will of God: therefore, we ought to long to find ourselves among those who delight themselves in the Lord, who are certain to have the desires of their hearts granted unto them (Ps. 37:4). To such desires the ears of God are open (Ps. 34:15).

15 The fact that God hears does not mean merely that He *listens* to us: it means that our petition is granted, though the answer may not come at once, and though, when it comes, it may not be what we expected it to be, or what we wanted it to be. "Everyone that asketh receiveth" (Mt. 7:8), though, when the Divine gift at last rests in our hands, it may be something far more wonderful than we had ever dreamt of getting. See on 3:22.

16-17 John has had much to say about love of the brethren: He now says that, if we love the brethren, we will pray for them, "what are men better than sheep or goats that nourish a blind life within the brain, if, knowing God, they lift not hands of prayer both for themselves and those who call them friend?" Especially, we shall pray for a brother who goes astray, believing with James that a Spirit-inspired prayer may turn a sinner from the error of his way (Jas. 5:16 and 20). The phrase "sinning a sin" occurs nowhere else in N. T.

There is, however, one sin in connection with which prayer should not be offered. John's words here are difficult of interpretation. The *sin unto death* should possibly be regarded as being the same as the sin against the Holy Spirit, of which Jesus said that the man who commits it is in the grip of an eternal sin (Mk. 3:29). Matthew Henry says of the sin against the Holy Spirit that "it is not all speaking against the person or essence of the Holy Spirit, or merely the resisting of His internal working in the sinner himself that is meant, for who, then, should be saved?" It seems to describe rather a *settled state* of sin, in which a man may go so far as to call evil good and good evil (Isa. 5:20) as the result of long-continued delight in and practice of sin; the character of such a person becomes fixed in evil. But then, how can we mortals, with our limited knowledge and insight, ever be certain that any man has reached that condition of soul? It ought to be observed that John does not say that the *sin unto death* can be definitely recognised as such. The practical conclusion, then, to which this passage leads us, is, possibly, that we ought to go on praying, exercising the judgment of charity. Dr. David Smith says: "There is a fearful possibility of a man putting himself beyond the hope of restoration: but we can never tell when he has crossed the boundary. If we were sure it was a case of 'sin unto death,' then we should forbear praying; but since we can never be sure, we should always keep on praying."[1]

---

[1] Dealing with John's words here, Dodd, with reference to the severe language used in the Epistle to the Hebrews with regard to apostasy from the Christian faith (Heb. 6:4—6 and 10:26—29) says that "it would seem likely that our present author too is thinking of

Two facts clear as crystal are to be borne in mind, and we should not try to pry further. (1). All unrighteousness is sin, however trival it may appear to be, and it needs cleansing and forgiveness. (2). There is sin not unto death, and the blood of Jesus is available for its cleansing (1:7). There is abundant scope, therefore, for intercessory prayer, and the Gospel of the atoning Redeemer encourages us to engage in it.

John has been dwelling on a dark mystery. There are twilight regions of truth where we feel uncertain. But there are grand certainties, and on three of them John dwells as he draws to close.

(2). *Three great Christian certainties* (5:18—20).

18 John begins each of these three verses with that trimphant *we know*. The first great Christian certainty is that of the eternal security of the child of God. John has just been saying that a Christian brother may sin a sin, may be guilty sometimes of an act of sin; now he says that whosoever is begotten of God sinneth not, in the sense

---

apostasy or denial of Christ as the sin that places a man beyond the pale. We know that he traced the presence and power of Antichrist in the denial of the Incarnation (4:2—5), and if a man had become identified with Antichrist it was perhaps natural to feel that he was past praying for." In connection with the suggestion made in the exposition that we should hesitate long before ceasing to pray for anybody, even for the worst of sinners, these further words of Dodd may be pondered: "The questions of the forgiveness of post-baptismal sin and of the restoration of the lapsed continued to agitate the minds of Christians for generations. The decision ultimately went in favor of the milder view, which admitted the lapsed to penance. The general sense of the Church has not endorsed the view that we are competent to decide that a given person has sinned himself beyond the pale of the divine mercy, and consequently is past praying for."

Dodd also reminds us that "it was not for nothing that the Church which preserved in its tradition the severe saying of the Lord about the sin of denying Him, also preserved the story of Peter's denial, of Christ's prayer for him, and of his ultimate recovery (Mk. 14:66—72, Lk. 22:31—34, Jn. 21:15—17)."

explained in the notes on 3:9. In that verse he had given
one reason why that is so; here he gives another reason — the
Eternal son of God *keeps him;* cf. the use of that verb *keep*
in 1 Pet. 1:5 and Jude, "kept for Christ Jesus." *Him* seems
to be the true reading.[2] The statement "the child of God
keeps himself" does not seem to be a very cheering one.
Calvin felt that when he wrote thus on this verse: "What is
God's work he transfers to us. For if anyone be the cus-
todian of his own salvation, the protection will be a miserable one." John, it would appear, does not teach here the
"miserable" doctrine that the child of God keeps himself.
There is a change of tense here which must surely be significant. The child of God is described by a perfect participle,
as in 3:9, 5:1 and 4, and also in Jn. 3:6 and 8 — whosoever
is begotten of God and remains a child of God. Then John
changes abruptly to the aorist participle never used by him
anywhere else of the same verb — He that was begotten
of God. The conclusion arrived at by Plummer seems to
be a sound one. "The perfect expresses a permanent
relation begun in the past and continued in the present;
the aorist expresses a timeless relation, a mere fact: the one
signifies the children of God as opposed to those who have
not become His children; the other signifies the Son of God
as opposed to the evil one." The Eternally Begotten keeps
him who is begotten by grace. We find some confirmation
of this interpretation in the fact that the second of John's
phrases, *He that was begotten of God,* is the same form of
expression that we have in the old Nicene Creed, "begotten
of the Father," where the reference is to the eternal generation of Him who is "God of God, Light of Light, Very God
of Very God."

The evil one does not lay hold on the man who is kept
by Christ. That man is beyond the reach of the grasp of

---

[2] *Keepeth himself.* We have the reading "keepeth *him*, in ℵ B and
the Vulg., and internal evidence seems to favor it. The Keeper is the
Eternal Son of God, the Only-begotten.

the evil one, for he is in the Father and in the Son, his life is hid with Christ in God (Jn. 10:28, 29; Col. 3:3).

19 Dr. G. G. Findlay says in an article in the English *Expositor* for 1899 that "it is a splendid, but it is an awful thing to say, 'We know that we are of God.' It is to be conscious that the hand of God has been laid upon us, to have felt the breath of the Eternal pass over our spirit to awaken and transform. It is to know that there is a power working within us each, at the root of our nature, that is infinitely wiser and stronger and better than ourselves; a Spirit planted in our hearts which comes directly from the being and the will of the Living God our Father, and links us individually to Him. To *know* this is to hold a distinction immeasurably above all earthly glory. It is to be charged with a principle of righteousness that can dissolve every bond of iniquity, that treads down worldly fear and pleasure, and makes us, living or dying, more than conquerors." It is that trimphant conviction which John declares to be the possession of all Christians.

The unbelieving world is not of God, it is dominated by the desires which are "not of the Father" (2:16); more than that, it lies in the arms of the evil one, whereas the child of God rests in the arms of the Father (Deut. 33:27).

20 The third certainty is the grandest of them all. It is, as Findlay puts it, the all in all of John's life and of his world of thought. It is the one on which he has insisted so emphatically right though the Epistle and to which he must give expression yet once more before he lays down his pen. "We know that the Son of God has come, and has given us insight to know Him who is the Real God; and we are in Him who is Real, even in His Son Jesus Christ" (Moffat). The word "understanding" or "insight" occurs nowhere else in John's writings: it occurs in Paul, in Hebrews and in Peter, who uses it in 1 Pet. 1:13 to describe the faculty of understanding or reflection which he exhorts his readers to brace up and to keep ever in use. All other gods so-called are figments of the human imagination: cf.

1 Cor. 8:4—6. The God and Father of our Lord Jesus Christ is the only Real God (Jn. 17:3), and to be in Him is to be in the realm of life, the life that is unfading and unwithering.

(3). *A final warning* (5:21).

21 The Apostle of love, in this final grave warning, addresses yet once more his readers as his *little* children; see on 2:12. The verb "guard" is used of the guarding of a flock in Lk. 2:8, of the guarding of a trust or a deposit in 2 Tim. 1:12 and 14; it occurs also in 2 Thes. 3:3. Christ is the great Guardian (2 Tim. 1:12), and He uses this verb of Himself in Jn. 17:12, where He also uses the verb "keep," which occurs here, in verse 18. But, while Christ is the great Guardian, the believer himself must exercise sleepless vigilance in the presence of the foe. The force of John's warning is: "Once for all be on your guard and have nothing to do with the idols." As already noted in 2:23, the false teachers against whom John wages relentless warfare in the Epistle did not worship the only Real God but a false image of their own thoughts. It is possible to do that still. If, as some have supposed, this Epistle is the latest in date of all the N. T. writings, it is very striking to find that this is God's last word to men: "Little children, guard yourselves from the idols." John may refer, partly at least, to literal idols of wood and stone, which were numerous enough in his day in Asia Minor and elsewhere, but in our day his words may be taken as referring to anything that threatens to take in the affections of our hearts the place which should be occupied only by the one living and true God.

> The dearest idol I have known,
> Whate'er that idol be,
> Help me to tear it from Thy throne,
> And worship only Thee.

THE SECOND EPISTLE OF JOHN

II John

1 The elder unto the elect lady and her children, whom I love in truth; and not I only, but also all they that know the truth;

2 for the truth's sake which abideth in us, and it shall be with us for ever:

3 Grace, mercy, peace shall be with us, from God the Father, and from Jesus Christ, the Son of the Father, in truth and love.

4 I rejoice greatly that I have found certain of thy children walking in truth, even as we received commandment from the Father.

5 And now I beseech thee, lady, not as though I wrote to thee a new commandment, but that which we had from the beginning, that we love one another.

6 And this is love, that we should walk after his commandments. This is the commandment, even as ye heard from the beginning, that ye should walk in it.

7 For many deceivers are gone forth into the world, even they that confess not that Jesus Christ cometh in the flesh. This is the deceiver and the anti-christ.

8 Look to yourselves, that ye lose not the things which we have wrought, but that ye receive a full reward.

9 Whosoever goeth onward and abideth not in the teaching of Christ, hath not God: he that abideth in the teaching, the same hath both the Father and the Son.

10 If any one cometh unto you, and bringeth not this teaching, receive him not into your house, and give him no greeting:

11 for he that giveth him greeting partaketh in his evil works.

12 Having many things to write unto you, I would not write them with paper and ink: but I hope to come unto you, and to speak face to face, that your joy may be made full.

13 The children of thine elect sister salute thee.

This short Epistle contains: 1. *Salutation* (1—3), 2. *Occasion of Composition* (4), 3. *An exhortation to love and obedience* (5, 6), 4. *Warnings against false teachers* (7—11), and 5. *Conclusion* (12, 13).

(1). *Salutation* (1—3).

1 The writer, who is almost certainly John the son of Zebedee, describes himself as *the Elder,*[1] as he does also at the beginning of Third John. Probably, because of his age and because he is the last survivor of the Apostolic company, John uses this designation. Westcott is probably right when he says that "there can be little doubt that it describes not age simply but official position." The Epistle was probably written to some lady of importance in one of the Christian Churches of Asia Minor: see Introduction. She is one of the elect of God, chosen in Christ unto etrnal life (Eph. 1:4; 2 Tim. 2:10; 1 Pet. 1:2). John loves her in truth, with the utmost sincerity of true Christian love, the love that is to endure for ever. The fame of this Christian lady had reached far, and all who had heard of her felt for her the same holy affection that John felt. True Christians are those who know the Truth (Jn. 8:32), and their common knowledge binds them closely together, though they may be separated far in time and space.

2 The Apostle and all believers love the elect lady *because of* the fact, *on account of* the fact of the abiding presence of the Spirit of Truth with them (Jn. 14:26) who enables them to abound in love and in all the rest of the fruit of the Spirit (Gal. 5:22, 23). Where the Spirit is there is the Truth of God in all the riches of its wonder-working power (1 Jn. 5:7).

3 In the salutations of Paul's Epistles we have usually "grace and peace;" here, as in 1 and 2 Tim., we have *grace,*

---

[1] In the Introduction the vexed question of "the elder John" is dealt with. The question whether "elect lady" is to be interpreted as referring to a person or to a Church is also discussed there.

mercy and peace; in Jude we have "Mercy unto you and peace and love be multiplied." Those are indeed richly blessed who have in their souls the grace of God that brings salvation unto them (Tit. 2:11), the mercy from which "all our hopes begin" (Eph. 2:4), the peace which guards their hearts as in a garrison (Phil. 4:7). These three heavenly gifts come directly *from the presence of* the Father and they come directly *from the presence* of Jesus Christ, the Son of the Father. The distinct Personality of the Son is implied and also His unity of essence with the Father. John emphasises with impressive fulness of language the Divine Sonship of Jesus, possibly in view of the false teaching to which he will refer presently, in vv. 7—10.

It is far more than a pious wish that John expresses here, it is a confident assurance, and assurance in which he includes himself — "shall be with *us.*" The words "truth" and "love" are very characteristic of John's writings, and nowhere is that more markedly the case than in this brief Epistle, where "truth" occurs five times and "love" twice as a noun and twice as a verb.

(2). *Occasion of composition* (4).

4 In the course of his Apostolical travels or, it may be, in Ephesus, John had met some of the elect lady's children who were true Christians: they were walking in truth, in accordance with the commandment which they received at the outset of their pilgrimage in the King's highway; cf. "heard" in 1 Jn. 2:7 and 24 and 1 Jn. 3:11 and "gave" in 1 Jn. 3:23, 24. The word "commandment" occurs four times in this brief Epistle. "Love, truth, obedience; these," says Plummer, "are the three leading ideas, which partly imply or supplement one another. Obedience without love becomes servile; love without obedience becomes unreal: neither of them can flourish outside the realm of Truth." Paul rejoiced when he heard that his converts were becoming fruitful and growing Christians (1 Thes. 1:2—10, etc.). John had a similar deep joy in his heart when he met these children of the elect lady. Does he mean to suggest gently that there are others of her children who are in danger of being contaminated with the errors to which he will refer presently?

(3). *An exhortation to love and obedience* (5, 6).

5 This verse and the following one seem to prove conclusively that the writer of this Epistle was the writer of First John. For "new commandment" and for "from the beginning," see on 1 Jn. 2:7.

6 *And the love is this,* the love to which we are called consists in this, practical obedience to the commandments of God. "In v. 5 obedience prompts love; here love prompts obedience. This is no vicious logical circle, but a healthy moral connection, as is stated above on v. 4. Love divorced from duty will run riot, and duty divorced from love will starve. See on 1 Jn. 5:3. The Apostle has no sympathy with a religion of pious emotions: there must be a *persevering walk according to God's commands.* In writing to a woman it might be all the more necessary to insist on the fact that love is not a mere matter of feeling." (Plummer). *The commandment is this,* it consists in this, that, in accordance with the first lessons which you received in the school of Christ, lessons which will never be abrogated, you should walk in love. True Christianity means walking in light (1 Jn. 1:6, 7) and it means walking in love (1 Jn. 2:10, Eph. 5:2 and here).

(4). *Warnings against false teachers* (7—11).

7 We Christians, John now says, need to walk on without swerving in the path of light and love *because* many deceivers are gone forth into the world, and it is our bounden duty to show to the world what true Christianity is. John has already branded the false teachers as liars (1 Jn. 2:22), as seducers (1 Jn. 2:26) as false prophets (1 Jn. 4:1), as the mouthpiece of Antichrist (1 Jn. 2:18, 22 and 4:3); he now brands them as deceivers. This word occurs again in N. T. only in Mt. 27:63, 2 Cor. 6:8 and 1 Tim. 4:1, but John uses the cognate verb, "to lead astray," in 1 Jn. 1:8, 2:26 and 3:7. The false teachers are quite likely the same as those described in 1 Jn. 2:19 as having *gone forth* out of the Church. They were leading unstable souls astray into dangerous regions of speculation and their teaching tended also to loose the bonds of moral obligation, for false theology and false living always go together. Their teaching denied Jesus Christ *as coming* in the flesh; if it were accepted, men could no longer believe in a true Incarnation of the Son of God; see on 1 Jn. 4:2, 3. It is worthy of notice again that John never speaks of Christ as coming *into* the flesh, but either as in 1 Jn. 4:2 and here, of His coming *in* the flesh, or of His *becoming* flesh (Jn. 1:14). To say that Christ came *into* the flesh would leave room for the teaching of John's heretics to the effect that the Divine Son was united with Jesus after He was born of Mary, and that would mean that there was no true Incarnation. Such teaching is undoubtedly the teaching of a dangerous deceiver, it is the teaching of a mouthpiece of the Antichrist.

8 John's meaning here is: "Look to yourselves, keep careful watch over yourselves (same phrase as in Mk. 13:9), lest these deceivers should nullify the good work wrought in you through our instrumentality; desire rather that you may receive the full fruit of it. Christians should seek the full fruition of the work of grace in their souls, in fulness of love (1 Jn. 1:4), in all the fulness of glory and honour and immortality (Rom. 2:7), when the crown of life (Jas. 1:12), the crown of righteousness (2 Tim. 4:8, the crown of glory (1 Pet. 5:4) shall at last rest on their brows. John is very seriously warning his readers, that, if their souls are infected with the poison of the false teaching, they may very easily miss something of their inheritance of glory in Christ.

9 The reading *goeth onward* is to be preferred to *trans-*

gresseth (AV).[2] John is here shooting a sharp dart at the "advanced" thinkers of his day. They claimed to be the possessors of a richer fulness of truth than the common herd of believers. Moffat translates: "Anyone who is 'advanced' and will not remain by the doctrine of Christ, does not possess God." Growth and advance there must be *in* the teaching of Christ, as the Spirit of Truth leads us step by step into all the fulness of its meanings and its implications, but to advance *beyond* the teaching of Christ is to wander about aimlessly in the misty region of unaided human speculation. To do that is to have no longer the only Real God as our God. He who abides in the teaching of Christ, as the well-loved home of his soul, has both the Father and the Son, and advances daily to closer and deeper communion with the Father and the Son. See on 1 Jn. 2:23.

10-11 Christian hospitality is not to be extended to such dangerous teachers as John has in mind, because to extend Christian hospitality to such would increase their opportunities for working mischief. Liddon says that John "is at once earnestly dogmatic and earnestly philanthropic; for the Incarnation has taught him both the preciousness of man and the preciousness of truth." A. T. Robertson remarks that "in a latitudinarian age these words may sound harsh or unfeeling, but a little knowledge of the situation will clear it up. It is not just a case of entertaining people who disagree with one on minor matters or an emergency case when true hospitality overrides ordinary difficulties. These propagandists of error were carrying on regular campaigns to destroy loyalty to Christ as Lord and Savior. People were called on to take sides for or against Christ. These 'deceivers' were also immoral in their lives. Suppose atheistic free-lovers were carrying on a campaign in your

---

2 προάγων is the reading in ℵ AB and some of the Versions, and seems to be the better attested reading. The word "goeth onward," like the phrase "and we are" in 3:1, is a precious part of the true text which has been restored to us by the researches of modern textual criticism.

town. Hospitality to such leaders would inevitably involve endorsement of their teaching and lives. John puts the matter sharply, but not more pointedly than the situation demanded." We should, however, be absolutely certain that men are as far astray from Christian Truth as John's heretics were before we think of meeting out to them such treatment as John here recommends.

(5). *Conclusion* (12, 13).

12 The close resemblance between this conclusion and the conclusion of the Third Epistle is worthy of careful notice. The two Epistles, quite possibly, were written about the same time. John explains the brevity of this short note by the fact that he hopes soon to appear before the elect lady and to speak to her face to face, literally, mouth to mouth, mouth answering to mouth. Paul has a different phrase in 1 Cor. 13:12, a phrase which means exactly what it says, face to face, face towards face. Their meeting, John says, will be a joyful occasion, and he entertains the hope that he may be able to help his friend to advance a little nearer to that *fulness* of joy which he wants the readers of his First Epistle to have (1 Jn. 1:4).[3]

13 Some nephews of the elect lady may have been engaged in business in Ephesus, where, possibly, John is writing, and they send their greetings to their aunt. It may have been these nephews who told John about the spiritual dangers that may have been facing some of the elect lady's children, the dangers referred to in the commentary on v. 4.

---

[3] *Paper and ink.* The word "paper" occurs nowhere else in N.T., but it is found in the LXX at Jer. 36:23. It means here, quite likely, Egyptian papyrus, as distinct from the more expensive "parchment" mentioned in 2 Tim. 4:13. But, as Plummer remarks, "both papyrus and parchment were costly, which may account for the Apostle's brevity." "Ink" is, quite literally, "black stuff." The word occurs again in 3 Jn. 13 and elsewhere in N. T. only in 2 Cor. 3:3. The "ink" may have been made of lamp-black and gall-juice, or more simply of soot and water.

THE THIRD EPISTLE OF JOHN

III John

1 The elder unto Gaius the beloved, whom I love in truth.

2 Beloved, I pray that in all things thou mayest prosper and be in health, even as thy soul prospereth.

3 For I rejoiced greatly, when brethren came and bare witness unto thy truth, even as thou walkest in truth.

4 Greater joy have I none than this, to hear of my children walking in the truth.

5 Beloved, thou doest a faithful work in whatsoever thou doest toward them that are brethren and strangers withal;

6 who bare witness to thy love before the church: whom thou wilt do well to set forward on their journey worthily of God:

7 because that for the sake of the Name they went forth, taking nothing of the Gentiles.

8 We therefore ought to welcome such, that we may be fellow-workers for the truth.

9 I wrote somewhat unto the church: but Diotrephes, who loveth to have the preeminence among them, receiveth us not.

10 Therefore, if I come, I will bring to remembrance his works which he doeth, prating against us with wicked words: and not content therewith, neither doth he himself receive the brethren, and them that would he forbiddeth and casteth them out of the church.

11 Beloved, imitate not that which is evil, but that which is good. He that doeth good is of God: he that doeth evil hath not seen God.

12 Demetrius hath the witness of all men, and of the truth itself; yea, we also bear witness; and thou knowest that our witness is true.

13 I had many things to write unto thee, but I am unwilling to write them to thee with ink and pen:

14 but I hope shortly to see thee, and we shall speak face to face. Peace be unto thee. The friends salute thee. Salute the friends by name.

This brief Epistle centres around three men, the first two evidently members of the same Church, a Church situated somewhere in Asia Minor. We have here (1) *Gaius* (1—8), (2) *Diotrephes* (9, 10), (3) *Demetrius* (11, 12) and (4) *a Conclusion* (13, 14).

(1). *Gaius* (1—8).

1 The Epistle is addressed to a man called Gaius: see Introduction. There is no greeting such as we have in Second John, but we may regard the prayer in the following verse as taking the place of such a greeting. For the phrase *whom I love in truth* see on 2 Jn. 1.

2 The word *prosper* occurs elsewhere in N. T. only in Rom. 1:10 and 1 Cor. 16:2. The word *health* refers to physical health, as in Lk. 7:10 and 15:27. The verb here used is used of one who is *sound* in the faith in Tit. 1:13 and of one who is *sound* in the graces of faith, love and endurance in Tit. 2:2. Gaius was surely a remarkable man. There was no doubt about the health and prosperity of his soul, he was having a fair journey spiritually, but his physical health, perhaps, sometimes left something to be desired. There are multitudes of people who are deeply concerned about the health of their bodies and who bestow the utmost care on the needs of their bodies, but they never give a thought to the health of their souls. How remarkable is the contrast in the case of Gaius! It may be that he was sometimes rather inclined to neglect his body in the intensity of his devotion to spiritual realities.

The order of the words in the Greek is impressive, with *all things* at the beginning and *soul* at the end of the sentence: *In all things I pray that thou mayest prosper and be in health, even as prospereth thy soul.* Perhaps the marginal rendering of Ps. 1:3 brings out the Psalmist's real meaning: "In whatsoever he doeth *he* shall prosper." In a marked degree Gaius exhibited the kind of prosperity described in that Psalm, the prosperity of the man who brings forth fruit in its season and whose leaf does not wither.

3 There is no doubt in John's mind with regard to the prosperity and health of the soul of Gaius, *for* from time to time various brethren who have visited the Church of which Gaius was a member have given glowing accounts of him. The Truth is *in* him and he walks *in* the Truth. See on 2 Jn. 4.

4 Gaius was one of John's spiritual children, and, as in the case of the elect lady and her family (2 Jn. 4), he declares again what it is that brings to his heart its deepest joy.

5 Gaius must have been a friend specially dear to John's heart, for he repeats here that affectionate form of address, *beloved,* which he had used in the second verse, and which he repeats again in the eleventh verse. Gaius was a man who would certainly hear at the end of the day his Lord's word of approval, "well done, good and *faithful servant*" (Mt. 25:21, 23), because of the *faithful* work which he was doing in entertaining from time to time the travelling evangelists who came his way. They were complete strangers to him but he recognised in them brothers in Christ,[1] and in entertaining them he was entertaining Christ Himself (Mt. 25:40).

6 These evangelists had borne witness to the practical Christian love of Gaius before the Church at Ephesus, where John possibly wrote this Epistle, and John gently urges Gaius to continue such good work, for it would always be needed. As A. T. Robertson reminds us, "the inns were abominable and travelling was difficult." John urges Gaius to continue the work of forwarding the evangelists on their journey, *in a manner worthy of God;* whose representatives they were, cf. Mt. 10:40—42. For that phrase "in a manner

---

1 *Brethren and strangers withal.* A. V. reads, "to the brethren and to strangers," but the true text reads καὶ τοῦτο ξένους (ℵABC, etc.) "to them that are brethren and *that* strangers," i.e., to brethren and those brethren strangers. The brethren and the strangers are not two classes of people, but are one and the same.

worthy of God", cf. 1 Thes. 2:12 and Col. 1:10. The verb *to set forward* occurs in Acts 15:3, Acts 20:38, Acts 21:5, Rom. 15:24, 1 Cor. 16:6 and 11, 2 Cor. 1:16 and Tit. 3:13.

7 These evangelists deserve all the help that can be given them, because the work which they have undertaken is a "labour of love." They deliberately refrained from seeking any monetary aid from the Gentiles, because to receive such aid would lay them open to misunderstanding. It was for this reason that Paul on occasion supported himself (1 Thes. 2:6—9, etc.). "The Gentiles" can hardly mean Gentile *converts:* cf. Mt. 5:47, 6:7, 18:17, the only other places where this word occurs. If there were false teachers who had *gone forth* (1 Jn. 2:19, 4:1, 2 Jn. 7) and were busily at work poisoning the minds of men with their pernicious teaching, there were others who had *gone forth* with far different aims and purposes. They had gone forth *for the sake of the Name,*[2] the Name that is above every name (Phil. 2:9). We have here the same absolute use of *the Name* that we have in Acts 5:41, "rejoicing that they were counted worthy to suffer dishonour for *the* Name;" cf. Jas. 2:7.

8 *We* therefore, in marked contrast to the Gentiles just mentioned, *ought,* out of a sense of moral obligation (same verb as in 1 Jn. 2:6, 3:16 and 4:11) to receive such preachers hospitably. In so doing, though we may not be able to preach ourselves, we shall be fellow-workers with these men unto the Truth. William Carey compared his missionary work to the exploration of a mine and said: "I will go down, if you will hold the ropes."

(2). *Diotrephes* (9, 10).

9 We know nothing of Diotrephes save what is told us here and he certainly appears in a very unfavorable light. John had written *somewhat* unto the Church of Gaius and Diotrephes, which possibly means that he had written a

---

² This is the reading in ℵ ABC, etc., and is certainly to be preferred to "for His Name's sake" in A. V.

short note to that Church. This note has perished; it may be that Diotrephes suppressed it. John says that Diotrephes does not *receive* him, in the person of his delegates; that is, Diotrephes flouts John's authority. Diotrephes was a man who *loves to have the first place*,[3] an expression which occurs only here. In utter contempt of the teaching of Jesus he wants to "lord it" over God's heritage (Mt. 20:25, 26; 1 Pet. 5:3). A. T. Robertson suggests that he was the kind of man who has sometimes been called in American church circles "the church boss," who wants to rule the church in accordance with his own desires and whims, a type of man who is not unknown in countries outside America. Robertson also says that he once wrote an article on Diotrephes for a Church magazine in which he developed the idea that Diotrephes was a typical "church boss," and the consequence was that some twenty deacons wrote to the editor cancelling their subscriptions because of the personal attack made on them!

10 John declares that, when he visits the Church of which Diotrephes is a member, he will deal in no gentle fashion with that arrogant man. He does not threaten the offender with excommunication, but he says that he will expose his conduct to the Church, directing public attention to it. The thunder tones, quite evidently, have not all departed from John's voice. The verb *prating* occurs only here in N. T., but the cognate adjective is found in 1 Tim. 5:13, where it is translated "tattlers." It comes from a root which was used of water boiling up or throwing up bubbles,

---

3 *Loveth to have the pre-eminence.* This phrase is represented by one word in the Greek *(φιλοπρωτεύων)*, a word which occurs nowhere else in N. T., but is found in several later Church writers. It is a compound verb, made up of a verb meaning "to love" and a verb meaning "to have the first place." It is rather interesting to observe that the second verb occurs just once in N. T., in Col. 1:18, where it is used of Christ, "that in all things He might have the preeminence, might have the first place." Christ is the only Head of the Church; there is no room in it for "little Popes," like Diotrephes.

and since bubbles are hollow and useless things, the verb here used came to mean "to indulge in empty or foolish talk," and the cognate adjective came to mean "garrulous, or babbling." The words of Diotrephes, however, were not merely the words of an empty windbag; they were *wicked* words, perniciously *evil* words (the adjective that is used of Cain in 1 Jn. 3:12 and of the devil in 1 Jn. 5:18, 19). Diotrephes had gone so far as to attempt to excommunicate those who were willing to give hospitality to the travelling missionaries or to special delegates sent by John: the present tenses *forbiddeth* and *casteth forth* may indicate that he had tried to exercise such tyranical power but that he had been foiled in his attempt. It is a most unlovely character who appears here before us for a few fleeting moments and then vanishes into deserved oblivion.

(3). *Demetrius* (11, 12).

11 From such an evil example John exhorts his beloved Gaius to turn away and to imitate not such an evil example but that which is good. The verb *to imitate* occurs again in 2 Thes. 3:7 and 9 and Heb. 13:7; the cognate noun occurs in 1 Cor. 4:16, Eph. 5:1, 1 Thes. 1:6, 1 Thes. 2:14 and Heb. 6:12. From the Greek word comes our word "mimic." He who *habitually does* good, walking in the steps of Him who went about doing good (Acts 10:38) gives clear proof that he has been begotten of God and that he belongs to the family of God; cf. 1 Jn. 3:10. He who *habitually does* evil has not seen God, he has never had any real vision of the Holy One, who is of purer eyes than to behold evil (Hab. 1:13) cf. 1 Jn. 3:6.

12 The example of Demetrius is a noble one to follow. Of him, as of Diotrephes, we know only what is told us here. That he was the silversmith of Ephesus who once made silver shrines for Diana (Acts 19:24) is only a conjecture, and, quite likely, a baseless one. He may have been a member of the Church at Ephesus who was commissioned by John to be the bearer of this Epistle and who needed this

warm word of commendation to Gaius, to whom he would
be a stranger. We have here a three-fold witness to
Demetrius; the witness of the community of Ephesus as a
whole *(all men);* the witness of the Truth itself: and the
witness of John and his fellow-workers at Ephesus *(we).*
That last witness Gaius had every reason to accept with the
utmost confidence, if he was, as is likely, one of John's
converts. The second and third witnesses should perhaps
be taken together, and the meaning of the somewhat obscure
statement that the Truth itself witnesses to Demetrius may
be that the witness of John is not the witness of an ordinary
man, but the witness of the Truth, the witness of the Spirit
of Truth, who speaks through him, as an inspired Apostle
of the Lord.

(4). *Conclusion* (13, 14).

13 For the very marked resemblance between these
words and the conclusion of Second John, see on 2 Jn. 12.
In the Second Epistle we had "with paper and ink;" here
we have "with ink and pen."[4]

14 John hopes *immediately* to see Gaius and to speak
with him face to face; there we have exactly the same phrase
as in 2 Jn. 12. Meanwhile, he invokes on his dear friend
at the end of his letter that Divine blessing of which he had
written at the beginning of his letter to the elect lady. "May
the peace of God, that inward peace of conscience which is
known by those who rest in God, be yours!" The
Christians at Ephesus send their greetings to Gaius, and
John wants Gaius to salute each of His friends in the vicinity
of Gaius by name, as warmly and individually as though
John had written down their names with his pen. The
description of Christians as "friends" is an interesting one.
F. W. H. Myers, in his poem "St. Paul", represents Paul as

---

4   The Greek word $\varkappa\dot{\alpha}\lambda\alpha\mu\rho\varsigma$, translated *pen*, here means "a reed,"
in which sense it occurs in the familiar phrase, "a reed shaken with the
wind" (Mt. 11:7 and Lk. 7:24). It signifies here a reed-pen, a writer's-
reed, as in Ps. 45:2 (LXX).

describing each one he has "won of sister or of brother" for Christ as "another friend in the blameless family of God." The friendship which binds together all the members of that family is to last for ever. If John uses this word as well as "brethren" and "beloved," as Farrar says, "it doubtless is from the remembrance of what he alone among the Evangelists has recorded, that the Lord Jesus had called Lazarus His friend (Jn. 11:11), and that He had said, 'Ye are my friends, if ye do the things that I command you' (John 15:14, 15)." The phrase "by name" occurs only once again in N. T., in Jn. 10:3, "He calleth His own sheep *by name.*" "The salutation," Plummer says, "is not to be given in a general way, but to each individual separately. John as shepherd of the Churches of Asia would imitate the Good Shepherd, and know all his sheep by name."

INDEX OF CHIEF SUBJECTS

INDEX OF SCRIPTURE REFERENCES

OLD TESTAMENT

INDEX OF SCRIPTURE REFERENCES

4:19	159	3:20	77	**JOEL**	
8:25-31	209	5:24	93		
10:12	103	7:6	43, 47	2:23	93
27:1	83	12	134	2:30	83
28:13	146	12:3	90		
		13:15	199	**AMOS**	
ECCLESIASTES		14:8	204		
		14:9	48		14
7:6	81	18:17	31	5:1-6	16
		23:6	150	8:4	47
ISAIAH		31:20	190	9:12	48
		31:31-34	162		
1:6	99	31:34	171	**JONAH**	
1:9	88	33:16	150		
1:11-17	193	36:23	232	4:8	31
1:15, 16	80				
5:20	221	**EZEKIEL**		**MICAH**	
9:18	60				
13:6	86	16:49	89	5:2	209
15:3	86	17:10	13	6:8	84
23:1, 14	86	18:12	47	7:19	103
29:13	80	21:15	90		
34:2	90			**HABAKKUK**	
40:7, 8	31	**DANIEL**			
40:26	89			1:13	238
41:8	54	4:35	89		
53	90, 111	7:15	52	**ZECHARIAH**	
53:7	112	9:7, 8	81		
54:5	77	12:12	94	2:5	45
54:11	30			3:1	148
57:15	79	**HOSEA**		12:6	60
59:7	86			13:1	143
60:19, 20	141		77		
61:1	171	6:3	93		
		6:4	83	**MALACHI**	
JEREMIAH		12:6	80		
2:3	36	13:15	31	3:5	43, 88

NEW TESTAMENT

MATTHEW		6:19	17, 86	12:6	53
1:18	62	7:1	16, 82	12:20	211
3:17	217	7:7	76	12:29	163
4:16	141	7:8	76, 193, 220	12:36	42, 96, 206
5:3	16	7:16	16, 64	12:37	42
5:7	49	7:20, 24	16	12:40	43
5:8, 9	71	8:27	178	12:44	61
5:12	94	8:29	52	13:15	101
5:21	94	9:36	191	13:19	162
5:22	62, 189	10:15	206	13:38	84, 162, 186
5:23	53, 189	10:22	27	13:43	180
5:27, 33	94	10:28	82	15:19	90
5:34-37	17, 96	10:40-42	235	16:18	98
5:38, 43	94	11:1	212	18:17	98, 236
5:43-48	207	11:7	239	18:35	49
5:47	236	11:20, 24	206	19:3	33
6:7	236	11:27	172	20:3, 6	53
6:13	84, 162	11:30	210	20:12	31

COMMENTARY ON EPISTLES OF JAMES AND JOHN

244

INDEX OF SCRIPTURE REFERENCES